HUMAROCK

Hummocks, Humming Rocks, and Silver Sands

By Fred Freitas

Rare 1892 photo by an unknown photographer looking from Third Cliff to Fourth Cliff courtesy of Jon Bond who found the photo.

Ridge Road and South Humarock Photo from the Author's Collection.

ISBN: 978-0-9910923-8-3

> *"In ordinary life we hardly realize that we receive a great deal more than we give, and that it is only with gratitude that life becomes rich."*-Dietrich Bonhoeffer

To: Chris, Julie, Bren, and Jillian who experienced life in Sea View/Humarock, and to Giovanna, who's just discovering it.

To the many, many people who made this book possible, thank you. Those of you who gave your time, your knowledge, your stories, and pictures, and, most importantly, shared your love of Humarock and Sea View with me, my eternal gratitude. A special thank you to my wife Jean who encouraged, supported, and cajoled me to finish this book even when the piles and piles of historic material strewn almost everywhere seemed to take over the house. To Dave Ball, my partner in historic crime, who supported, encouraged, and pushed me to finish this project also a special thanks. This book is dedicated to them. Finally to Ray Freden, Chris Brown, and the many people I interviewed and gave me photos, stories, advice and materials: Cynthia Krusell, Arthur Brown, Bob Branca, Bob Graci, Janet Fairbanks, Captain Robert Paine, Roger Crawford, Linda Hughes, Rob Mitchell, Pat Arnold, Ruth Wile, Keith Dobie, Jane McNamara, Bob English, Russ, Gina, and Dan Clark, Peter Noyes, Doctor and Charlie Mahanor, Mary Ellen Mastriani, Michael Callahan, Dolly Snow Bicknell, Tom Callahan, Bob Gallagher, Paul Armstrong, Bill Frugoli, Janet Peterson and countless others whose names would fill several pages – I can not express how grateful I am to you.

To three individuals who are no longer with us but who shared a love of and passion for Humarock: Marjorie Mahanor, Richie Mahanor, and Bob Brian. Marjorie, Bob, and Richie, it is finished! Thank you for all the stories, materials, and refreshments as we shared our love of Humarock. God Bless You All!

Contents

Introduction

No synonym for God is so perfect as Beauty. Whether as seen carving the lines of the mountains with glaciers, or gathering matter into stars, or planning the movements of water, or gardening still all is Beauty! -John Muir

I have lived in the Humarock area for forty-five years and have witnessed many changes over those years. But the one thing that hasn't changed over this span of years has been my gratitude at having chosen this for my home. The beauty and variety of the natural wonders during all seasons astounds me daily. A large blue heron had decided this past summer that our

backyard garden was a perfect spot for a takeout meal. If you are a chipmunk or a small rodent, you enter this garden area at your own peril. My wife photographed this heron catching and devouring a chipmunk and later observed him catching a mouse. As I startled the heron one morning, a long, harsh squawk of annoyance erupted as his six foot wingspan majestically lifted and sped him off into the far marsh to seek an alternate meal. Over the years I have become an avid bird watcher as small birds of all varieties arrive to feast on my wife's bird feeders, or in the case of some bigger birds to pick at the leftovers that have spilled onto the ground. Recently hummingbirds have zeroed in on some new plants my wife Jean had purchased just for this purpose.

The marshes that surround my property are alive with all types of birds depending on the season. When the marsh hawk arrives, the smaller birds disappear in short order and await his departure. Two of our birdhouses have become favorite birthing facilities. We have observed different birds making new nests in them twice this past summer. Activity abounds around these houses all summer as residents first construct new homes, incubate the eggs, and then feed their young when hatched. Finally the young, under watchful parental eyes, take flight and are now on their own. Another interesting sight is to observe the bird bath. Some birds dive right in, splash around shaking the wings in a wild dance while others sit sedately on the edge and politely dip in a beak for their afternoon refreshment. Some uncouth louts arrive at the bath and land so that they face away from the water and use it as their personal latrine. Birds are only some of the observed life.

Another favorite time for me is sunset. The myriad hues as the sun sets with blue turning slowly into grays and pinks with clouds acting like an artist wildly blending colors on his

palette then adding them to his canvas thus creating a spectacular image, is truly awe-inspiring. I sometimes wish that I had the talent to capture on canvas the marsh grasses as they slowly begin their change from the green hues of early spring and summer to golden yellow of autumn, as well as the trees as their leaves fill in during spring,

turn bright green with summer, and then become a feast of color for autumn eyes. The bite of winter cold and its starkness have a beauty all their own as the winter sun slowly sinks into the west. I once remember walking over to the ocean after several weeks of bitter January cold only to find that the ocean had frozen over out more than a quarter of a mile. What a strange sight to see waves trapped under the ice, yet still progressing to the shore while changing the ice's shape with its movement. Stranger yet was the sound, or the lack of a sound, as I watched transfixed with the waves rolling in under the ice.

Over the millennia, three visitors to Humarock have had an impact on this land. The first visitor was the last glacier about 15,000 years ago, which by its movement shaped and molded this land. The second visitor, was actually a set of visitors; they were nomadic Native Americans who hunted and settled along the North and South River valley. During the winter their habitat was nestled around the ponds that are now in Pembroke, and then as food became more abundant, they moved and summered along the coast in what is now Scituate and Marshfield. The final set of visitors at first came from Europe and Africa. They began to arrive in the late 16th century and into the early 17th century. Later other visitors journeyed here from many other parts of the world. All these groups of visitors and their interactions affected the land that we now call our home - Humarock. This book will attempt to narrate their many and varied stories.

Aerial view of Humarock from ocean looking at main bridge with Holly Hill in the background - Date unknown, photo courtesy of Scituate Historical Society

Visitors to Humarock

"There's always a story. It's all stories, really. The sun coming up every day is a story. Everything's got a story in it. Change the story, change the world." — Terry Pratchett

Glacial Impact

As I gazed out my front window and watched the sun slowly rise out of the ocean and blanket marsh, dunes, hill and river with a majestic coating of color, I reflected on the vast span of years and the many stories, known and unknown, that have unfolded over this landscape. The story of Humarock began long before the colonial period with its European dominancy; even before Native American tribes roamed and settled this land.

Our story began in the dim past, millennia ago, as the last glacier, like a Titanic Rodin, continuously sculpted and contoured the lands of North America, particularly the lands we call today Scituate and Marshfield. The North River valley, the North and South rivers and tributaries, cliffs, hills, marshes, sandy peninsulas, and barrier beaches were the results of this glacial sculpturing. To appreciate Humarock's story one must begin with an understanding of the effects of the last glacial epoch.

"The Laurentide glacier pushed south or southeast across Plymouth County.... The ice covered our landscape for a million years. As the glacier melted, the run-off (melt-water) became the North and South rivers and their tributaries. Large blocks of ice that broke off and melted also formed kettle ponds. The hills of Marshfield, Pembroke, and Duxbury are called moraines. The deposits are known as Glacial drift and bowlder clay. There was lots of sand mixed in, too. If the hills were egg-shaped they were called drumlins.... The four Scituate cliffs are drumlins with the seaward sides washed away by waves (Vinal, p.26)."

As previously stated, Fourth Cliff was one of many drumlins that were formed beneath the great ice sheet. Colman's Hill in Scituate is an example of an east-west terminal moraine, yet another glacial creation. Both are good examples of continuity and change in nature. As the centuries have passed, Mother Nature through erosion has substantially reduced the size of drumlins, eskers, and moraines. Man has also had a hand in these changes as well. There are many residents who have seen old pictures of Eaton's Hotel perched high above Greenbush and many more who remember the Boston Sand and Gravel operation on the Driftway. But as the years pass, fewer and fewer inhabitants know the stories of what happened to the Colman's Hill that Thoreau once walked upon.

As the glaciers disappeared, the next agent of change, Native Americans, arrived on the scene.

Top: View of the Eaton Hotel with its 100 steps to the top in Greenbush on Colman Hills. Bottom: Eaton Hotel on hill in distance with Old Oaken Bucket pond and Mill (next to Ice House) in Greenbush in foreground.

Thoreau Brothers once walked here

Driftway: removal of Colman Hills

Holly Hill from Humarock

The Site of the Boston Sand and Gravel Company

In 1914, the Boston Sand and Gravel Company bought mining rights to the Coleman Hills and began to remove them. The sand was loaded on train and by barge, headed for Boston to create the foundation for Logan Airport. In the two pictures from this page we see the Boston Sand and Gravel vessel Noble-Maxwell leaving the North River with sand for Boston. Between 1922 and 1931, the company removed 48,000 tons of sand and gravel, or 2,000 tons per day for

Noble-Maxwell steaming through the new inlet; Fourth Cliff in foreground. C.1920s

six days a week. From 1947 to 1963, barges towed by tugboats **(see pictures on the next page)** moved 200,000 tons per year. Most of Colman's Hills, that once stood forty feet high, disappeared entirely. A network of roads evolved and moved with the operation, sliding along the Driftway to meet the needs of the latest excavation. In all, 14,000,000 tons of sand were transported to Boston. The complex network of trails and access to the ocean made it an ideal landing-place for illegal bootleg liquor in the late twenties. Almost anyone with access to a power boat during Prohibition could travel the two sea miles to offshore, and even when the Coast Guard increased its surveillance, Scituate's drinkers were seldom thirsty. By the early sixties, the open-pit mine had pretty much played out, and on July 18. 1963, the buildings caught fire in a fire second only in townspeople's memory to the Cliff Hotel blaze.

Noble-Maxwell in North River 1930s

Today, the new Massachusetts Bay Transit Authority Greenbush commuter rail station, the town's recycling and transfer centers, and the Widow's Walk Golf Course stand where George H. Eaton once thought he'd find his fortune. The Driftway Conservation Park offers picnic tables and a boat launching site where once lobster boats unloaded cases of Canadian Club. The remains of the old docks now overlook the salt marshes that first attracted the Men of Kent over 375 years ago.

Off to Boston - Pictures of Boston Sand and Gravel - February 28, 1960 (Notice 4th Cliff in the top photo)

Native Americans

Humankind has not woven the web of life. We are but one thread within it. Whatever we do to the web, we do to ourselves. All things are bound together. All things connect.

- Chief Seattle, Duwamish (1780-1866)

The story surrounding the Native Americans who first populated North America is a narrative that is constantly changing as new archaeological sites are discovered and explored, and old theories of migration debated, then changed or debunked, or finally modified reflecting new understandings. Added to this academic debate is the fact that most Americans' knowledge and understanding of Native American tribes is poor, based on myths, or simply wrong, which has led to a misrepresentation of the past, particularly in the writing of local history. Again, this book is not an attempt to explain the complex social, economic, cultural, and political world views of the many tribes that composed the various geographic regions of North America, nor is it an attempt to explain the complex relationships between Native Americans and the first Europeans and Africans who came here, but simply to tell the story of Humarock's history in a simple, truthful, and understandable way.

But first, several misperceptions of Native Americans needed to be addressed. The first is that there is no one, universal Native American culture. Native Americans adapted to their habitats and environments. Their ways of living and beliefs reflected their adaptation to their particular land. Hence southwestern native beliefs, ways of living, and languages were different from northeastern ones. Most of the Native Americans living in the Scituate and Marshfield area were Algonkian. This is not a culture, but a language group. Many tribes of the northeast region spoke Algonkian; the other large language group there was Iroquoian. Over North and South America there are 25 language families of which Algonkian and Iroquoian are but two. A second misperception about Native American cultures is about cultural areas or divisions. To help geographers and

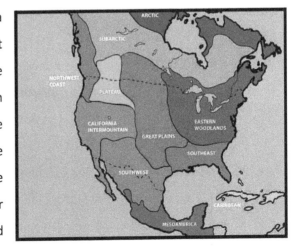

anthropologists study Native American groups, ten culture areas, or rough groupings of contiguous peoples who shared similar habitats and characteristics, were established. The culture area of particular interest to us was called the Northeast. It stretched from the east coast of Canada all the way south to North Carolina and inland to the Mississippi River valley.

"Its inhabitants were members of two main groups: Iroquoian speakers (these included the Cayuga, Oneida, Erie, Onondaga, Seneca and Tuscarora), most of whom lived along inland rivers and lakes in fortified, politically stable villages, and the more numerous Algonquian speakers (these included the Pequot, Fox, Shawnee, Wampanoag, Delaware and Menominee) who lived in small farming and fishing villages along the ocean. There, they grew crops like corn, beans and vegetables.

Life in the Northeast culture area was already fraught with conflict—the Iroquoian groups tended to be rather aggressive and warlike, and bands and villages outside of their allied confederacies were never safe from their raids— and it grew more complicated when European colonizers arrived (http://www.history.com/topics/native-american-history/native-american-cultures)."

The third misconception that must be remembered is that with the arrival of Europeans in the late 16th century things were changed radically. So radically that historians and anthropologists called it the Columbian Exchange. This exchange impacted the whole world in many ways both for the good and for the bad. For Native Americans the encounter left an estimated 90% of them dead because they lacked immunity from European, Asian, and African diseases. In addition Colonial wars repeatedly forced the region's natives to take sides, pitting the Iroquois groups against their Algonquian neighbors; in some cases pitting tribe against tribe in their own confederacy. Meanwhile, as white settlement pressed westward, it eventually displaced both sets of indigenous people from their lands.

Let us examine the tribes of New England of interest to us. Thirty tribes made their homes in what today composes Massachusetts, Connecticut, Rhode Island, and New Hampshire. (Massachusetts then was made up of today's Maine and Massachusetts). Some of the larger tribes were the Wampanoags, Narragansetts, Pequots, and Nipmucs while some of the smaller tribes like the Podunk, the Pocasset, and Mohegan were caught between their more powerful neighbors. Place this in the context of a larger struggle between Iroquoian speakers and Algonkian speakers and the arrival of Europeans with very different motivations for settlement, and a recipe for disaster is present. Therefore, it is important to understand the complexity of our story as it unfolds.

With this broad overview, let us begin with Samuel Deane in his History of Scituate, Mass., from 1831, to view his perception:

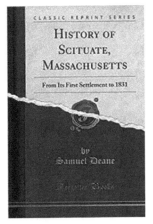

"Scituate, like most of the towns in Plymouth Colony, had been nearly depopulated of the natives by the small pox, a few years before the English made a permanent settlement on this coast. But there were many evidences left, that is, that it had been thickly peopled. They were the Matakeesetts, and controlled by the chief or sachem of the Massachusetts. The principal encampment of the remnants of this tribe at the time Scituate was settled, was about the ponds in Pembroke. They visited the sea shore often for fishing and fowling, but not many resided here.... (Deane, p. 143)."

Deane extolled the early settlers of Scituate saying that even though the region was almost devoid of Native Americans, they, the settlers, were conscientious enough to purchase Indian title to the land for a fair price. He then proceeded to cite two documents to prove his point. He concluded his Aborigine section with,

"It has been very common for people to lament over the fallen fortunes of the Natives of these shores, and to criminate the forefathers for driving them from their wonted forests, and occupying their lands by force or purchasing them for an inadequate trifle. As general remarks, we believe these to be the cant of very superficial readers and reasoners, and certainly without the least truth or pertinency so far as respects Plymouth Colony. The lands were purchased whenever a tribe could be found to allege the slightest claim. The sums paid were small, but they were a sufficient compensation to the few wandering natives whom the pestilence had spared, and who could make no use of the lands; nay, they were often above the full value of the lands to the English. These lands were a dangerous and uncultivated wilderness, and had they been received without compensation, they would have been a perilous and costly possession. Plymouth Colony claimed not a foot of land but by fair purchase, save the little districts of Pocasset, Showamett, Assonet and Mount Hope, and these were dearly won, if ever lands were so won, by conquering an unjust and unrelenting enemy. There is reason to lament that the authorities of Plymouth yielded to the imaginary necessity of executing the brave Anawon, and especially that they sold into slavery Metacomet's (Philip's) youthful son: but the justice and humanity generally shown to the natives, will be more apparent, the more we examine the subject. "Philip's Boy goes now to be sold," (see letter from John Cotton, March 19, 1676-7, Cotton papers) (Deane pp. 145-146).)

What was your reaction to the above sources? What did you learn? To me, Deane seemed to make a point that the English settlers paid a fair amount to wandering natives for their land. As the centuries have passed, we have found that his story, so seemingly simple, was much more complex then Deane's could ever have imagined.

The first point is that our knowledge of Native Americans has been limited by time, biases, and lack of information and understanding of what constituted the lives of Native Americans. Today, what we have ascertained is that some tribes of Native Americans wintered in the area of today's Pembroke around the ponds located there, and during the summer they moved their homes to the seashore where food was more abundant and easily acquired. They farmed corn, beans, squash and tobacco extensively, but relied on fish and shellfish during the summer months. During the cold months of early fall, winter, and early spring the native peoples supplemented their food supplies by hunting. Because of their nomadic life styles, a well-defined network of transportation had also developed. This network followed streams and routes that had the easiest terrain, as Native Americans traveled either by foot or by water. This system of trails, paths, and waterways evolved and changed over the period before the European arrival. Paths and trails connected these seasonal camps and settlements where in the spring plants were gathered, cornfields planted, and fish caught. There has been much evidence of this Native American activity from arrowheads to woven fish weirs found from Mattakeesett ponds, along the North River banks, to the Scituate seashore over time, as well as the presence of goods clearly acquired by trade networks that stretched all over North America.

A second point integral to our understanding is that the Native Americans were decimated by diseases brought from Europe, Africa, and Asia. Scholarly estimates are that 90% of the indigenous people died from diseases carried by unknowing visitors. Jared Diamond, in his best-selling book *Guns, Germs, and Steel,* raised in Chapter 1 what he called Yali's Question: "Why is it that you white people developed so much cargo and brought it to New Guinea, but we black people had little cargo of our own? It was a simple question that went to the heart of life as Yali experienced it. Yes, there still is a huge difference between the lifestyle of the average New Guinean and that of the average European or American. Comparable differences separate the lifestyles of other peoples of the world as well. Those huge disparities must have potent causes that one might think would be obvious. . . . Thus, questions about inequality in the modern world can be reformulated as follows. Why did wealth and power become distributed as they now are, rather than in some other way? For instance, why weren't Native Americans, Africans, and Aboriginal Australians the ones who decimated, subjugated, or exterminated Europeans and Asians (Diamond, pp. 14-15)?" The answer for me has already been answered – Germs! Europe, Africa, and Asia had several things going for them that the Americas did not; population in Europe, Africa, and Asia combined had a much larger population than the Americas. If you have more people, you will have more diseases. Second, Europe, Africa, and Asia had more domesticated animals like pigs, cows, dogs, sheep that were not in the Americas. This meant that more diseases were able to make the jump from animals to humans in Europe, Africa, and Asia than in the Americas. Finally, when diseases struck for the first time the number of people who died was extreme, but the survivors passed on resistance to these diseases to their children. Because of the geographical isolation of the Americas, diseases that had routinely made the rounds of Europe, Africa, and Asia had never been to the Americas, so when the first Europeans, Africans, and Asians came to the Americas all the mixed diseases took a fearful toll of lives. In return, the America's farmers had crops that were very healthy, nutritious, and vegetarian, like corn and potatoes, as well as a well-balanced diets. The result was that disease-resistant Euro-Afro-Asian became even healthier. What did Native Americans receive from the exchange? Coffee, sugar cane, and bananas, but the problem here was that these crops required much hard manual labor, which led to enslavement of the Native American workers. Then with Native Americans dying both from the diseases brought over to them and the hard manual labor of plantation life, Europeans needed a new labor source who would be disease-resistant. They found them in Africans, which in turn explained the vast number of Africans forced into the Americas as slaves on sugar, tobacco, and cotton plantations. The Small pox virus, the pig, potato, and a kernel of corn are really more important historical characters in the chronicle of the Americas than Columbus, Cortes, Moctezuma, and Pizarro. Why should we know about the Columbian Exchange? It explains why we have tomato sauce on our pasta; why European nations became the most wealthy and powerful nations in the world; why Portuguese is spoken in Brazil while Spanish is spoken in most other South American countries; and finally what you think about American history may be all wrong.

After the passage of over 150 years Samuel Deane, a Congregational minister, still justified the taking of Indian land and the subsequent victory in the Indian wars of the 17th century by the English. Do Deane's justifications for the taking of Indian lands, because they did not make use of them and because they were an unrelenting enemy, resonate positively or negatively with you today? Especially in light of the fact that maybe the success of the Pilgrims and Puritans was not that their God was on their side to give them good health and fortune, but that their immune systems were the difference.

What did the Native Americans of the Humarock area leave as their legacy besides evidence of their settlements and artifacts? Three answers sprang to my mind: their love of and respect for the land, their Native names, and the paths from their seasonal camps to their settlements. Some modern apologists mythologized the Native American life style and impact on the land by stating that they were a peaceful people who did little to change the land. This disguised the conflict between not just tribes of the Iroquoian and Algonkian language groups, but conflict among the language groups themselves. Secondly, native peoples did have an impact on the land, but not as great as European settlers. A Native American custom of regularly burning the leaves under the trees in Fall or Spring prevented the growth of a dense thick underbrush. Later, as beaver skins became highly valuable as trade items, Native Americans hunted them near to extinction. Native American respect for the land came from the very flexible tribal boundaries and their belief that no one owns the land. This belief would become one of the main sources of conflict with European settlers.

Native American names are still with us, from some of our states' names (Alabama, Alaska, Connecticut, and Massachusetts) to names of our mountains (Mount Greylock, Taconic), rivers (Merrimac/k), lakes, falls (Niagara), animals (Caribou, moose, raccoon), fish, cities, towns (Scituate, Cohasset), counties, parks, and byways (Mohawk Trail, Cherokee Hill Byway, Geronimo Trail Scenic Byway) throughout the region, and finally barbecue (Taino), skunk (Massachusetts), kayak (Inuit), and hammock (Taino). My favorite is Lake Chargoggagoggmanchauggagoggchaubunagungamaugg, or today's Lake Webster. It, too, was formed by a glacier and it, too, has a name that it is still debated.

Native Americans' final legacy was their paths and trails throughout the area. Many of these trails and paths were later adopted and enlarged as cattle paths and to colonial bridle paths and eventually highways in modern days. In the Humarock area the main highway for native use was the North River, but two other main trails or paths were utilized.

"Soon needing an overland route along which to drive their livestock from Plymouth to Marshfield, the settlers began to use an ancient Indian way that led along the edge of Plymouth Bay. It followed the beach in North Plymouth through present-day Kingston, crossing the Jones River at the old Wading Place near Rocky Nook, and continuing through Duxbury west of present Route 3A/Tremont Street, to enter Marshfield at the Duxbury line at Careswell Street. This old way continued through Marshfield, crossed the South River at a narrow place known as the Valley Bars, and ran along the foot of Snake Hill to a ferry crossing of the North River near the present Humarock Bridge. This early road was recognized and formally designated by the Plymouth Court on 10 May 1637. It was, quite possibly, the first court-ordered road in America. It was called the Green's Harbor Path, since it led to Green's Harbor. In Marshfield it was often referred to as the Plymouth Path or the Scituate Path, depending on which direction the traveler was headed (Krusell and Bates, p.6)."

This path would later become a recognized public cartway during the 18th century. When John Hiland in 1726, claiming ownership of the southern section of Fourth Cliff from the North River to the ocean, put a fence across to block access, he was ordered by a Justice of the Peace to tear it down because it was the "Common Road" between Scituate and Marshfield. When the Town gave the Fourth Cliff Land Company a quitclaim deed to all the land or Hummocks below Fourth Cliff between the North River and the ocean to low water mark in 1884 and after the Fourth Cliff Land Company had the land surveyed and a plan of house lots was drawn up by Frank Wadleigh in February of 1882, it became imperative that a road be laid out. This came to fruition with a meeting held on April 9, 1889 at the Hotel Humarock. "On petition of Charles A. Jackson, J.S. Greely, E.P. Welch, E.H. Bonney and others that a town way be laid out and opened to the public from the northerly end of Fourth Cliff and running over the Fourth Cliff and Humarock association's land to Marshfield Avenue so called The Selectmen notified the resident owners of the land over which the way would probably be located. They would meet at the Hotel Humarock on the ninth day of April at 10 o'clock a.m. 1889 for the purpose of laying out Said way also posted names of Parties notified J.S. Greely W.O. Merritt and Fourth Cliff land company, April 9th the Selectmen met at Hotel Humarock according to notice given and after hearing what parties interested had to say proceeded to lay out Said way."

Central Avenue to the left. Tapley house on the right. View from the Post Office.

Another path from Humarock went over Fourth Cliff across the barrier beach to Third Cliff along the Driftway to what is today Route 123 to River Road to Hanover Four Corners and on to the ponds at Pembroke. "Doubtless, the migrating Indians came along this route in their seasonal migration, intent on fishing, hunting or trading with various other tribes and settlers. Artifacts, many more than 5,000 years of age, are being unearthed along the river banks and inland even now by archaeological groups. While there was actually a well-defined network of trails and roads crisscrossing the colonial land grants, the present state roads were laid out with the advent of motorized transportation. Their somewhat erratic design attests to their heritage and origin.... With these facts in mind, one particular individual in Scituate decided that perhaps special attention could be brought to the history and heritage of this extensive and meandering roadway." Bob Ladd, an avid history buff, organized his information and forwarded it to his representative at the time, Frank Hynes who took it from there. On April 16, 1985 a state law was passed that designated "...route 123 in the town of Scituate, presently known as Cornet Stetson Road, shall be designated and known as Old Satuit Trail (Scituate Mariner pp. 3-4)." Here was a clear connection between the past and present.

The Third agent of change to Humarock was the European, Asian, and African connection of the Columbian Exchange. The cultural and ecological impact of this third agent continues to the present day and will into the future. Individual chapters will highlight some of these changes in more detail.

Left photo: Bob Fagan 1930 Humarock Beach. Right photo: Humarock Beach 1930. Pictures courtesy of Pat Arnold. Used with her permission.

Above: Barrier Beach Connecting Fourth and Third Cliff – Shown from Fourth Cliff. Below Women on barrier beach looking toward Fourth Cliff.

What's In A Name?

"What's in a name? That which we call a rose
By any other name would smell as sweet." Romeo and Juliet (II, ii, 1-2)

'What is in a name? Very much if the wit of man could find it out.' The anonymous writer who penned this well known saying undoubtedly had it right. What better place to begin than with the name Humarock, or is it Hummocks, or is it Sea View, or is it some other appellation that has yet to stand the test of time? Communication is the act or process of using words, sounds, signs, or behaviors to express or exchange information or to express your ideas, thoughts, feelings, etc., to someone else. Because of Humarock's history of settlement by different groups, we need to realize that the first settlers, the Native Americans, had many different language groups. Even though some tribes and subtribes spoke Algonkian, the different dialects were not understandable by some subgroups. Then, after the first European settlements, the Puritan settlers mispronounced, misheard, and misreported what they heard. In some cases the first Native American words were heard by terrified, prejudiced Puritans. Finally, consider that, according to a compilation of New England Indian Place Names written in 1962, the author stated that 300 years from the Pilgrims' landing at Plymouth the Wampanoag, Natick, Nipmuck, Narragansett, Pequot, Mohegan, Wappinger, Mahican, Pocumtuck, and Pennacook tongues had all disappeared. Take the Swampscott as an example. The native term Musquompskat became Swampscott. Now add the fact that 17th century Englishmen spelled their own names six, seven, or eight different ways and the chance for error has exponentially increased. Finally, include the opportunity for someone to perpetrate a hoax or joke like Larry Daly, an editor of the Webster Times, did sometime around the 1920's regarding what Lake Webster's name meant. The popular, but inaccurate, translation of the lake name is: "You fish on your side, I fish on my side, and nobody fishes in the middle." A more accurate translation seems to be something like: "English knifemen and Nipmuc Indians at the Border or Neutral Fishing Place" or "Englishmen at Manchaug at the Fishing Place at the Boundary." This example illustrates the danger in quoting a Native American source as well as a story's general reliability.

With all this in mind, let us consider 'How Humarock got its Name". In two sources I found the following: Humarock (Wampanoag) - "shell place" or "rock carving". This first source was **Wikipedia.org/wiki/Humarock** - it added that, "etymology can be traced back to Edward Rowe Snow . . . ." The second source was *Indian Place Names for New England* compiled by John C. Haden printed in New York by the Heye Foundation for the Museum of the American Indian in 1962 p. 71. The entry was:

Humarock Plymouth County, Mass.? *Wampanoag*? "shell place"? or "rock carving"?.

In the introduction to his book (pp. xii - xiii) Haden explained how to read the above,

> "....The form used throughout this listing presents the Indian place names in boldface type, using the most-commonly-seen spelling; this is followed by any secondary term in lightface . . . ; then the location is given by county and state for all place names included. When followed by ?, this indicates that the place name has been found in early documents, but that its actual place is not known for certain today. The dialect or language is indicated in italics; if doubtful, that doubt is shown by ?. Suggested translation of the name, and any comments are then given, followed by variant spellings or cross-references, the latter in boldface. Thus all actual place names are in boldface, linguistic terms are in italics, and the balance is in lightface type throughout the listing.
>
> Selection of the names to be included has been primarily based on the occurrence of names on historic or quadrangle maps, their appearance in a historical document, or in any generally-accepted work of literature...."

Well, so much for Name version 1.

Name version 2 is that Humarock developed from "The Humming Rocks". Willard de Lue in a series of articles on the South Shore explained this version. According to this version the crash of the surf on the rocks accounts for this name. Another version of this story is placed in colonial times. A group of Tories arrived at Humarock at night and slept along the beach and were awakened to the Humming Rocks in the morning. Well, do you like Willard's version?

Name version 3 is that the area is Humarock, Seaview, or Sea View. In an early 1950's article about Humarock, Raymond W. Beecher of Reading, who had summered in the area for eight years as a boy and young man, wrote to Williard de Lue, "You said that you believed there once was a hotel at the road which ends at the Humarock oceanfront when the railroad station, the village, and even the beach was just plain Seaview." He continued, "There certainly was a hotel there. . . and today, right across from where it stood, is the oldest cottage now on the beach, belonging in 1897 to a Mr. Jackson. There were only about a dozen cottages on Humarock Beach at the time." De Lue also heard from Herbert I. Jackson, an old acquaintance and the son of Mr. Jackson mentioned by Beecher. "My father organized the company that built the bridge from White's Ferry to Humarock. I was marooned there for three or four seasons." He added, "The marooned being his idea of beach life for a young fellow in the early days . . . though he says that later on there was a skating rink - about where the post office is now." (Note: Post office in the 1950's was located in Clark's store, not where it is today in 2018.) Many

news articles in the late 1890s and into the early 1900s interchanged Humarock, Seaview, and Sea View, which led to false assumption that the emerging resort of Humarock and the Marshfield village of Sea View were the same, or worse that Sea View was an extension of Humarock. This assumption is incorrect and does

a disservice to Sea View's long and illustrious history. This misrepresentation continued to be perpetuated as Humarock continued to be developed. The brochures of the Hotel Humarock advertised, "The Hotel outside and its environments has also received attention. New walks have been added; the drives to and about the hotel rejuvenated, and this season the hotel will be connected, by the extension of one of the most beautiful drives in the country – the famous Jerusalem Road, an almost unbroken drive from Hull and Nantasket to the Humarock." This appeared in the 1891 brochure. The 1900 brochure stated, "Beautiful country drives to Marshfield Hills, Scituate Harbor, Peggotty Beach, "Old Oaken Bucket," Jerusalem Road, Nantasket, Home of Daniel Webster, Miles Standish Monument, and to all haunts around Historic Plymouth." It later added, ". . . [The Hotel] is one mile from the station at Sea View, over a good road with beautiful country scenery a grand view of ocean and north." Notice that there is no real mention of how historic and vibrant with its own cultural life Sea View was. Add to this that new transplants to the area, myself included, were ignorant of Sea View's rich

history; even when told of Sea View's historic past some transplants stubbornly cling to being part of Humarock. Is it any wonder that a long-time resident of Sea View in frustration demanded, ". . . Now back to Sea View, the lost village of Marshfield. It disturbs me to the bone how Humarock has eroded the historic Sea View along the formally North River and now South River. Humarock was practically unknown when Sea View was a thriving industrial village. Many ships were built at the Hall, Keene shipyards & White's Ferry yard. Humarock was known to duck hunters and a passage across the river to Boston. Sea View's boundaries are defined in my street listing of 1897 by the Post Office one used. The Northern line, shows the residences of Summer Streets & Flower Hill Lane went to the Sea View P.O. The Western line was at about Pleasant Street & Eames Way, also used the Sea View P.O., now, Ferry hill & Holly Hill were in the village of Sea View, along with Bayberry Point, Julian St bridge area to the Coast Guard station. The Bridgwaye is in Sea View along with Crawford Boats & the Yacht Club. That area all using the Sea View P.O. Tell me just how does Humarock deserve to claim historic Sea View??? Most Sea View residents don't know where they live.   "As a forty-five year plus resident of Sea View, I reject this version."

Finally, Version 4 and the one I believe is the most probable. In maps I have viewed back from the late 1800's to the late 1700's, the beach area is marked Shore Hummocks, Shore Hummock, Hummock Flats, Humock Flatt, Hummock Beach, and other variants. The 1831 map of Scituate was the only one labelled Humarock stretching from the base of fourth cliff to the old mouth. Hummock is a noun and has three meanings, two of which apply for us:

1. an elevated tract of land rising above the general level of a marshy region.
2. a knoll or hillock.

Many locales have a suffix "-rock". However, Hummockrock would be a difficult word to pronounce, but is clearly plausible as a variant of "Shore Hummocks." We have many such examples from our own history. Think of Charleston, South Carolina; originally it was Charles Town after England's King Charles II who had granted the land to eight of his loyal friends.

Which version do you prefer? Maybe you have your own version, variation, or an entirely new account. An acquaintance of mine came up with a humorous version. According to his tale, the first Native American who arrived here stubbed his toe on a stone as he stepped from his dugout canoe. Turning to his friends he stammered, "Hummm, a rock!" Take your pick, you have a lot to choose from.

Spectators on Humarock Bridge watch boat races

E. L. Josselyn, Sea View, Mass.   RIVERSIDE HOUSE, HUMAROCK BEACH

Top photo: Is the Riverside House in Humarock, not Sea View. Middle photo: Is Upland Road on Holly Hill but in Sea View. Bottom photo: Janet Clark 1938-39 Webster's oldest daughter with 1930 Ford Victoria sedan on the bridge.

Residence of E. A. De Witt, Holly Hill,   Humarock Beach, Mass.

THE BRIDGE, HUMAROCK BEACH, MASS.

Humarock's Geography

"(Media question to Beatles during first U.S. tour 1964)
"How do you find America?"
"Turn left at Greenland." — Ringo Starr

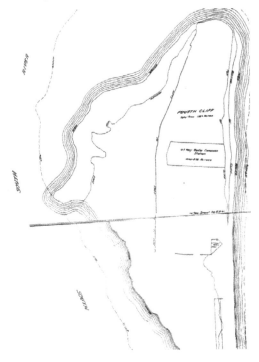

Humarock now is composed of three distinct geographic forms, but before November 26, 1898, there were four. Today moving southward from Third Cliff, there is the New Inlet of the North River, the Fourth Cliff, and rest part of a barrier beach that stretches from the base of the cliff to the Marshfield boundary at Rexhame Beach. Prior to November 26,1898, the sections were: a barrier beach that joined Third and Fourth cliffs, Fourth Cliff, another barrier beach stretching from the cliff's base south while the final section was outlet to the sea where the North and South Rivers merged and emptied into Massachusetts Bay.

> Looking south to the mouth of North and South rivers from the glass cupola on the top of the Hotel Humarock prior to 1898.

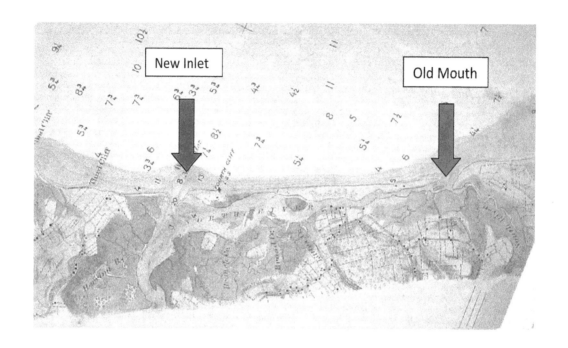

New Inlet

Old Mouth

Above picture 1903 chart showing Humarock as an island. Below picture of barrier beach between the cliffs

Today looking from 3rd Cliff to 4th Cliff –New Inlet

There have been many groups or associations that governed the activities of Humarock in the past as well as today. The governmental agencies are: the Town of Scituate, the State of Massachusetts, Plymouth County, and the Federal government. Residents' input and action have been represented by: the Fourth Cliff Land Company, The Fourth Cliff Club, The Humarock Beach Improvement Association, The South Humarock Civic Association, and the Scituate Coastal Coalition. As the times and needs changed over time, so did the activities of these citizen organizations. For example, today the government's recreation area is for all military personnel for leisure activities where as during World War II it was part of our coastal defenses with ordnance perched atop the cliff, ready for action. Note: The Julian Street Bridge was constructed to bring that ordnance to Fourth Cliff since the main bridge could not support its weight. One group has disbanded, the Fourth Cliff Land Company; however, this group was active in developing house lots in Humarock. They also met with the Selectmen of Scituate in the Hotel Humarock in the late 1880s and laid out Central Avenue from the southern base of Fourth Cliff to Marshfield Avenue. The Tapley family members of the Fourth Cliff Land Company were also instrumental in Humarock's development plus giving to the Town of Scituate land for a firehouse, parking area,

Stock Certificate HBIA Real Estate Trust

and tennis courts for recreational purposes, as well as public access to the beach. One HBIA fundraising activity was to offer shares in the Humarock Beach Improvement Real Estate Trust for $100.00 per share in 1926. Number 16 share was issued to Edward M. Peters, witnessed the 24th day of November 1926. The HBIA was active in the late 1920s and early 1930s in dealing with the issue of parking in Humarock. The purposes for which the HBIA was incorporated was to "promote the interests of the citizens and owners of property on Humarock Beach and localities adjacent thereto by aiding and securing social and municipal improvements in said localities and to provide social and recreational activities, and any other activity permissible under the current laws of the Commonwealth of Massachusetts." It is still active today. The South Humarock Civic Association, which has been active for 65+ years, is a non-profit organization whose headquarters is located at the Julian Street Bridge. Its fundraising activities have supported various civic and charitable causes in the area since 1945. Its many activities included dances for all ages, Bingo, yoga classes, July 4th races, Horribles Parade, and many other activities. Who could forget "The Horribles Parade!" My girls (late forties) still talk about the dances they attended at the South Humarock Civic Association building and being dressed up for the parade while we older folk remember the bingo nights and more recently the yoga classes for those intent on keeping physically fit and flexible. Having been a teacher, the Horribles Parade was the signal that summer was over for me and time to get back to work. Today I am retired, but still look forward to a rite of passage for me – the end of summer and the beginning of fall. When I was a Vice President of the Scituate Historical Society, the records of the Fourth Cliff

Club were donated to the Society, how active this group is in Humarock now is unknown to me, but following is some of the information I gleaned from their records. The Fourth Cliff Club, according to their records, was started in 1946. Boundaries of membership "shall be Central Avenue, north from the apex of Central Avenue and Cliff Road (with affiliated members)" from the apex and Atlantic Drive – 8/21/82 Cliff Road, River Road, and Silver Road. The purpose of the organization was twofold: 1. Civic improvement, 2. Social activities and the maintenance of recreational facilities. They also established that two meetings per year would be held. Under Civic improvement, they listed that a boardwalk to the beach is to be maintained by the Club, barrels for clean-up would be provided and paid to be emptied, members to be kept informed of town developments, an annual bloodmobile drive in Humarock, and an annual picnic to be held.

There were 32 paid members in 1950. The annual meeting was held at 4 o'clock on Sunday August 6th on the 'float.' The meeting lasted 55 minutes with the following motions voted on:

- Motion was made and seconded that two benches be built on the raft. Motion passed.
- Discussion followed whether to install lights or reflectors on raft. Motion made and seconded to have reflectors. President Thomes to handle the matter at his own discretion. Motion carried.
- Motion made and seconded to look into the matter of new road going up hill on waterfront. Committee of eight to be appointed by President. Four members to be natives and four non-residents. Motion carried, committee to stay on job until it has been accomplished.
- Some discussions about a sea wall matter to be taken up at a later date.
- Election of slate of officers: same officers were elected for another year: Willard Thomes president, Mike Lumenti, vice president, Chas. Blake, treasurer, Wilfred J. Croteau, secretary.

Included in the records donated to the Scituate Historical Society by Fourth Cliff Club was a letter from the Plymouth County Electric Company dated September 13, 1954, addressed to Mr. Kenneth E. Whiting of 710 Pleasant Street, Belmont, Mass. From L. J. Bradbury, Supt. Of Distribution. Mr. Bradbury wrote, "Dear Mr. Whiting: This is to acknowledge receipt of your letter of September 10, and to inform you that we realize that the load in the Humarock section of Scituate has been growing and and we plan to convert our primary circuit in that area to operate at 4160 wye volts instead of at 2400 volts delta as at present. This will give increased capacity to this circuit and should help to improve voltage conditions. We plan to have this work completed before the next summer season. In regard to adequate transformer capacity, if you are referring to any particular location it will be helpful if you will let us know, and we will have an engineering study made of those locations to determine if any changes in the transformers are necessary. Thank you for bringing this matter to our attention. Very truly yours, L. J. Bradbury.

The Fourth Cliff Club on October 22, 1966, petitioned the town that between #254 and #276 on Central Avenue – water accumulates and does not drain off. There have been many occasions when automobiles have become stalled in the water and had to be towed, according to Mr. Covell of the Humarock Garage. This petition was signed by eleven permanent residents. On November 17, 1966, the town responded. Mr. Bamber, Superintendent of Public Works, stated that the problem was caused by fill blocking the prior natural drainage to the marsh. His recommendation was to survey, study, and have cost estimate made. He added that he would try to include this in the budget for 1967. Lester J. Gates, chairman signed the town's response. In a November 8, 1966, letter from Gladys Hennigar to Mary Mulvey, Gladys wrote, " Dear Mary, I am enclosing the list to you as not having seen you I am afraid we may be too late sending it in as their budget may be all figured out for next year. Evidently another house is going in down near the others on the river side as the lot says "Sold" So guess we shall have to get some oars to cross the road. How did you like the storm last Sun.? It was awful down here. Best regards to all the family. Sincerely – Gladys H."

The second meeting of 1971 focused on the newly formed Humarock Community Council goals, which were that the parking lot at the center be restricted to Scituate residents only; that zone D for fire insurance instead of zone B; and the Scituate exchange used for the telephone.

In 1972 a motion was unanimously passed that Fourth Cliff Club stay separate and not be a party to any other group (Humarock Beach Improvement Association discussed – marina at Hatch's.)

1973 floodplain control approved at March 1972 Town Meeting: from Fourth Cliff to Newell St. there can be no building in general, except for piers, subject to a public hearing.

1977: Unanimous vote to stay as the Fourth Cliff Club to protect their identity. Also the walk and float on Jerry Sherman's land open to everyone was noted. Their final item was to approve $60 to repair the walk to the beach. Gerard J. Mulvey, president of the Fourth Cliff Club wrote a letter to David A. Nellis, Chairman regarding the public hearing scheduled for

August 18, 1977, at 9:00 pm pertaining to the rebuilding and repairing of the cat walk on the property of Mr. and Mrs. Alton Sherman. Mulvey wanted to go on record along with Mr. and Mrs. Alton Sherman, Mulvey and his wife Mary, the members of the Fourth Cliff Club, and residents in the area, as strongly in favor of this walk being repaired and rebuilt. He cites the history of the walk and maintenance records that proved the use and maintenance of the walkway. "This walk is the only access that the residents in the area have to the South River. . ." Mulvey added that Mr. and Mrs. Alton Sherman who own the land have assured everyone that they will continue to allow people to cross their land to enjoy the river. Since the walk is raised and no part rested on the marsh, Mulvey failed to see what damage could be done to the environment.

1981: The issue of tearing down the pier, which was built in the 1940s, was under discussion. After voted 22 votes for keeping it and 3 to tear it down.

1982: A meeting was held on Saturday July 3, 1982, at 3:30 pm at the home of Brad Dooley. The four officers were: Brad Dooley, president, Vincent George, vice-president, Sally Thomas, secretary, Cheryl Strazdes, treasurer. The Executive Board was composed of the four officers and John Thomas. The Annual Picnic was scheduled for August 7, 1982, and the Annual Meeting August 28, 1982. Annual dues were $5.00 per family – payable to the treasurer by August 1, 1982. The agenda was lengthy with reports on: acceptance of minutes, Treasurer's and Town Meeting Report, Off-Road Vehicles. There was also a discussion on By-Law change, Beach Clean-up, Board Walk Area Project and the Annual Cook-out. The final items included a Nominating Committee and Old and New Business.

FOURTH CLIFF CLUB RULES

1–SMALL CHILDREN OR CHILDREN WHO CAN'T SWIM ARE NOT ALLOWED ON THE FLOAT, WITHOUT SUPERVISION.

2–DO NOT PUSH OTHERS ON THE FLOAT INTO THE WATER

3–NO BOATS ARE TO BE TIED UP TO THE FLOAT, OR THE WALK TO THE FLOAT, AT ANY TIME.

4–LIFE PRESERVERS AND THE ROPE ON THE LIFE PRESERVERS ARE NOT TO BE TAMPERED WITH.

5–DO NOT THROW STONES ON THE BEACH.

6–PLEASE KEEP THE BEACH CLEAN. DO NOT BE A LITTERBUG.

7–RESPECT THE PROPERTY OF OTHERS.

8–PLEASE DO NOT BRING BOTTLES OR GLASS CONTAINERS TO THE BEACH.

9–CLEAN THE FLOAT AFTER CLEANING FISH. OTHER PEOPLE USE THE FLOAT, BE CONSIDERATE OF OTHERS.

THANK YOU FOR YOUR COOPERATION.

These groups' activities have waxed and waned dependent on membership, issues, and residents' interest. Currently the Scituate Coastal Coalition is pursuing its goal "to unite the voices and actions of the ten beach associations in order to work more effectively on issues of particular importance to the population living along Scituate's coastline. Among those issues are public health, public safety, flood mitigation measures, storm preparedness, and regulatory constraints as they pertain to coastal properties. Our stated goal will be to address concerns through the sharing of information and, when necessary, by taking action to interface with town and state officials on behalf of the coastal residents and property owners." As we age, trying to pass on our legacy to younger generations through civic organizations becomes difficult.

There are several ways to arrive in Humarock. One way is by boat if you own one. There are marinas, boat-landings, and launching sites on both sides of the river. The most common way of entrance is by truck or car over one of the two bridges that lead into Humarock. The main bridge into Humarock was named the Sea Street Bridge and was built in 1952 and replaced the one built in 1882. Before 1882, White's Ferry provided the only transport to Humarock from the Marshfield side. In 1998, in honor of the 100th

Main Bridge into Humarock built 1952 in 1998 renamed Frederick Stanley Bridge

anniversary of the Portland Gale the bridge was renamed the Frederick Stanley Bridge. Stanley was the long tenured keeper of the Fourth Cliff Life Saving Station that later became the Fourth

Cliff Coast Guard Station before it burned to the ground. Many local residents had enlisted the state and county officials to name the new bridge after Frederick Stanley. When the new construction was completed in December, 2008, the new bridge was The Frederick Stanley Bridge. Hopefully, the bridge will last for another 50 or 60 years. The second bridge called the Julian Street bridge was mentioned before. It had been built during World War II because the main bridge could not sustain the weight of the ordnance being brought to Fourth Cliff as part of the

Boston Harbor defense system. It had sustained damage from storms and was closed. Repairs were made, but before the new Frederick Stanley bridge was rebuilt, a new Julian Street bridge was needed. This was done before the main bridge was closed in 2007. The new bridge was

2 views of the Francis R. Powers Bridge: Top from River Road; Bottom: from Bayberry Road.

named the Francis R. Powers Bridge and was dedicated on September 15, 2008. Frank was a Dorchester boy, for over 30 years the long-time superior clerk of Plymouth County, a World War II hero, and a long-time Humarock resident. Jim Moran, project coordinator, postman, and neighbor came up with idea of naming the bridge after

Powers said Clare Sheehan Powers his wife. Clare and many neighbors led the movement to name the new bridge after Powers. Support came from many sources at the time: Scituate Selectmen unanimously voted for it, Senator Robert Hedlund and State Representative Frank Hynes both said support from the neighbors was great. The legislation went through in record time said Hynes.

The final way to enter Humarock is to walk in over the Rexhame Beach dunes to the beach, or stroll along the South River's edge through marshes, grasses, and plants.

Top: Along the edge of the South River near Old Mouth Road.

Right: Over the dunes in Rexhame to the ocean then along the shore.

Humarock's Happenings

- By the early 17th century, the lower reaches of the North River west of Scituate Beach and the Fourth Cliff was called New Harbor or New Harbor Marshes. In 1681 the 40 ton bark Adventure wintered in the lee of Fourth Cliff before making her way to the West Indies. Proceeding from New Harbor halfway to the mouth was a settlement on the Marshfield side of the river. Started in 1638 by Jonathan Brewster, it passed through several owners until Benjamin White, grandson of Peregrine, gained ownership in 1712. From this point on it would be known as White's Ferry until the ferry was replaced by the bridge built by the Fourth Cliff Land Company in the late 19th century.

- On November 14, 1709, Joseph and Sarah Woodworth of Scituate, John Hyland's aunt and her husband, sold him fourteen acres of upland at the Fourth Cliff for 94£.

- On August 14, 1736, John Hyland transferred ownership of the northerly half of the Fourth Cliff, some fourteen acres, bought off of Joseph Woodworth, and two acres given him by his mother, to Cornelius White of Marshfield. A marginal note reads reconveyed to said Hyland…. This latter reference shows that the land was back in John's possession on April 28, 1746. The deed was not registered until after the death of John's son, William, in whose possession the land then lay. On July 6, 1742, John received 40£ from his five sons, James, John jr., Thomas, Benjamin, and William Hyland, for a ten-acre lot in Conihassett, which they later used in an exchange with James Merritt.

- Washington, January 20, 1854, a letter was sent from the Secretary of War, Jefferson Davis, to the Speaker of the House of Representatives, Hon. Linn Boyd that communicated the results of a report of a survey of Scituate harbor and North river. Davis wrote, "In compliance with the resolution of the House of Representatives of the 16th instant, 'that the Secretary of War be directed to communicate to this House the report of a survey of Scituate harbor and the North river, in the State of Massachusetts, ordered by the last Congress,' I have the honor to submit herewith a communication from the Colonel of Engineers, enclosing the report of the survey called for, and stating the reason why it could not be completed and furnished to Congress at an earlier period. Very respectfully, your obedient servant, Jeffn. Davis, Secretary of War." There was a two-fold issue here: first to make Scituate harbor a harbor refuge and second to dig a canal from Scituate harbor to the North River. The report done by J.G. Barnard, Brevet Major of Engineers was sent to Gen. J.G. Totten, Chief Engineer of the Army Corps, Washington, D.C. In his report Barnard wrote, "No doubt many things could be done, which would be very useful to the local interests, for less money; but these, I conceive, it is not the business of the government to undertake. The canal is not indispensable to the project for a harbor of refuge. Still, it would be an advantage to the harbor; and if there is really yet timber for ship building about the North river, (a matter which I have heard called in question,) it would be of great value to the surrounding country. Regretting that I am unable to give anything but this general outline of a project, I submit to you, with a request that, if the matter becomes of any practical importance, it should be referred to successor for further study." Not a very ringing endorsement, is it? Now add this to the story: Ex-President John Quincy Adams, then Representative to Congress, was induced to ride down to Marshfield and visit the spot where the new cut was desired. But after a hearing from the citizens, pro and con, the authorities thought it not feasible, chiefly on account of the injury it was claimed would be caused to the meadows near the upland and islands by overflow or strong tides. Without Adams or the Army Corps of Engineers' support, a large number of locals decided to take things into their own hands. They "gathered together, and with picks, hoes, shovels, axes, etc., etc., with plenty of ox teams and horse teams to convey them, marched in the darkness of the night, with lanterns in hand to the beach, and there they began operations, dug and toiled throughout the vigils of the night. They dared not undertake the task in the day time, because it would be a criminal offense to be caught infringing against the rights of property vested in the United States.

Morning came and the party journeyed back to their homes . . ." not being successful. The hard meadow bank was an obstacle, for it was as hard as rock. A short time later the river had filled it up again. The Portland Gale of 1898 solved their problem, but the far reaching consequences of this solution destroyed the salt haying industry and an increased salinity far up the river into Pembroke that killed all the white cedar trees there is a testament to the unforeseen consequences of our actions. Today, the skeletal remains of white cedar trees are still to be seen from the highway that passes nearby.

• Calvin Jenkins of Scituate sold about 3 ½ acres of land, more or less, of meadow on Fourth Cliff for $59 to B.J. Greely, J.P. Newell, and C. E. Jackson, trustees of the Fourth Cliff Land Company. The date of the deed was February 17, 1881.

• On December 10, 1881, Bela T. Jacobs of South Scituate for $337.50 conveys to Gilbert A. Tapley of Danvers ten acres, two quarters and twelve rods of salt meadow plus another 3 acres of salt meadow bounded on the north by a meadow Tapley already owns to a beach known as Broad Neck all the way to beach on the ocean.

• Then in 1882 the same Calvin Jenkins in consideration of one dollar paid by the same trustees of the Fourth Cliff Land Company turns over 2 acres, more or less, of beach. As mentioned before, the Town of Scituate gave to the Fourth Cliff Land Company trustees a quitclaim deed to all of the beach, shore hummocks from the southerly base of Fourth Cliff to the mouth of the North River; this recorded in Book 551 pages 561 -562. What I was interested in is found on page 562. It states, ". . . to the said Greely, Newell, and Jackson trustees as aforesaid and their successors and assigns, to their own use and behoof forever, as joint tenants and not as tenants in common, But in trust nevertheless for the uses and purposes and with all the powers and subject to all the provisions named in said deed of Walter A Tapley to said trustees recorded in said deed of Walter A. Tapley to said trustees recorded with Plymouth Deeds, Book 478 pages 79, 80 & 81 to which reference is to be had for full description of the trust."

• On April 26, 1884, Howard Hamblin of Boston and trustee of the Humarock Hotel Company in consideration of one dollar and other valuable considerations paid by Benjamin L. Greely, John P. Newell, and Charles E. Jackson as they are trustees of the Fourth Cliff Land

Company quitclaim to them seven lots with the buildings on them being "lots numbers 49, 50, 51, 52, 53, 54, 55, also the rear portion of lot 64 bounded as follows –commencing at the corner where lots No's 51, 52, & 64 join and running on the dividing line No's 64 & 53 westerly 50 feet to lot No. 63 thence turning and running right angles southerly on the line of lot No. 63 twenty-five feet; thence then turning and running at right angles Easterly on a line parallel with but distant 25 feet from the first mentioned boundary fifty feet to said lot No.51:thence turning and running Northly along the line of said lot 51 twenty five feet to the point of beginning."

• March 21, 1899, Gilbert A. Tapley, Charles E. Jackson, and Nahum T. Greenwood, trustees of the Fourth Cliff and Humarock Beach Company, sold to Walter A. Tapley of Danvers

for the sum of $5000 16 lots of land with buildings. The lots being numbers 49, 50, 51, 52, 53, 54, 55, 56, 57, 58, 59, 60, 61, 62, 63, and 64 all from a plan drawn by J. F. Wadleigh, surveyor, dated February 25, 1882. Bounded on Marshfield Avenue 400 feet, on Central Avenue 300 feet, on Harvard Street 400 feet, and on the beach 300 feet – containing 120,000 square feet of land.

- April 27, 1901, Tapley sells to Merrill for one dollar and other considerations 16 certain lots of land with buildings: 49 through 64 on Wadleigh's 1882 plan. Book 818 page 558.

- Book 816 page 598, Merrill sells to Tapley for $9000 at 5% interest payable semi-annually on demand, 16 lots of land numbers 49 through 64; Bounded on Marshfield Avenue 400 feet, on Central Avenue 300 feet, on Harvard Street 400 feet, and on the beach 300 feet – containing 120,000 square feet of land.

- June 20, 1904 – Tapley acknowledges full payment of mortgage by Merrill. What do you think has transpired?

- Town Report 1939: 5 volunteer callmen at Humarock. Bituminous resurfacing and patching: On Marshfield Avenue in Humarock section, a great amount of difficulty has been experienced in providing a stabilized surface, due to the nature of the base. 1880 yards of bituminous concrete cushion was applied and has given excellent results to date. This street is a direct approach to Humarock Beach and it is believed the present surface will serve for many years to come.

When the water system at Humarock Beach was taken over by the Scituate Water Department, all of the water lines were small and were covered only from 6 inches to 18 inches with sand. This meant shutting off water service and draining the pipes in the fall, and turning on the water again in spring with considerable repairs and cleaning every year, at the expense of the Water Department. Replacement of these small lines has been started and this spring the section south of Marshfield Avenue and the east of River Street was completed, allowing 12 months' service to all of the houses in that section and eliminating the cost of draining and repairing small lines.

- 1940 – Report of the Fire Department. A new problem presented

Central Avenue running north toward Fourth Cliff; North River; then Ferry Hill

itself at Humarock Beach shortly after the Board took office. A large building development was started increasing considerably our fire hazard in this district. The older residents of this part of the Town demanded adequate protection of their properties. The only possible way to meet their needs was to place a permanent man of the department in charge at this point. This was done and is being continued at this time, since your Board feels that it is absolutely necessary for the protection of the locality. In addition to fire hazards, your permanent man has been able to give valuable aid in several instances to victims of immersion. The saving of life in itself has warranted our additional expense at this point . . . . In considering our budget for 1941, we shall not increase the budget over that of this past year, with the exception of the amount needed to take care of our problem at Humarock Beach . . . .

Board of Health: Development area at Fourth Cliff – special regulations governing sewage disposal at this point were put into effect to conform strictly to the State Department of Health and Sanitation. No cesspool, septic tank, or plumbing can be installed unless permit be obtained from our Plumbing inspectors and locations for tanks, cesspool and drainage must meet the approval of the Inspectors.

Plumbing Inspector's Report: 111 permits. The development of Fourth Cliff and Humarock Beach with the constant increase in the number of houses presented a particular problem in the matter of the disposal of sewage. This was met by your board through the establishment of Rules and Regulations calling for purification by septic tanks, leaching drains and cesspools specified to give the best results in accordance with the location which the particular disposal

Post Office and General Store, Humarock Beach, Mass.

was to be made.

Police officer – full time service June 15th to September 15th. Officers at Humarock Beach and North Scituate Beach provided with one of the department's motorcycles in order to better cover the territory assigned.

- Report of the Special Committee – Erection of Fire and Police Station - Humarock Beach. Your Committee selected the site for the Fire and Police Station on town-owned property abutting the town parking space off River Street, Humarock Beach. Plans and specifications were drawn and bids invited by advertising in the Scituate Herald. An effort was made to interest local contractors to enter bids, without success. The contract was awarded to the low bidder Walter S. Robbins of Falmouth, Mass. The supervision of the construction of the building was delegated to Mr. Frank Westerhoff, whose experience as a building contractor and the deep interest he showed in the supervision of the work was of great value to the committee and the town. The contractor was paid a bonus of $30 early completion of the building before July 15, 1941. He was paid $10 per day for being three days ahead of schedule.

Fire and Police Station, Humarock Beach, Mass.

- Special Police Service. Regular intermittent Police Officers were placed on nine hour per day shifts from May 30th to Labor Day at Humarock Beach and North Scituate Beach. This service was rendered following a petition from residents of these two districts. The Board of Selectmen, Advisory Board, the Police Department, reviewed the request as reasonable and necessary to augment the regular police services at these points.

- Special Town Meeting, 1942. Article 10. Recommended; To see if the Town will vote to accept the layout of the County Commissioners making Julian Street at Humarock a public way and raise and appropriate the sum of $300.00 to defray the expense of land damages caused by said layout. Decree No. 1015. Plans on file at the Town Clerk's Office, or act thereon.

- January 29, 1943. Report of Scituate Rationing Board No. 271. The Board started operations in January, 1942. The first articles to be rationed were tires and tubes, these being followed by gasoline, sugar, typewriters, bicycles, men's rubber footwear, coffee, fuel oil, and stoves.

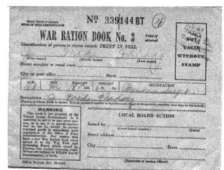

- Friday, February 4, 1944. Scituate Herald, North River Pilot section. "Many of our readers will remember Robert Boles of Humarock who formerly conducted the marine shop and boat yard at Humarock. We received a long letter from Bob last week; he is now somewhere in the combat area in the Pacific, on the USS Schuylkill, which is a large Navy oiler. Bob is now a Lieutenant U.S.N.R. We think Bob is the chief navigating officer on this ship as he speaks in his letter of getting the old girl around to her different points' destination. He also speaks of seeing his brother, Orlo, several times. Frank Romano, another one of the boys who used to be at Bob's yard was recently on furlough. Frank took an active part in the severe fighting at Tarawa, displaying bravery for which he was decorated. Frank tells some interesting things connected with this epic struggle in the far Pacific."

- Friday, April 21, 1944. Scituate Herald. North River Pilot section. "We hear that flounders are caught from the bridges in Humarock."

- Friday, April 13, 1945.   OUR LEADER PASSES – FRANKLIN DELANO ROOSEVELT. Headline in the Scituate Herald with a quarter of the front page with the above heading and his picture and part of Whitman's poem *O Captain My Captain*.

Colonial Living: Farming, the Hylands, and the Marshes

The Western yeoman had to work as hard as a common laborer or a European peasant, and at the same tasks. Despite the settled belief of Americans to the contrary, his economic status was not necessarily higher. But he was a different creature altogether because he had become the hero of a myth, of the myth of mid-nineteenth-century America. from *Virgin Land*

If you asked your grandparents how they got their food, they might have a different answer than you think? Why is this? It's because agriculture has changed throughout history. We have mythologized many parts of American history. One particular myth that has long endured has to do with agriculture and is that of the yeoman farmer. He was independent, self-sufficient, living an ideal existence on the land. This image and influence came from John Locke and Thomas Jefferson and other intellectuals and was later reinforced through Romanticism and Agrarianism. According to the Yeoman - American Studies @University of Virginia,

"The creation of the United States of America coincided with a time when European intellectuals were reassessing the place of agriculture in society. The concept of farming (and the farmer) was taking on a new, elevated status in the minds of the day. This notion of the noble cultivator became a part of the foundation of the new democracy. The garden would be tilled by free citizens, possessing all the virtues bestowed by the Creator upon the husbandman.

The yeoman became a feature in American politics very early. The Federalist and Agrarian forces in government were divided in opinion just following the Revolution. The Federalists, led by Alexander Hamilton, were in favor of a strong central government with most power in the hands the landed few, and looked to commercial and industrial expansion. The Republicans, led by Thomas Jefferson, believed in the primacy of local government and a mainly agrarian national economy, based on small independent farmers.

The American yeoman farmer had become a symbol of the Agrarian philosophy articulated by Thomas Jefferson and later embraced by "The Farmer's Calling". Horace Greeley writes that above all professions, he would recommend farming to a son. Among his reasons is that farming is "that vocation which conduces most directly to a reverence for Honesty and Truth." "

But where does the truth lie? When we look back to the past and our farming heritage, do we do so with rose-colored glasses? Has our vision of this bucolic, rustic past become mythic, bored, and unreal? Have we relegated this past to some form of Rockwell image; homey, feel good, and long ago? I

43

believe the best description was given by John D. Long summarizing his early impressions of early Hingham, but could easily apply to early residents of Marshfield and Scituate:

> The picture of the early time, if it could be reproduced, would present a body of men and women engaged in the ordinary activities of life, cultivating their farms, ploughing the seas, trading with foreign lands and among themselves, engaged in near and remote fisheries, maintaining the school, the train-band, and the church, holding their town-meetings, - a people not without humor, not altogether innocent of a modicum of quarrel and greed and heart-burning, yet warm with the kind and neighborly spirit of common and interdependent fellowship. The Massachusetts settlers indulged in no mere dream of founding a Utopia or a Saints' Rest. They were neither visionary philosophers nor religious fanatics. Their early records deal with every-day details of farm and lot, of domestic affairs, of straying cattle and swine, of runaway apprentices and scolding wives, of barter with Indians, of whippings and stocks and fines for all sorts of naughtinesses, of boundaries and suits, of debt and legal process and probate, of elections and petty offices, civil and military, and now and then the alarm of war and the inevitable assessment of taxes. They smack very much more of the concerns, and the common concerns, of this world than of concern for the next. They are the memoranda of a hard, practical life [...]. [p. 142-143, Bangs, Seventeenth Century Town Records of Scituate Massachusetts.]

Well, what did the farmers of Marshfield and Scituate do to meet their basic needs? So they farmed the land, raising animals and crops to meet their needs. They also cut the grasses from the

marshes for feed for their animals and insulation. As Freemen of their towns, they also shared in the use and division of the common lands. Farmers also needed to develop other skills necessary to survive in their environment. Because of the poor farmland, some used new skills for fishing, shipbuilding, trade, etc. Others learned to tan and make shoes. Still others learned to make and use metal. Still others were clockmakers. Colonial men did not have one job. They had many at different times of the year. In the winter when they could not farm, they utilized skills they had developed. This might be as simple as hiring themselves out as day laborers, or tanning hides and then preparing to make shoes. Usually farmers' sons learned the skills that their dads possessed and taught to them, but in some cases sons were apprenticed so that they could learn a trade. Some like Israel Litchfield of Scituate taught himself how to make and repair watches. The story of early Scituate,

Marshfield, and Humarock is about people, and people then and today are similar, unique, and unquestionably interesting because like us they had biases, prejudices, failings, weaknesses, and strengths. They can be good as well as bad, sometimes both at once. One look at four court records supports these images.

First, in the 26 October, 1686, Court of General Sessions and Common Pleas, Mary Sutton of Scituate confessed to fornication with one Joseph Booth and was fined 5 pounds or to be whipped. Mary took an oath that Joseph Booth was the father of her child, and she charged him with having "Divers times bodily and Carnall Knowledge of her within the months of April and May in 1686." The court ordered Booth to pay maintenance for the child. Mary would keep her child until it reached eight years of age, and Booth, would pay to the selectmen of Scituate eighteen pence a week for the first year and twelve pence a week for the next seven years. Presumably at the age of eight a child was considered to be able to earn his own living. Second, at the 4 July 1673 Court in Plymouth under Governor Winslow, ". . . Information was given and complaint made to the Court by Isaac Chittenden against Humphrey Johnson, of Hingham, in the government of Massachusetts, for that the said Johnson hath, contrary to order of Court, cut down or plucked up a stake set as a bound mark of land layed out by the committee of Scituate to the said informer at or by a swamp near the land of Thomas Hiland, Senior. The case was tried by a jury of twelve men, whose verdict on the case is as followeth: We find for our sovereign lord the King, Humphrey Johnson having broken the law of this government in cutting down a stake that was sett up as a land marke, which law is in the Book of Lawes, chapter the third, number the twenty-one – Upon consideration of the boldness and insolency of the said Johnson coming into this government, who is one of another government, to do this act, and his pragmatical management of the same, the Court saw cause, for this fact so circumstanced, to amerce him in the sum of five pounds, to be payed as a fine by him to the use of the colony." Third, at the March 1687/88 session, John Merritt and his wife Elizabeth of Scituate were fined fifty shillings and costs for premarital fornication, their child "being born twelve weeks too soon, That is to say, at twenty-seven weeks after marriage or thereabouts." The final example is John Hiland Jr. (Scituate Labourer) v. James Coleman (Scituate Joyner). Case, for £100 damages for defendant's "Assult on the Body of the plaintiff...which putt him to Great pain and Caused the Loss of Much of his Blood and Rendered him uncapable of Bisness for a Long time." Defendant pleaded not guilty. Jury verdict for plaintiff, 40s. and costs, taxed at £4.18s.6d. Before you jump to conclusions about Scituate morals and life in that town, the court records are full of such stories from all towns, not just Scituate. . I used Scituate examples because of the focus of our book being Humarock, but I could have chosen any of the other Plymouth County towns and the court cases would have been similar: illegal selling of spirits, women pregnant but not married, masters mistreating apprentices or servants, and cases of physical and emotional abuse. As I researched daily life, one other interesting fact surprised me – the volume and number of the transfers of land. Most of the town records are filled with land sold, exchanged, or rented. If the freemen thought that their land was too straight or too rocky, they sought remedies either through the town's committees or in the courts. A perfect example of this was Timothy Hatherly's petitioning the Plymouth Courts for more farming land for the town because the "lands of Scituate were too straight." The Court sent out a committee to examine the situation themselves. They agreed with Hatherly and granted Scituate a two mile long by one mile deep section of land on the Marshfield side of the North River (the Two Mile). I became intrigued when I discovered that John Hyland stubbornly argued from 1726 to 1742 that the marsh grass that he cut around the Fourth Cliff was his property while the town of Scituate claimed otherwise. The battle between these two

A North River gundalow containing marsh grass is pictured on the site of Roht's Marine, Rte. 3A just up river from the Fourth Cliff.

heavyweights has been preserved in Plymouth Court records, countless Scituate town meetings, committee reports, and reports from specially-appointed agents. All of which devoted time and energy to resolving this question of land ownership. His stubbornness was one thing, but as the story unfolds, other questions and issues arose which led me to see him as a supremely human person, and as such both flawed and heroic. It also illuminated a historic problem regarding sources: what happens when all the evidence recorded supported only one side of argument. With that thought in mind begins what I called "The Salt Marsh Saga of Fourth Cliff: Subtitled My Grass, Not Yours!" The background of our story began with the deaths of Thomas Hiland senior and junior and how valuable marsh grass was in the early eighteenth century to farmers. Regarding the importance of marsh grass, William Gould Vinal wrote,

"The saga of salt haying is of historic interest for several reasons: first, because those who went down to the salt meadows in hay carts or gundalows are fast disappearing; second, because there are scant records of those hardscrabble days of Scituate farmers; third, because no continuous account with its significance has ever been published." Vinal continued by saying that these hardy men may never have heard of a thermos bottle, but they knew how to keep water cool and drinkable when the container was buried in a bushel basket of hay. They may not have used the word insulation, but they certainly knew that "banking their houses" with salt hay or seaweed kept out the winter cold. Vitamins were not in their daily ken but they had been versed from time immemorial with the importance of salting cattle. Finally, and not the least important, was that salt haymakers proved to be the best of neighbors, for they were always ready to help the other fellow out who had figuratively become stuck in the mud. "Salt haying had its day, it left behind the imprint of work well done, it has gone its way. Let's pause, then", give these salty days the recognition they deserve. The settlers arrived at the southern base of Coleman's Hill in 1636. Their new Meeting House on the hill of Meeting House Lane overlooked New Harbor Marshes. There was a good lagoon back of Fourth Cliff for mooring vessels. It had to be agreed by joint consent, according to families and stock, what portion

Marshfield Meadows, Massachusetts. Martin Johnson Heade

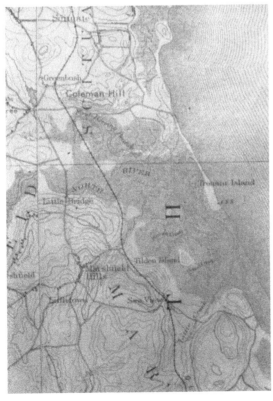

each landowner would receive. Salt meadows were divided into grants and later came the division of uplands and swamps. I will interject an interesting story here about Wills Island and how it received its name. Many people at the time were embroiled in a controversy concerning two issues: one, over whether the minister should be paid by taxing freemen or all rateable inhabitants, and second the mode of baptism. The result was that 22 families left Scituate for Barnstable. John Cooper was the head of one of these families. William Wills, freeman, purchased Wills's Island and marshes from John Cooper in 1639. Mr. Wills erected his house on the island. One of Captain Bill Vinal's favorite stories was to share in a trip to Wills's Island. He lived in what he described as an isolated section of South Scituate (Mt. Blue). He said the journey in a hay cart over bumpy roads was not exactly a balloon tire experience. Riding on a dead axle i.e. with no pretense of springs, made a rattling good trip. Wills's Island was only five miles as the crow flew and, at most six and half miles by the winding highway. He said their mph was as slow as molasses in January. By the time they got out of Neal Gate Road, down the lane with the bars put up, and slumped through slough holes in the tide pool meadow, they had burned up two hours. By the time you arrived, your bones need a rest and your muscles needed to be stretched. You then tied up the horse and put a blanket over her to keep off the mosquitoes and horseflies. Bill diverged then as he explained the stops along the way, especially the stop at Andrew J. Litchfield's country store where they were allowed one stick of licorice or a peppermint; one apiece. Capt. Bill added that a small sized farm made a subsistence farmer a jack-of-all-trades. He was engaged in salt haying yes-, but along with it went the teaching of fishing, hunting, and seamanship. Bill's family owned two meadows near Wills Island. At noon they shook out their lunch pails and drank their switchel made with milk, molasses, and water seasoned with a dash of ginger or vinegar. His mother sometimes sent along tarts or turnovers to be shared with "guests." After lunch, all hands turned out to work. They used all tools except the scythe, which was only used by Bill's father. These tools the boys used included the rake, fork, and hay poles. When done loading the hay in the wagon and hitching up the horse, it was time for home. Bunching, poling, tedding, raking scatters, pitching, stomping the load, and wearily plodding home are now obsolete performances. The words haymaker, pitching, and heckling have taken on new meanings. We no longer talk about sweet grass, cut grass, or black grass. Nor do we say salt hay, fresh hay, and English hay. Hay is hay, meaning timothy, red top, orchard grass, and hers grass, which were brought separately from Europe by way of England. The Men of Kent found natural meadows waiting to be used. Salt-haying was never agriculture. It was harvesting a wild crop rather than planting and tilling the soil. The huge tracts of God-given salt-hay lands required no clearing, grubbing, rolling out boulders, plowing, manuring, planting, hoeing, or weeding. Is it any wonder then that salt meadows were mentioned in nearly every official document in the Plymouth County right up to the Portland Gale of 1898.

What about those salt marsh ditches viewed from Little's Bridge? How were they dug and why? One answer was to mark boundaries. These were done to prevent the indiscriminate cutting of hay. The meadow lands were marked off into rectangles because this was an old English custom. The winding rivers and curving upland shores, however, presented problems, which leads us to John Hyland's story.

So who were the Hylands, particularly who was John Hyland, and what makes John's story so compelling? John Hyland (*the family name is spelled three different ways in the records: Hyland, Hiland, Hilland*) was the grandson of Thomas Hyland, who according to Deane's 1831 history of Scituate, Mass., was one of the first Men of Kent who settled in Scituate. "According to John Lothrop's church records list, there were 171 people who lived in Scituate between 1633-1639; Thomas Hiland was one." Thomas' farm was on the Fourth Cliff while his home was near the Driftway. Thomas was, not only one of the Men of Kent, but also one of Timothy Hatherly's Conihasset partners and therefore, entitled to the land divisions of this group as well as a share in the town of Scituate's division of the common land. As a freeman of Scituate, he also had a vote at town meeting, and as a member of the Conihasset partners, he had an equal voice in any decision made there as well. However, the freemen of Scituate, who were not Conihasset partners, had no say in what occurred with the partners. This was source of irritation between these two groups. [*The last meeting of the Conihasset partners was held in 1767 when it was disbanded.*] When John's only brother, Thomas Junior, died in the Quebec expedition in the war of 1690, John became the heir to the Hyland estate.

The facts that we know are that John Hyland, son of Thomas, was born March 17, 1670/1, and baptized August 6, 1671. He was one of five children: the youngest son, his older brother was Thomas born January 25, 1662/3, Elizabeth was born 1665, Mary was born May 15, 1667, and Ruth born June 15, 1673. There is good circumstantial evidence that John's wife was Elizabeth James, daughter of William James of Boston and Scituate and his wife Mehitabel; they were Quakers. John and Elizabeth married at Scituate in January 3, 1694/5. On June 14, 1709, John Hyland's name appears as one of those who have purchased a pew in the new meetinghouse of the First Church of Scituate called the Northerly Society of Scituate on the 14th day of June 1709. The Hyland pew was next to the east door on the right hand going in at the East end of the Meeting House. Elizabeth Hyland, wife of John, was baptized there on March 8, 1710/1, and on April 1, 1711/2, was joined to the Church. We know they had a large family and while Elizabeth's family worked at sea and most her family eventually moved to Rhode Island, John and Elizabeth, however, stayed in Scituate with John working the land. As a means of exchange John used hay, Indian corn, and beef and sheep to pay his bills, purchase shoes for his family, and finally pay his legal bills. John and Elizabeth's children were: Ruth – 1695, Elizabeth – 1697 (not listed in his will), James – 1701, John – 1704, Sarah – 1706, Thomas – 1708, Ann – 1710, Benjamin – 1711, Mehitabel and William (listed in his will). John died at Scituate on December 15, 1753, while Elizabeth's death occurred sometime after December 8, 1748, because she is mentioned in her husband's will of that date. John also functioned as an active member of town as he served as one of the surveyors of highways in the years 1703, 1719, and 1723. He also served as an administrator to several wills and as a witness to Henry Chittenden's will. The records also show him paying taxes on his sons John, Thomas, Benjamin presumably all older than sixteen. He also appears on the tax records for both real estate and livestock in 1730. One final record shows him receiving a payment of ten schillings from his aunt's husband. John also appears in land ownership, land transfers, with members of his family as well as on several deeds with individuals like James Merritt, Joseph Woodsworth, Samuel Holbrook, and others. Putting all the above together, we get a picture of John as a worker who farmed the land, raised livestock, bought and sold land, all in order to provide for a large family.

There is another aspect of John which begins early in his life. It appears that John was no stranger to involvement in the court system of his era. A few cases will prove the point. In September of 1687 Captain John Williams of Scituate sued Thomas Hyland "for his said Thomas Hylands son John killing of said Williams his horse beast." A not guilty plea was entered. However, Williams was awarded 50 shillings plus cost of the suit. In September of 1707, John sued Amos Turner of Scituate for "trespass and ejectment." Few details survive for us to know what the final decision reached was. Another case in 1726 finds John Hiland, yeoman, James Hiland, labourer, John Hiland Jr., labourer, and Elisha Jones, cordwainer, all of Scituate v. James Coleman (Scituate Joyner) in court facing £1,000 damages for exhibiting a complaint to John Barker, JP, at Scituate that the plaintiffs "had Cutt of the Ears of a Certain horse of his the said Coleman…[and defendants] did prevaile with John Read who was the Kings Attorney at that time to Exhibett a Complaint to the Generall Sessions of the peace…." Defendants pleaded in abatement. Abated. Appealed by plaintiffs with Peter Collamer (Scituate Yeoman) and Elisha Bisbe (Pembroke Attorney at Law) sureties. [Pleaded in abatement is a type of plea that is made by certain people who are accused of a crime or a tort. In such a plea the defendant does not deny the claim made by the plaintiff. Instead, they merely state that they disagree with the time, place, or form of the accusation. Finally, James Briggs (Scituate Cordwainer) v. John Hyland, John Hyland Jr., James Hyland, and Thomas Hyland (all of Scituate…Husbandmen). Trespass for £18, due as treble damages for cutting 6 loads of sedge grass at Hummock Flat in Scituate, contrary to provincial act of 13 Geo. I. The defendants pleaded that "they Cutt No Grass Nor Sedge on any Island of Flat in the North River but they cut Three Loads on the Meadow Joyning to the Beach Next the said Hummocks and had Ridght So to Do." Jury verdict for plaintiffs., £10.16s. and costs, taxed at £7.6s. Appealed by defendant, with Eleazer Morton (Plymouth Cordwainer) and John Sprague (Duxborough Yeoman) sureties. A different picture of John emerges.

Thomas, senior, seems to have been land rich being not only a freeman of Scituate but an equal member of the Conihasset partners. He was, as well, active in town affairs. John's father was also named Thomas but he died in 1706. But as I examined the town records after John had become sole heir of Thomas's estate, I noticed that he began to sell all of his grandfather's Conihasset land. Why? My guess was that he must have fallen on hard financial times. Marya Myers in the New England Historical and Genealogical Register for July 2003 makes a convincing case about my guess. She stated,

"The Hyland household was in financial difficulty by mid-1728. During the next five years John Cushing, Jr., Ebenezer Simmons, Benjamin Stockbridge, and Nicholas Litchfield each brought John to court for loans and mortgages not paid. Hugh Caldor, a Boston shopkeeper, sued for the 21 pounds + owed him, presumably for goods. Scituate saddler Joseph Turner demanded payment of an outstanding balance of 4 pounds 13 shillings for mending "one male Pilleon and one Crooper," plus a saddle, bridle, and other leather goods. John had made partial payment with beef, mutton, cheese, sheepskins, and cash. In December 1730 the Commissioners of the provincial bills of credit brought a large number of actions before the County Court. Among those sued was John Hyland of Scituate, yeoman, who failed to appear at court, but was ordered to pay the 68 pounds 11 shillings 6d due within two months or relinquish possession of the land." Another case on 2 January 1732/33 by Thomas James of Hingham claiming that he was owed £8 for six boatloads of English hay by John Hyland was heard by the Superior Court in Boston for the County of Suffolk went in Thomas' favor. John's failure to comply led to an arrest warrant issued in August 1733.

The answer to why is found in the court records under a "Riot in Scituate"; and in the July 2003 New England Historical and Genealogical Register article by Marya C. Myers titled: "The Great Sedge Grass Caper"; and what I called "The Salt Marsh Saga of Fourth Cliff: Subtitled My Grass, Not Yours!"

To understand the story we actually need to begin at Scituate Town Meeting of 14 July 1703. At that town meeting it was agreed "to hire or let out the flatts or common mowing ground belonging to S[ai]d Town in the North river and Herring brook . . . for the term of seven years." This was followed until 1726 when John Hyland went to the Hummock Flat and began cutting sedge grass. To the people who had leased the land and to the town fathers, John was trespassing. John, however, saw it differently. To him this was his land. For the next sixteen years, court case followed court case with countless town meetings, special committees, and special agents trying to resolve the dispute. Piecing the puzzle together by the late-1720s it appears that John Hyland ran into financial problems. An examination of the records of Town Meetings of Scituate, Plymouth Court Records by Konig, Massachusetts Historical Society William Cushing Papers, and Marya C. Myers research presented the readers with some answers and more questions. The argument presented by the Town's Attorney, John Cushing Jr., has been preserved. John Hyland's position has not been preserved, but can be ascertained by the arguments presented by Cushing.

Basically John Hyland's arguments for the taking of sedge grass were threefold: First, the land was his, passed down to him through his family. Second, that the ancient records proving his claim were lost when the town's records were burned in old Mr. Lothrop's days. Thirdly, that the mouth of the river had altered over time and was in 1742 about half a mile more to the south than formerly.

Cushing challenged each of these points first by stating that nothing proved John's title to land that was being cut. When John in 1726 ran a fence from the falls of the cliff to the sea, he was ordered by the Justice of the Peace to remove it because it was the "Common Road" from Scituate to Marshfield. When a witness stated that he bought wood from Thomas Hyland on the Hummocks by White's Ferry, Cushing challenged him by asking how cutting by White's Ferry could give anyone possession of land two miles distant was hard for him to reconcile. Cushing's retort about the changing mouth reiterated the 1682 agreement that Scituate and Marshfield had decided that the channel would be the bounds between them. Also Cushing challenged that Hyland had no proof to where it ran in 1682. As to the town's records being burned, Cushing dismissed it saying, "But for him to pretend by ye loss of his bounds and ye records (which by ye way he can't prove) he is unlimited and may challenge what he pleases is too frantic a notion to deserve a solid answer." Cushing maintained that John had proved only that he had title to the Fourth Cliff and its meadow, nothing else. Cushing also concluded that John Hyland's chief business was to travel from tavern to tavern at Pembroke, Plymouth, and other places especially Marshfield spreading his unhappy case before all persons who would listen, thus greatly prejudicing many people. Thus Cushing challenged the validity of a Jury that had visited the area and had reached an erroneous decision. This, Cushing concluded, led to more turmoil and lawlessness as Hyland and his supporters were encouraged by a false decision that "might have ended in bloodshed and death."

At the Scituate Town Meeting a group of men (John Cushing, David Little, Thomas Bryant Esqr., James Hatch, Nehemiah Randall, Stephen Clap, Peter Turner, Samuel Turner, David Clap, Ensign Otis, and Joseph Tilden "equally & poverally to be their agents in their Town's name and to appear at said next Superior Court Judieature & to be held ninth within and for ye County of Plymouth. On the Tuesday immediately proceeding the last Tuesday of April next. Then and there to defend them aginst the action of review of a plea of ejoynmt which John Hiland of said Scituate has comisnd agst them then and there to be tried and all others of matter & things whatsoever & to act & doe all things relating _9?) premises as fully as daid town could doe if present with power substitution."

In the Town Record book (C-3) labeled Humock Flatt Beach May 29, 1738, it is written: "Recently repossessed from John Hyland at last Superior Court now committed to Thos. Bryant and Capt. Caleb Torrey to administer as agents for the town."

John Hyland died on 15 December 1753. John's son James upon his father's death became the heir to his great-grandfather's estate. Because little provision had been made for his brother John in his father's will, James gave to John two parcels of land in his possession, the Fourth Cliff and its meadow and a tract of land called Bailey pasture. One interesting fact about James was that he was chosen constable 6 April 1733, but he refused to serve. This was at the height of the disagreement between the town and his father.

At a town meeting on November 11, 1839 a report was filed by the committee chosen at the 1838 Town Meeting. "That in the opinion of your committee the beaches from the north end of the great pond to the beach claimed by Marshall Litchfield – from the southerly end of the Third Cliff to the northerly end of the Fourth Cliff to the mouth of the North River belong to the town. Your Committee are not aware that any individual claims any of the aforementioned beaches and we have therefore assumed the ownership in behalf of the town so far as to demand payment for trespass thereon. It is the opinion of many individuals that the beach claimed by Marshall Litchfield belongs to the town – that beach is very valuable on account of the great quantity of sea manure that washes ashore and if it is the property of the town your

Committee believe that it would be for the interest of the town to claim and take possession of it. . . ."

Further they added, individuals that trespass on this land and take these items should pay for this privilege. They turned over ninety dollars that they had collected from several persons who had trespassed. One person, Henry Hobbs, refused to pay twenty dollars demanded of him. They added "from the best information we have been able to obtain, said Hobbs is not a responsible person and the town is not likely to obtain damage for the trespass." The committee recommended that the town get the advice and opinion of counsel, learned in the law, upon any questions relating thereon. They concluded by stating that "the only way to stop irresponsible persons from trespass was to arrest them in the act and on the spot. A great quantity of stone has been taken to the great injury of the beaches in as much as it weakens the defence against the Sea and if continued, destroy a large amount of property owned by our citizens." The Committee recommended that the town petition the state legislature to pass a law that preserves and prevents the taking of the stone, sand, or gravel from any of the beaches in Scituate. The report is signed by Gideon W. Torrey. Chairman.

Voted: that the same committee be the standing committee with the addition of Walter Foster, Ichabod R. Jacobs and Shadrach B. Merritt -

Voted: that the Committee be directed to pay over to the Town Treasurer after deducting their necessary expenses, all monies now in their hands in that they may hereafter receive –

Voted: that the Selectmen be instructed to petition the Legislature for a law in conformity with the above report. [Town Records 9 1821-1845 pp. 272-273].

Some other milestone dates in the history of Humarock are included below:

- March 3, 1884, Voted that Treasurer give a quit claim deed to the Fourth Cliff Land Co., of the land and beach below the Fourth Cliff, under the direction of the Selectmen.
- April 5, 1884, Voted that the Town in consideration of one dollar authorize its Treasurer to give the Fourth Cliff Land Co. a quitclaim deed of all the land or hummocks below Fourth Cliff, between North River and the Ocean to low water.
- March 1, 1886, Voted to raise and appropriate $300 for repairs on the road leading from Third Cliff to Fourth Cliff.
- March 4, 1889, Article 30 of Town Warrant: in regard to accepting the bridge across the North River built by the Fourth Cliff Land Co. Referred to Selectmen.

- March 30, 1889, Selectmen notified of hearing on petition for layout of town way from northerly end of Fourth Cliff to Marshfield Avenue.

Hotel Humarock from Marshfield side of the bridge (present day Bridgwaye Inn)

- March 2, 1891, Voted that the town raise and appropriate $2500 to build the road at Fourth Cliff as ordered by the County Commissioner and that the Road Commissioner put the building of said road out by proposals. Notice of said proposals to be posted two weeks before the unsealing of the same.

Looking towards Fourth Cliff - Humarock

BIRDSEYE VIEW OF HUMAROCK BEACH, MASS.

From Ferry Hill Marshfield looking across Sea Street Bridge to ocean

Humarock, Mass. looking South.

How Colonial Humarock Became Modern

You know you're from Humarock if driving back over the bridge out of Humarock, you can't wait to come back!!

As we have read previously, Humarock from settlement times until the late 19th century was used primarily for farming of both crops and cattle, and also for its marsh grasses. We also learned that even though most people would declare their main occupation as farming, they were engaged in many other activities as well. Finally to meet their basic needs, land was constantly being sold, leased, or utilized in ways to foreign to us today. In 1872 John Tilden Junior, also called Captain John Tilden, lived on 35 acres of land on the Fourth Cliff. He was born on 26 July 1897 and died 15 April 1882. Captain John Junior was married to Sally Vinal of Scituate, who died on 18 August 1863. He then married Wealthy Beaton Wood on 13 December 1864. Wealthy died in Boston at the age of 80 on 30 December 1891. What we know about John Tilden Junior was that he was appointed by the Governor of the State as Commissioner of Wrecks, with advice and consent of the council, and for ship-wrecked goods within and for the said County of Plymouth, 6 July 1852. Besides land records, the other piece of information about him was that he, with George H. Weatherbee, Junior, Elisha W. Hall, and their associates and successors formed a corporation named the Tilden Free Bridge Corporation to build a pile bridge from Fourth Cliff in Scituate to Trouant's Island in Marshfield on April 1, 1872. There were four sections to the corporation (See Chapter 166). Section 1 laid out the Corporators and their powers and duties. Section 2 stated that the bridge would be across the North River and built of suitable materials and be at least twenty feet wide. The capital stock of said corporation shall not exceed twenty-five thousand dollars into shares of one hundred dollars each with the right to purchase and hold such real and personal estate as may be necessary, but not exceeding that sum. The bridge would have to have a suitable draw of at least twenty four feet for the passage of vessels. It was to be kept in good repair and subject to the approval of harbor commissioners according to the fourth section of Chapter 146 of the acts of the year of this act, 1866. Section 3 stated that the bridge had to be completed within five years. Section 4 stated that the act shall take effect upon its passage, which as stated above was April 1, 1872. The other two facts we know are: that first on October 1, 1872 John Tilden of Scituate took out a mortgage of $4500 from Gilbert A. Tapley with the provisions that if "upon any default in the performance or observance of the condition of said mortgage to sell the said premises with all improvements that might be thereon at public auction in said Scituate first publishing a notice as therein required and to convey the same by proper deed or deeds to the purchaser or purchasers absolutely and in fee simple; and whereas there has been such default and notice has been published and a sale has been made as will more particularly appear in and by the affividavit here to be subjoined." Second, on the sixth day of October 1877 it stated, "We hereby certify that we were this day present and saw John Tilden the mortgagee named in a certain mortgage deed given by Gilbert A. Tapley to said Tilden dated October 1, 1872 and recorded in Plymouth County Registry of Deeds, Book 393 page 110-111 make an open, peaceable, and unopposed entry on the premises described in said mortgage, for the purpose by him declared, of foreclosing said mortgage for breach of condition there of. The witness whereof we hereto set our hands this day. Robert H. Hall James W. Tilden. Then personally appeared the above named Robert H. Hall and James W. Tilden and made oath that the foregoing certificate by them subscribed is true. Before me. Chas. A. Cole. Justice of the Peace. Rec. October 20, 1877 at 8 a.m. and recorded. Mr. S. Danforth Reg." On this day, I believe, Modern Humarock began to emerge.

The facts are simple enough. Tilden took out a mortgage for $4500 to develop his Tilden Free Bridge Corporation using his property on Fourth Cliff as collateral. Whatever he planned to do with this money failed and he was foreclosed on five years later. Now, let's examine some facts about the 1870s to deduce what possibly might have happened. First as the United States entered the late 19th century, a period of great industrial, urban, transportation, and social change, work and leisure, particularly leisure, began to be viewed differently than ever before. Locally the railroad was expanding through the South Shore. In a schedule for the South Shore Railroad, it stated "on and after Monday, May 2, 1859, three trains for Boston leave Cohasset at 6:55 a.m., 10:00 a.m., and 5:05 p.m. while trains leave Boston for Cohasset at 8:30 a.m., 2:10 p.m., and 6:30 p.m. A footnote adds: Stages for Cohasset, Scituate, and Scituate Harbor upon arrival of every train. Stages leave for Marshfield upon arrival of 2:10 p.m. train. and on

Saturdays of 2:10 and 6:30 p.m. trains." The Duxbury and Cohasset Railroad was built in 1870, "before the summer people began to know where Scituate was, when the Sand Hills were just

Eaton Hotel Greenbush

sand hills and called "Barker's Beach" and the old light house, the Barker farm house, Patrick Wherity's fishing house, a few mossing houses, and the Turner farmhouse were the only building near, when the roadway, such as it was, went through the barnyard of the Barker farm, and the question of beach rights was being agitated in the town meetings

and in the courts, George H. Eaton a young Boston business man, bought property and conceived the idea of a summer hotel and cutting the rest of the property into cottage sites (p.71 Joseph Merritt. *Old Time Anecdotes of the North River and the South Shore*)." His hotel was built 150 feet above sea level on the west side of Colman Hills. There were 100 steps to the top; carriages used a side road. His plan was for 65 cottage lots on Colman Heights (Greenbush) Scituate, Mass. Access to these lots would be from Colman Avenue which was to be 50 feet

wide and intersect with Union Street where the Duxbury and Cohasset Railroad tracks were. Hatherly Street, Water Street, CresCent Avenue, Gertrude Avenue, Eaton Street, Dale Street, Glen Road, Dot Street, and Highland Street would be the main thoroughfares around which the cottages would border. Open space was provided and called Eaton Reserve, Read Reserve, and

several areas of open space. On Eaton Reserve at the top was Lake Hatherly while surrounding the Hotel Grounds and Flag Staff were a Croquet Ground and Bowling Alleys. Easily reached by proceeding down Water Street was the Greenbush Railroad Station. If you looked diagonally across the river and marshes toward the ocean, what did you see? The answer was the Fourth

Cliff. Upon Fourth Cliff Merritt continued, "a lone two-story building and an old barn were for a long time the only structures to be seen. This was the Fourth Cliff House, one of the first summer boarding houses on the South Shore. Long before the days when summer people were coming in any number to Scituate and Marshfield a few families who had discovered the place and liked the quiet were in the habit of spending their vacations there. . . . Later in the season when shore birds came, the house was filled with gunners for several weeks. . . . The Howards of Hanover ran the place for a few years and were followed by Mr. and Mrs. William O. Merritt who came in 1879 and stayed thirteen years. The house was burned in 1902." With all of this activity going on around him, it wasn't surprising that John Tilden thought that this was an opportunity for him as well. The problem was an economic one; it was called the Panic of 1873.

"A major economic reversal began in Europe and reached the United States in the fall of 1873. The signal event on this side of the Atlantic was the failure of Jay Cooke and Company, the country's preeminent investment banking concern. The firm was the principal backer of the Northern Pacific Railroad and had handled most of the government's wartime loans (Civil War), using a widespread sales campaign backed by advertising to sell bonds to people who had never before owned securities.

Cooke's fall touched off a series of events that encompassed the entire nation. The New York Stock Exchange was closed for 10 days. Credit dried up, foreclosures were common and banks failed. Factories closed their doors, costing thousands of workers' jobs. The volume of destitute people soon overwhelmed the abilities of charities to function. Most of the major railroads failed.

The public tended to blame President Grant and Congress for mishandling the economy. The causes were much broader, however. The postwar period was one of frenetic, unregulated growth with the government playing no role in curbing abuses. More than any other single event, the extreme overbuilding of the nation's railroad system laid the groundwork of the Panic and the depression that followed. Recovery was not realized until 1878.

In addition to the ruined fortunes of many Americans, there developed from the Panic of 1873 bitter antagonism between workers and the leaders of banking and manufacturing. This tension would erupt into the labor unrest that marked the following decades (http://www.u-s-history.com/pages/h213.html)."

But as we know timing is everything. With the Panic striking the United States and with banking, railroads, businesses bankrupt and closed and people out of work, Eaton's grandiose

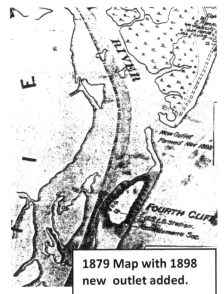

1879 Map with 1898 new outlet added.

plans went up in flames and my guess is so did John Tilden's. One of the results of the Panic was that capital was concentrated in the hands of fewer and fewer people. If you had the money, you could now use it to your advantage over competitors who were at an economic disadvantage. People like Carnegie and Rockefeller did just that. David Blanke, a professor of history at Texas A & M, in an article about the Panic states, "George K. Holmes reported that, by 1890, 71% of the nation's wealth belonged to less than 9% of the public – an unhealthy and lopsided disparity of wealth distribution that has only been equaled, in this country, in the past twenty years." So who was able and had the capital to take economic advantage of this situation in Humarock? They were called the Fourth Cliff Land Company. A look at the 1879 Scituate map shows 5 structures on the Fourth Cliff of which two are labeled and one of labels is incorrect. The one in error shows the Mass Humane Society Building at the southern base of Fourth Cliff and the U.S. Life-Saving station on the top of the cliff. The rest of Humarock is shown on Plate 32 Humarock Beach (see image on next page). It shows house lots from Concord Street to Hawthorne Street. The 1903 Scituate map is based on the Portion of Section No. 3 Plan of land in Scituate, Mass. Belonging to Fourth Cliff Land Co. J. F. Wadleigh, Surveyor, Feb. 25, 1882. The 1879 map of Scituate (above) shows one house on Fourth Cliff labeled G. A. Tapley. We now know that Gilbert A. Tapley gave the $4500 mortgage to John Tilden that was foreclosed on when Tilden's property was sold at auction on October 1,

1877 to Nathaniel P. Merriam of Danvers in the County of Essex for $4500. Trustees of the Fourth Cliff Land Company included: Gilbert A. Tapley, Benjamin J. Greely, Charles E. Jackson, Walter A. Tapley, Nathaniel P. Merriam, et. al.

It would be the Fourth Cliff Land Company that would be the first of the developers to begin the planned development of Humarock. This development would began with The Hotel Humarock, which appears for the first time in Scituate' tax records in 1885. In 1885 the Fourth Cliff Land Company of Boston holdings of land and buildings was assessed at an aggregate value of $24,195 and paid a tax of $362.91. Their land holdings from the tax records indicates 84-½ acres of land plus 200 acres of land and beach and eight structures: House, Barn, Mamm. Barn, Mamm Shed, Hotel Humarock, Skating Rink, and a New House. The Hotel Humarock was worth the most at $15,000.

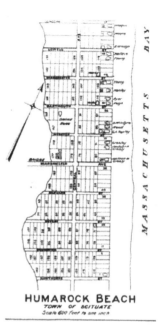

HUMAROCK BEACH
TOWN OF SCITUATE
Scale 600 feet to one inch

" *The sea is a mighty invigorator.*"

Hotel Humarock, Humarock Beach

POST-OFFICE & STATION
SEA VIEW, MASSACHUSETTS

SIXTH SEASON
FREDERICK MERRILL, *Proprietor*

A House of many attractions. Overlooking a most Charming View of the Beach and Ocean, where families are contented and happy — the entire season.

The Hotel Humarock

The following appeared in the Cambridge Chronicle, 7 May 1887. HOTEL HUMAROCK. Humarock Beach, or "The Humarocks," as it has been known from time immemorial, is conceded by every lover of nature to be one of the most charming and picturesque locations for summer resort that can be found on the entire Atlantic Coast. It combines the grandest features of ocean scenery, with fine views of river and quiet country; and its situation, owing to its many natural advantages, offers to the summer pleasure seekers every opportunity for land and water recreation.

The Humarocks, an old Indian name for this retreat, comprises the peninsular forming the Southern extremity of the town of Scituate, in the county of Plymouth, Mass. It is bounded by the broad Atlantic on the East, and the beautiful North River on the West, which is about one-fifth of a mile wide, and is navigable for more than twenty miles into the interior; upon its banks, fertile fields and wild woodlands.

On its front the superb Humarock Beach, than which there is none finer in the world, is about three hundred feet wide, and extends from the towering cliffs of Scituate, with its rocky shore to the point below the Hotel where the North and South rivers pour their united streams into the sea.

A substantial bridge – a structure 650 feet long – spans this gracefully winding river and connects the Humarock with main land, and with the quaint old town of Marshfield, the "Home of Webster," which is about six miles distant by a charming country road.

About five miles distant to the north, nestles the village of Greenbush (Scituate), with it an inspiration which gave to the world that immortal poem, 'The Old Oaken Bucket.' Ten miles down the coast lies the historic town of Plymouth, venerable memory.

Hotel Humarock is one of the finest, most commodious, and for its size, most thoroughly built hotels on the coast; contains over one hundred rooms, each lighted by gas, with mattresses and woven wire springs new this season, nicely furnished, with inside blinds, steam radiators have just been added to heat the dining room's cold mornings, and the guest parlor is heated by wood fire in a large, open fire-place. The house is located almost at the water's edge and its broad verandas command fine views of the ocean and hills. The air is very pure as the southerly breezes coming over the land pass first over a river 1000 feet wide before it reaches the Hotel thus purifying it and reducing the temperature eight to ten degrees. The life in the air is a great restorer to invalids, many of whom testify to the effects upon the system for months afterwards. The dryness of the atmosphere is a subject of comment. Malaria is unknown, mosquitoes are an exception and not the rule.

A large new, fine stable about 2000 feet from the hotel with fine carriages and horses to let is worth the attention of those wishing to drive to places of interest. Horses are boarded at reasonable rates.

The cottages and hotel are exempt from all attractions for the carousing element, that is so distasteful, and is met with at all other beaches. The whole beach is owned and controlled by the Fourth Cliff Land Co., and it is determined that no nuisance shall be tolerated.

The fruits, meats, etc., come from the best of markets daily; vegetables and products of dairy supplied from neighboring farms. Fish and lobsters caught daily from off the shore and served at the table directly from the sea, and the table service will be maintained at the highest standard. The well supplies the house with delicious drinking water and the drainage is absolutely perfect.

Splendid Surf Bathing on the sandy beach, perfectly safe from undertow, while quiet bathing in the still waters of the river and of a warmer temperature can be enjoyed at pleasure.

Excellent fishing can be had either in the river or "out at sea" as the waters around the peninsula are justly celebrated for the abundance and variety of fish.

Safe Boating is assured at all times in the river only twenty rods from the house.

Bowling Alleys and Billiard parlors connected with the house, and Telegraph in the office to all parts of the world.

Full particulars as to route and terms sent on application by addressing A. M. Mills, Proprietor Hotel Humarock, Sea View, Mass., or J. L. Greely, 19 Congress Street, Boston.

Hotel Humarock on Marshfield Avenue

Approaching bridge to Hotel Humarock (large building right on beach after bridge) on Sea St. Sea View

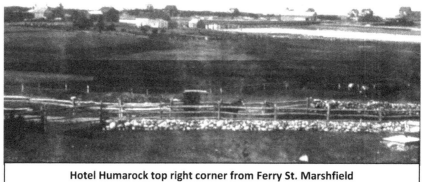

Hotel Humarock top right corner from Ferry St. Marshfield

The Hotel Humarock's Ad

The Hotel Humarock with its broad piazzas fronting the sea, stands close to the water's edge, on a peninsular which comprises the southern extremity of the town of Scituate.

On the east is Massachusetts Bay with its grand ocean view, and on the west the beautiful North River, which winds its way through the hill into the interior and is navigable for more than twenty miles.

The Beach

There is no finer beach in the world than Humarock Beach – three hundred feet wide and extending as it does from the towering cliffs of Scituate to the point below the Hotel, where the North and South rivers pour their united streams into the sea.

The sandy beach and grand surf make bathing a delight, while those who enjoy a milder temperature can indulge at pleasure in the quieter waters of the river. The beach is entirely free from the carousing element.

Lovely drives among the hills connect the hotel with Marshfield, "the home of Webster," – five miles to the north, the village of Greenbush with its "orchards, the meadow, the deep tangled wildwood," and the old well which gave inspiration to the immortal poem, The Old Oaken Bucket, - ten miles down the coast is the historic town of Plymouth.

The Hotel

The Humarock has been put in thorough repair inside, the rooms freshly tinted and painted, while in the kitchen new ranges with all modern improvements, new steam tables, and in fact everything necessary has been added, thus assuring hot and well cooked viands. A new nurses' and children's dining-room has also been added.

The Table will receive particular attention. A prominent Chef has been secured who will have charge of the cuisine.

The Humarock contains over one hundred rooms, each lighted by Gas and Nicely Furnished, and is one of the most commodious and thoroughly built hotels on the coast. Electric bells in all the rooms.

The Hotel outside and its environments has also received attention. New walks have been

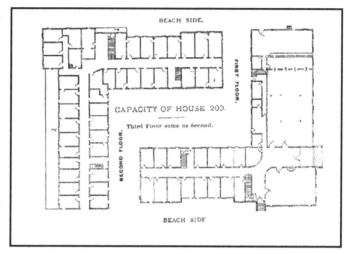

added; the drives to and about the hotel rejuvenated, and this season the hotel will be connected, by the extention of one of the most beautiful drives in the country – the famous Jerusalem Road, an almost unbroken drive from Hull and Nantasket to the Humarock.

MUSIC EVERY EVENING FOR DANCING.

The hotel is provided with running water, and the new system of drainage is perfect. The dryness of the atmosphere is remarkable; the land breezes being purified by passing over the river 1200 feet wide. Our well supplies the house with delicious drinking water.

MALARIA IS UNKNOWN.

Fishing

Excellent Fishing can be had in the river or out at sea. Sail-boating is assured at all times in the river only twenty rods from the hotel.

Tennis Court, Bowling Alleys and Billiard Parlors connected with the house, and Telegraph in the office to all parts of the country.

The Skating Rink will be utilized as a playground for the children.

Elm Street Sea View. Belanger's Farm is on the left. At the top of the hill Elm Street leads down to Sea St.

Route

The Humarock is thirty miles from Boston on the Old Colony Railroad. Express Trains from Boston to Sea View Station, connecting with coaches to Hotel Humarock by a delightful drive of about a mile.

Six trains to and from Boston daily. Be sure to call for Hotel Humarock ticket. Terms $2.50 and $3.00 Per Day. Special rates by week or month.

The house will be open for inspection after May 15th.

During the season entertainments of various descriptions will be inaugurated by the management.

The 11:20 a.m. trains from Boston, returning 2:34 or 5 p.m., will be found most convenient to those desiring to examine rooms.

Stabling and horses to let at reasonable rates near the hotel.

The information contained in the above portion of text (not the photos), came from the 1891 season brochure (pictured at the top) W.S. Sawyer , Manager. The information below comes from when the hotel was owned by Fred Merrill of Avon and was culled from the Fifth and Sixth Seasons brochures.

By 1900, in addition to being lighted by gas and having electric bells in every room, it now has telephone. It boasts of Perfect Service, Comfort, Rest, Quiet, and Health and No Mosquitoes. Its patrons are of the best families of Boston, New York, and from all over the United States. It continued to offer boating, bowling, billiards, tennis, croquet, etc., while music, parties, concerts, and hops are provided. The sixth season began on June 15th. The Hotel is still advertising Stable accommodations of buckboards, surreys, traps, etc. can be obtained at moderate prices. Guests desiring to bring their own private teams are assured of first class service. What I found of most interest was the ad now states that The Hotel is upon an island five miles in length, which reflects what had

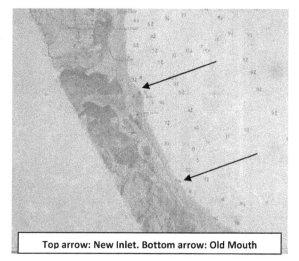

Top arrow: New Inlet. Bottom arrow: Old Mouth

happened during the Portland Gale of 1898 with the new inlet and the Old Mouth still open.

From a series of articles written by Willard de Lue, Article VIII continued, "You said that you believed there once was a hotel at the road which ends at the Humarock oceanfront," writes Raymond W. Beecher of Reading.

Scarcely had Beecher's letter arrived (and there'll be more from it) when I heard from an old acquaintance, Herbert I. Jackson of Hyde Park . . . who turned out to be the son of the Mr. Jackson mentioned by Beecher.

His father was Charles E. Jackson, prominent Boston conveyance, and a resident of Jamaica Plain; and the family cottage is exactly as Beecher remembered it – right at the present seawall, on the left, and at the end of Marshfield Ave., which cuts across Humarock from the main bridge.

AN ACT TO INCORPORATE THE WHITE'S FERRY BRIDGE CORPORATION. *Ch.* 294.
Be it enacted, &c., as follows:

SECTION 1. William H. Eaton, Horace P. Flint, George O. Brastow, their associates and successors are made a corporation by the name of the White's Ferry Bridge Corporation; with the powers and privileges, and subject to the duties, restrictions and liabilities set forth in the general laws which now are, or hereafter may be in force relating to such corporations.

SECTION 2. Said corporation may construct a pile bridge across the waters of North River, between Marshfield and Scituate, at or near the place now known as White's Ferry, and the capital stock of said corporation shall not exceed twenty-five thousand dollars, divided into shares of one hundred dollars each, with the right to purchase and hold such real and personal estate as may be necessary and convenient for the purposes of this act, not exceeding that sum.

Said bridge shall be well built of suitable materials, at least twenty feet wide and floored with planks, with sufficient railings on each side and shall have a suitable draw in the same for the passage of vessels, all of which shall be kept in good repair at all times: *provided*, that the structures built under this act shall be subject to the determination and approval of the harbor commissioners, as provided in the fourth section of chapter one hundred and forty-nine of the acts of the year eighteen hundred and sixty-six.

SECTION 3. If said corporation neglects for the space of five years from the passage of this act, to build and finish said bridge, then this act shall be void.

SECTION 4. This act shall take effect upon its passage.
Approved June 2, 1871.

"My father organized the company that built the bridge from Whites Ferry (Marshfield) to Humarock," Jackson said. That means that it was front of the hotel, which faced the ocean – a building four-storied at the corner, topped by a glassed-in observation cupola; with two big wings of three stories above a half-basement, one wing facing the ocean, the other running back along Marshfield Avenue to where it intersected Central Avenue.

"There were two hotels on the site," Jackson recalls. One was there in the early 1880s. Jackson says he took a photo of it in 1885. "It was burned in the 1890's and then, was rebuilt, but burned again after a few years. Moses Sargent ran the first one." Note: My research has the hotel burning to the ground three weeks after it opened in 1882. It was completely rebuilt and opened in 1883. It burned to ground again in June of 1901. A second hotel was built in the early 1900s.

It must have had some pretense of fashion, for Jackson recalls that Sargent employed [African American] waiters in his dining room.

Now back to Beecher's account: "On the left, just across the bridge, where now stands a garage, was a livery stable where my father used to hire a horse and buggy, and sometimes a 'surrey with a fringe on top.'" I believe that the back part of the garage is the same, long, comparatively narrow building that housed the stable. [When I moved to the area in 1973, this was Covell's Garage. It has been since then a distributor of lobsters, a fish market, and now I am not sure.]

"The road that now turns left at the garage and goes up to Fourth Cliff was then a pretty rough one, but it did go way over to Third Cliff before the storm of 1898. I remember the '98 storm very well, being 17 at the time; and not only did the sea break through the low strip between Fourth and Third cliffs, but it chewed off about 200 yards of Fourth Cliff itself. I had a

MOTOR BOAT ON THE RIVER

snapshot of cows grazing on a part of the cliff which doesn't exist now."

In a June 13, 1954 letter to the editor, John F. Smith from Marshfield Hills wrote the following: "In his South Shore articles, Mr. de Lue mentioned the opening of a new mouth of the North River in the storm of 1898, and the closing of the old one. The old mouth did not close until some years later.

In the Summer of 1899 I ran the first gasoline motor boat on the South Shore, at Scituate, where I was born, for my father Captain John H. Smith. The next year it was sold to Fred Merrill, who owned the Hotel Humarock, and I went with it in the summer of 1900 to carry parties of his guests. Our trip was from the old wooden Humarock bridge down to the old mouth of the river and out into the bay, north to the new mouth, and back inside to the bridge.

We were ready for the Summer of 1901 but the hotel burned June 16 at noon, and all the baggage of the guests, which had come on the train, was burned with it. The old mouth of the river closed some years after that during a heavy northeast storm in the winter." John Smith continued his letter by explaining his connection to Scituate and how his father had a roller skating rink brought from Provincetown to Scituate Harbor by packet boat. After his father's death the skating rink was sold to George F. Welch, who cut the rink out from the rest of the building and used it to make a lumber

shed out back. He finished the letter by explaining he graduated from Scituate High in 1899, left Scituate to work at the Boston Post Office in 1906 and where he retired from in 1933. This made him to be in his early 80's when he wrote this letter.

Now came the development boom of the early 20th century and growth.

The picture below was contributed by W. Ray Freden from his collection.

Humarock Beach

Comparatively few people in our great metropolis are aware that within an hour's ride from Boston on the New York, New Haven and Hartford Railroad, there is one of the finest beaches on our New England coast, nearly five miles in length, adjoining Marshfield (the home of Daniel Webster) and within easy driving distance of Plymouth, Scituate Harbor and Light, Miles Standish Monument, The Old Oaken Bucket and many points of historical interest in the old County of Plymouth.

Humarock Beach has been known to many for years; a large hotel, recently burned, having been a popular resort for visitors from all over the country. There is quite a large colony of summer residents from Boston and neighboring cities who have built cottages upon this beach, and the season of 1904 was remarkable for development along lines of improvement, mainly by the introduction of pure running water in abundant supply from a neighboring hill, thereby increasing fourfold the natural advantages of perfect drainage and sanitary conditions. Every house was occupied last season and not a dwelling could be hired for any price shortly after the season opened. Buildings are being rapidly constructed on the site of the old Humarock Hotel, and in the vicinity, and the season of 1905 promises large accessions to the present colony which consists of the better class of residents, owing to judicious restrictions in the sale of shore property and the barring out of objectionable features, such as beach fakirs, the sale of liquors, etc.

Mr. J. L. Greeley, the well known real estate dealer, who has made a specialty of beach property for years and who has occupied his cottage directly on the beach for many seasons, has charge of the sale of this property in lots to suit purchasers. Plans and photographs may be seen at his office, 161 Summer Street, Boston, and information regarding the property will be given. He may also be found on the premises at Humarock Beach during the summer months.

BIRDS EYE VIEW FROM POST OFFICE, HUMAROCK BEACH, MASS.

"You have to go out, but... You don't have to come back."

Humarock: Life-Saving a Priority

"I drew him out of the water." – The seal of The Humane Society of Massachusetts.

The 17th and 18th centuries were part of the Age of Sail. As vessels plied their trade along New England's rugged coasts, they were subject to the vagaries of New England weather and geography. The result was a tale of wrecks and deaths as vessels pounded by Mother Nature and holed by the many treacherous rocks and ledges left crews adrift in frigid water or ashore on desolate beaches. There, in either place these poor helpless survivors soon succumbed to the horrific elements of cold and exposure. A group of philanthropic men from Boston concerned about the needless deaths resulting from shipwrecks and drowning and who wanted to find ways to save lives, met to establish an organization patterned after the British Royal Humane Society. "Formally established in 1786, The Humane Society of the Commonwealth of Massachusetts elected James Bowdoin, the governor of Massachusetts and the founder of Bowdoin College, to be its first president. The other original trustees were Rev. John Clarke, Dr. Aaron Dexter, Rev. Dr. Simeon Howard, Rev. Dr. John Lathrop, Rev. Samuel Parker, Dr. Isaac Rand, Dr. John Warren, Dr. Thomas Welsh, Dr. Benjamin Waterhouse and Judge Oliver Wendell. In 1791, The Humane Society was formally incorporated in the Commonwealth of Massachusetts. From the outset, The Humane Society focused on recognizing selfless lifesaving rescues and preventing such tragedies. It established an awards system with a financial stipend for those who risked their lives to save others and presented its first award in 1786. By

sponsoring public lectures and publishing research studies, it encouraged innovative lifesaving techniques and resuscitation measures. Its resources financed a number of firsts in the country: lifesaving huts and rescue boats along the coast, swimming instruction for Boston public school students, instructional posters on resuscitation methods and funding to create Massachusetts General Hospital, McLean Hospital and the Boston Lying-In Hospital. (http://www.masslifesavingawards.com/history/)."

Because of its remoteness, isolation, and scene of numerous shipwrecks, the first house

built and sustained for the use of shipwrecked men was in Scituate in 1787. It was called Scituate Charity House and was located 1 mile south of the Fourth Cliff near White's Ferry. By 1806 there were 18 huts along the coast and Nantucket and Martha's Vineyard. The house of refuge was provided with simple furniture, food, clothing, utensils, and means for making light and fire, so that if any were cast ashore at this spot in storm and cold he might not perish until local people could come to their rescue. This had happened too many times in the past.

"The Humane Society recognized that even more people could be saved if boats could be launched to go through the surf. Intrigued by a new design for a lifesaving boat, the Trustees provided funds for the construction of the first lifeboat in America. It was completed in 1807 and housed in Cohasset. With additional funding provided by the

Commonwealth of Massachusetts, the number of lifeboats and boathouses along the coast expanded. [Scituate would contain several of these boat houses].

By 1871, when the US Life-Saving Service (USLSS) was created, The Humane Society was responsible for 78 lifeboats and 92 huts, boathouses and other structures.

U. S. Life Saving Station, Humarock, Beach, Mass.

Volunteers manned these facilities and all were eligible for medal awards. Many of these volunteer leaders were the first to be hired for the new USLSS. For several years, the USLSS and The Humane Society co-existed and often competed to be the first on the scene of a disaster. During major storms, their joint efforts meant that more lives were saved because neither organization could respond to all of the needs.

In 1915, the USLSS and the Revenue Cutter Service were merged to form the US Coast Guard. The Humane Society continued to maintain lifeboats and lifesaving stations along the Massachusetts coast through the 1930's and disposed of the last of its lifesaving equipment in 1946 (Ibid)." The United States Life-Saving Station # 28 was built and located at the southern base of Fourth Cliff.

Humarock has claim to both a history with the Mass. Humane Society with the first hut of refuge being constructed there. Later the United States Life-Saving Service built station #28 there, and finally in 1915 the new United States Coast Guard was housed in the same building.

Let us begin our Humarock lifesaving odyssey with the United States Life-Saving Station

Fourth Cliff Coast Guards Drill, hauling out heavy line, Humarock, Mass.

at Fourth Cliff. The U. S. Life-Saving Service built the Fourth Cliff station, an 1876-style that is shown in the picture on the previous page. It was the only one of its kind on the Massachusetts coastline. The surf men from this station patrolled southward to the mouth of the North River, and northward across a barrier beach toward Scituate Harbor. The station burned to the ground in 1919, leaving the lot at the southern foot of the hill that remains empty today.

What was the daily routine like at the Fourth Cliff station? First look at Form 1809 below:

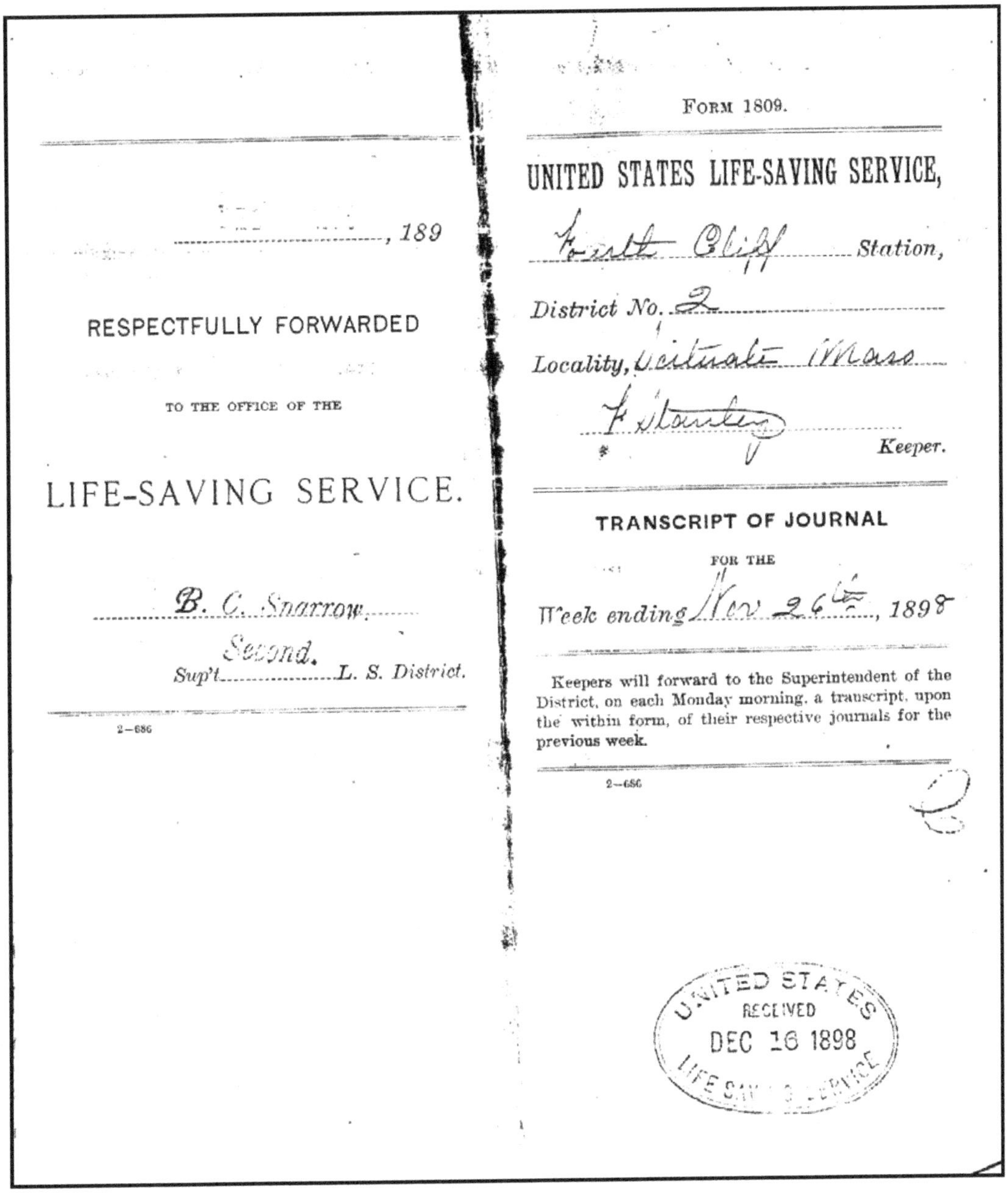

_____, 189

RESPECTFULLY FORWARDED

TO THE OFFICE OF THE

LIFE-SAVING SERVICE.

B. C. Sparrow
Second.
Sup't_____L. S. District.

2—686

FORM 1809.

UNITED STATES LIFE-SAVING SERVICE,

Fourth Cliff Station,

District No. _2_

Locality, _Scituate Mass_

F. Stanley Keeper.

TRANSCRIPT OF JOURNAL

FOR THE

Week ending _Nov. 26th_, 1898

Keepers will forward to the Superintendent of the District, on each Monday morning, a transcript, upon the within form, of their respective journals for the previous week.

2—686

UNITED STATES
RECEIVED
DEC 16 1898
LIFE SAVING SERVICE

The first thing learned is that the keeper of a life-saving station had to fill out a weekly report detailing the occurrences for the previous week from his respective journals and forward these reports on each Monday morning to the Superintendent of their district. We also learned from this document that F. Stanley was the Keeper of Fourth Cliff Station, which was in District No. 2, and that the Superintendent of District 2 was B. C. Sparrow. The final fact was that this transcript of the journal was for Week ending November, 26, 1898.

Notice that the Journal is to be filled out by the Keeper after recording the Station, District, Month, Day, and Year, the Keeper wrote observations of: Condition of the Surf, Direction and Force of wind, as well as the Reading of the Barometer and Thermometer four times a day (Midnight, Sunrise, Noon, Sunset). He then listed the eight patrols noting who did each of the patrols. Several questions were then asked and his response written next to the question. Stanley was then required to fill in the number of vessels from each of six classes that passed the station that day.

He then completed his report for this day by putting remarks in under GENERAL REMARKS and signing the form. "House swept throughout – All brass and iron work cleaned." His General Remarks for the rest of the week are as follows:

- Nov. 21st "House swept throughout – All brass and iron work cleaned. Visited North Key post – changed No 1 Key for No 1 found Safe and Key in good condition.
- Nov. 22nd House swept throughout. All brass and iron work cleaned. Omitted exercise with boat beach too rocky.
- Nov. 23rd House swept throughout. All brass and iron work cleaned. Practised with Signals. Visited South Key post did not change Keys.
- Nov. 24th House swept throughout. All brass and iron work cleaned. Omitted exercise with apparatus on account of wet weather.
- Nov. 25th House swept throughout. All brass and iron work cleaned. Exercised with beach apparatus. Exercised restoring the apparently drowned.
- Nov. 26th House swept throughout. All brass and iron work cleaned.

Sounds like a pretty routine week, right! Wrong! Listen to Stanley's written report for Sunday,

USLSS Station at Fourth Cliff

Nov. 27th 1898. Condition of Surf – he checked off the highest rating possible for the four times very high; Direction and force of wind, four times he recorded North East – Heavy gale – Snow. Thermometer: Midnight, 32; Sunrise, 32; Noon, 25; Sunset, 20. Barometer: Midnight, 29.66; Sunrise, 29.25; Noon, 29.25; Sunset, 29.48. Under Patrols he wrote, "impossible to patrol from 8 pm to 4 am. Under General Remarks this is what was written, "During the gale this day the flag pole was blown [down] the out-building was moved of[f] from its foundation and a lot of shingles torn off and the platforms were washed away with the steps of the Station, and a Key post with one Key. The beach a little north of this Cliff is cut through so that it is impossible to get across except with a boat and then only occasionally. Patrolled the beach all day as far as it was possible to go as there was a large quantity of wreckage washing ashore all day." The cut that Stanley mentioned was the new inlet for the North River. A break had been blasted through the shingle beach and

Three Days After Great Storm of 1898

the course of the river dramatically altered. What he witnessed possibly had not been seen since the Great Hurricane of 1635. Stanley was finally able to reach Scituate Harbor on Tuesday, he informed the citizens that their coastline had been changed forever. On November 28th Stanley wrote, "Spent the day in clearing away the wreckage about the premises and looking for any bodies that might come ashore." On the 29th he remarked, "Four of the crew spent this day trying to find the bodies of four men that were lost from a gunning stand in the river. The rest kept a lookout along the beach for bodies. Visited South Key post – changed No 3 Key for No 2 found Safe and Key in good condition. The 30th he reported, "Sent 2 men across the cut in the beach to keep a lookout to the northward while the rest patrolled the beach to the South. Was compelled to send two men North together as one could not get across alone." For the remainder of the week his general remarks were the same, "House swept throughout and All brass and iron work cleaned." Let me give you one more fact from the U.S. Department of Agriculture, WEATHER BUREAU for the Month of November, 26 – 27, 1898 records, "11 am a hurricane of terrible violence began on the night of the 26th and continued through the 27th Steamer Portland and 100 lives lost off Cape Cod Wind reached velocity of 85 miles an hour. $500,000 dollars worth of property lost along Cape Cod Coast."

The complete story of what happened to some of those trapped in the marshes around Fourth Cliff is told below.

The new inlet three days after storm above; New inlet below today .

Richard Wherity was a veteran lifesaver who signed on with Josiah James in 1889 and served at the Fourth Cliff Station for 10 years from 1890 1900. Richard Wherity recalled the Storm of '98 this way, "The station cancelled all leaves and the crew went on around the clock watch." His first task was to warn gunners in a shack back of Fourth Cliff. Later in the afternoon

he took off one of gunners [a Webster boy] in a boat. The four remaining gunners were reluctant to leave their sport. By now you know who these four young men were. During the Gale Wherity had duty which took him to Hatch's Gunning Stand [south of the Fourth Cliff Station]. He rescued Mr. David Sears and they hiked back of the breakwater to Humarock Bridge, then a drawbridge. The bridge was weaving back and forth because of the gale and the water. [Thomas Tilden told his children that the evening tide on November 26, 1898, never ebbed, and that the next tide came in on top of it.] Wherity got Mr. Sears across the bridge which, because of the new breakthrough, was practically an island. Wherity fought his way across the bridge which managed to hold all during the storm. Finally he reported back at the lifesaving station.

On a more positive note, can you imagine being told that three of your family members

"So. River Gunning Shanty"
Richard Clapp, Everett Clapp, Wm. H. Clapp
(all brothers)

had been killed in a storm surge during an incredibly powerful storm. Then, hours later, they walk in the door alive and well. This happened to Ann Rossini Clapp of Greenbush. The Clapp brothers (Richard, Pete, and Bob) had gone to their gunning stand at the base of Snake Hill in Marshfield. According to a letter from Ann Rossini Clapp to her daughter Helen:

"When the water was up to their armpits they tried to leave their shanty in their small boat, but were in danger of sinking when the Lord took a hand. A stray gundalow came drifting past them. They immediately leaped into it as their small boat sank. Having no oars and with water up to their waists, the craft drifted to the Marshfield side. Before the Clapp brothers arrived there, they heard cries for help and saw the Henderson brothers being swept away in their boat. Frustrated because they could not maneuver the gundalow to aid them, the Clapps were forced to leave the Hendersons to their fate. When it was close to land,

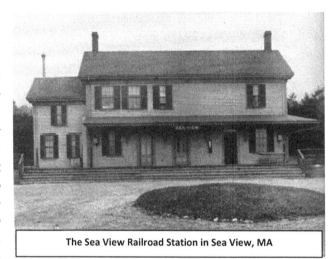

The Sea View Railroad Station in Sea View, MA

the men leaped for the shore. Then they made their way to the Sea View Railroad Station. Richard, being pretty well benumbed, they had to cut his boots off and his feet rubbed to keep him well and good. Brandy was downed by them all and warmed them up. Then they started for home. When they got to the bridge [Little's] the debris and breakage with water running too quickly to swim across, so they headed for the Union Bridge. There they swam across and headed for Greenbush. They got home about 3 pm. They had been in the water from nine until two. We had received news that they and their shanty had gone hours before they appeared. And there was rejoicing when they opened the door on us. I haven't got over trembling yet. Then to cop the climax Little Elijah started two hours before to get to the life savers at Fourth Cliff but couldn't get there it was like a sea and he had a hard time to get back from where he was. He had to crawl on his hands and knees to get back.

"Four of the boy gunners there to the bottom at the same time our boys and young Webster landed. They were Emma Tildens son, Joe Fords son and two Hendersons sons. Oh it is so dreadful, Our boys have been searching with others for their bodies fortwo days. Some men found the Ford body. I expect the boys any moment and I hope they have found them all...."

Dave Ball and I have uncovered other primary sources that filled in the blanks. A man named George Woodman, who had been on Trouant's Island during the storm, recalled the Henderson camp was just north of the island on a low rise. He observed the boys out hunting on the marsh that afternnon. He saw they had shot some geese and since Woodman and his friends had not, he decided to go to their shanty and see if he could buy one for Sunday dinner.

He went, but when he got there Woodman found that one boy had left and taken the geese with him. Actually Richard Wherity, a surfman from the Fourth Cliff lifesaving station, had used the station's boat and warned them about the threatening weather forecast. George Webster left with him and returned to the Fourth Cliff station, the others decided to remain. Woodson noted that on Monday morning, "Our house was the only one left and it washed off our piazza. about 11 o'clock we saw a boat coming down the river filled with men. They saw us and you can visualize their feelings when they saw that the Henderson house had been washed away, but apparently the four boys were safe on the island. It was a very different story when they came ashore. Two of the men were too weak to walk. Very distressing."

All the drowning victims' bodies from the Henderson shanty were discovered. Albert Tilden's body was found on December 1 and the Hendersons were found December 2. The joint funeral for the Henderson brothers and Albert Tilden was held on December 3rd because they were such close

friends. There was a private funeral held for George Ford in Marshfield. A poem written by Miss Edna Clapp was read at the joint funeral; she would later marry Harry Henderson (Fred and Bert's brother) in 1903. Reverend T. Thompson, minister of the First Parish Church, in his eulogy said,

> We cannot even afford to have such young men leave us for the better opportunities of the earthly life. We need them and they have been taken from us, and while we must submit, we can but lament their taking off.

> They were also young men of skill and bravery which would have been sufficient to have extricated them from many a peril such as would appall others. But it seems certain that no amount of skill could have saved them in the desperate situation in which they found themselves upon that terrible day when wind and wave combined and stout ships went down with all aboard.

I am not satisfied to say of the loss we have suffered. "It was to be," or "It is all for the best." I submit, when I must to calamities such as this, or even of lesser moment. To so acquiesce may easily become an excuse for little thought and may prevent future precautions that at another time might avail. Let us but say, "It was to be,' but rather, "It shall not again be."

The funeral home record from page 3 reads, ". . . triple funeral in the church. Procession formed with Bert in my hearse. Fred in my small hearse and Bert Tilden in Marshfield's hearse. Met by Phoenix F & A.M. of which this one was a member [Bert Henderson] and escorted to church. Church was full. Masonic service at grave."

It was a service those in attendance never forgot and never wished to witness again. A young man speaking of their fate said, "It is hard on us who had been associated with them often in labor and in sport. We knew them as others could not because of this intimacy." He continued, by saying that the boys were so companionable. They won and retained the esteem and love of others through their conversation and deportment. "All who knew them will be deeply affected. They can never be forgotten."

One final irony of this story, the gundalow that saved the Clapps was owned by the Henderson brothers! It had broken loose during the storm!

As the Keeper and surfmen of the Fourth Cliff Station soon found out, they were an island. The only mainland link was the Humarock Bridge, that connected Sea Street Marshfield with Marshfield Avenue in Humarock. Today, there are two bridges that connect Humarock to Marshfield and the Old Mouth has long since 1898 been filled in. Until 1998 the main bridge into Humarock was called the Sea Street Bridge while the smaller bridge was known as the Julian Street Bridge until June 22, 2008. Today the Julian Street Bridge is the Francis R. Powers bridge named after the Clerk of Courts for Plymouth County and long time Humarock resident while the Sea Street Bridge was renamed the Captain Frederick Stanley Bridge after the long time Keeper of the Fourth Cliff Life-Saving Station.

Captain Stanley was born in Boston January 27, 1845, and died of Diabetes on September 10, 1915. He married Julia A. Flynn on September 16, 1868. They had seven children and lived on Allen Street in Scituate. Both he and his wife are buried in Union Cemetery on Stockbridge Road. His age at the time of his passing was 70 years. His obituary in the Boston Globe for 11 September 1915 read, "In Scituate, September 10, Captain Frederick Stanley, 70 years, 7 months, 24 days. Funeral at late residence, Allen St. Scituate, Sunday at 2 pm. Relatives and friends invited. At the age of 12 he followed the sea and made voyages from Boston to

CAPT. FREDERICK STANLEY.

Scituate and commanded several vessels later, among them the bark Valparaiso. He made Scituate his home for 12 years previous to entering the life saving service. His son Thomas Stanley is the proprietor of the Stanley House at Scituate Harbor. His three daughters are Miss Ellen Stanley, Mrs. Edward Tobin and Miss Margaret Stanley. Captain Stanley is a man of many friends among the native people and summer residents of the South Shore. He is popular in the ranks of the life savers. Stanley was appointed as a surf man on January 17, 1880, shortly after the Fourth Cliff Station opened. The 1910 Globe article continues, "The station then as now, had a crew of seven men, among them being Capt. George H. Brown, who is now in charge of the station at North Scituate beach and who recently reached the quarter century mark in service. In October of the same year Captain Stanley was placed in charge of the station with the rank of Captain, succeeding Capt. John Smith, now a resident of Scituate Harbor. He has served as captain ever since, so that the silver anniversary of his captaincy will be marked by October 1 of the present year. During his service Capt. Stanley has aided 34 good-sized vessels, and a large number of small craft. Among them was the fisherman M.H. Norton, which came ashore bottom-side up near his station on November 25, 1888. Fourteen lives were lost at the time, but there was one survivor, Martin Allen. He lived inside the vessel during the interval from the time she was upset to the time that the life savers discovered her, and stepped ashore after she was beached without being discovered until sometime after. He was at Austin & Stone's Museum shortly after the wreck, and remained some time.

In a brief article about people of Scituate in the Boston Globe on August 4, 1912, it opens with "Captain Stanley Begins His 33d Year as Superintendent of Fourth Cliff Life-Saving Station." Then three years later in the weekly transcript journal for March 23, 1915, the general remarks written by Matthew Hoar were, "Keeper Frederic Stanley retired, and I have taken charge as Acting Keeper with Richard Graham as temporary surfman. M. Hoar, Act-Keeper." So ended one of the great careers in the history of Massachusetts Life Saving. Captain Frederick Stanley left a long legacy of dedication, duty, and concern for others.

For the final story for this chapter I could have chosen many of the heroic actions and rescues achieved by Keeper Stanley and the Fourth Cliff Life-Saving crew, but for me, one stands out, the wreck of the Helena. Let's begin!

Imagine that you are captain of a vessel carrying thousands and thousands of board-feet of pine from the South to Maine. You are caught, as you are nearing what you think is a safe haven, in the blinding snow of a furious gale that has been pounding you for hours. Visibility is near zero when suddenly you see the bright flash of three distinct colors that you instantly recognize as a Coston flare. With sickening realization you comprehend that you are near to shore with immediate danger confronting you. As you try to shout orders to your crew to try to avoid this catastrophe, the ship suddenly is pounded onto rocks and the horrible sounds of your ship bottom being gouged, ripped, and torn assail your ears. Instantly you realize you and your crew's one hope for salvation lies in the rigging. Quickly, you shout orders to the crew to get up the masts and into the rigging and lash themselves there and pray the light you briefly saw was nearby help. This imaginary tale came true on January 30, 1909, at the Fourth Cliff station Humarock.

Our story commenced when the night patrol of the Fourth Cliff station had just completed his walk up the beach and was entering the station when the lookout yelled that a schooner was coming on the beach.

Jumping up from the breakfast table the crew rushed to the boat room and swung open the door prepared to launch their boat. But as they did the vessel surged and plunged forward before the howling storm. With a thunderous crash which seemed to shake the vessel from stem to stern, she plowed her way over the huge boulders with

rendering that seemed to tear out her bottom. Captain Stanley immediately determined that the surf-boat was not necessary because the vessel was so close to shore. He ordered that the breeches buoy would be better used, so the wagon and the gun were hauled out and dragged with much exertion up the cliff until it was directly opposite the stranded vessel.

Breeches Buoy in use at Sandhills, Scituate

The vessel's crew could be seen lashed to the rigging but the intense noise of the storm and thundering surf made communication by megaphone impossible. However, the crew ascertained what their rescuers intentions were and distributed themselves in the rigging to receive the line. On the second attempt Captain Stanley's shot fell directly over the main mast. The vessel's crew quickly made the line and hawser firmly attached to the head of the mainmast; this was followed quickly by the block and tackle. The thankful crew was now ready to make the trip to shore over a swaying rope with flying spray and stinging snow assaulting them as they were drawn toward the cliff. The cook, J was the first - with the rest of the crew following one by one. The last man across was the vessel's commander Captain John Cummings. The steward of the Helena, Orlando Crowley, telling of his travail said," I have a wife in Boston, and I tell you when I struck this beach almost exhausted after a tough night's work, I felt pretty good. It was my first experience in the lifebuoy, and I don't care for another one under the same conditions right away."

Wreck of the schooner Helena on the Fourth Cliff, Scituate two miles from proposed harbor of refuge.

The crew and captain were soaked to their skins, and the life savers fitted them out with dry clothing which, if it did not fit, the crew said was all right, and they voiced their gratitude to Captain Stanley and the crew of the station, who, they said, treated them like brothers. The life saving crew also gave the Helena crew warm food. Miss Elsie Barker and Mrs. Edith Mills, who came from Marshfield, did much to assist the sailors.

An hour after the Helena's crew had been brought to shore the life-boat of the Massachusetts Humane Society, No. 29, manned by a crew of hardy Scituate "mossers" and with Capt. Christy O'Neil at the steering oar, pulled manfully down the beach to aid in the rescue. They came ashore later and seemed disappointed at not having had a chance to assist in the work.

Captain John Cummings, whose vessel was twelve miles off course, said, "We struck bad

Wreck of the Schooner Helena, Jan. 31, 1909, Scituate, Mass.

weather when off Nauset about midnight, the wind piping a stiff gale from the southeast with driving, blinding snow, the storm increasing in violence with a shifting wind which finally came around to a fierce gale from the northeast. It was thick as mud, there being absolutely no observation. We kept the vessel well up for Boston Light, hoping to make the harbor, but the fierce wind and current must have set us in shore far beyond my calculations, and the first thing we knew breakers were right under our bow. Although I put the helm hard up we went ashore bow on with a hard crash and here we are, piled up on the rocks, but thankful, to be ashore alive, thanks to the brave life savers." Most of the members of the crew were sent to Boston by the evening train, Captain Cummings and the steward alone remaining at the life-saving station. Capt. Stanley and Capt. Cummings of the Helena will keep a sharp watch through the night, but indications favor a lessening of the wind and sea.

The Helena was a comparatively new vessel, being built in Bath in 1900 for New York parties. She was 504 tons net burden, 168 feet over all, 35 feet beam and 13 feet draft. She was deeply loaded with 500,000 feet of yellow pine for Portland. It was consigned to the Wilson Irwin lumber company of this city [Portland]. Her cargo was insured. The schooner was owned by Capt. Charles Hodgkins of Lamoine, Me, although she hailed from New York and was managed by A. H. Bull & Co. of that city.

On February 2, 1909, the Boston Water Front Items, it was stated that serious doubts are expressed over saving the schooner Helena, which was driven ashore at Scituate during the blizzard Saturday. The tug Confidence with the wrecking lighter Salvor went there early yesterday but the sea was so rough that the tug could not approach near enough to work. An attempt will be made to lighten the deckload, and when this is done, if the vessel holds together, an effort will be made to drag her off the beach. Capt. Cummings paid off the crew of the vessel at the office of his agents on State St. Most of the men will join other vessels at this port.

Before we finish our story of the wreck of the Helena and the Fourth Cliff Station, two additional stories need to be told: one serious and one light. The first story comes from the

92

Weekly Transcript of Journal Fourth Cliff dated January 31, 1909, the day following the wreck of the Helena and her crew's rescue. F. Stanley, Keeper, wrote under general remarks, "The Capt. Of Helena ashore near this station fell out of the rigging. Surfmen Quinn and Carlton with an outsider James Ward jumped into a dory and tried to get him but owing to the sea running

around the bow were unable as every sea would sweep them back on the beach finaly when the Capt. Was compelled to let go of the rope the sea swept him round the bow. The surfmen left the dory and Carlton and Quinn caught him just as I arrived on the scene. We took him on to the beach. He was unable to walk, so surfmen Barber, Carson, and six outsiders picked him up and carried him to the station where I had him stripped, rubbed down wrapped him in blankets, gave him hot drink and put him to bed with bottles of hot water round him and he soon fell asleep. In 3 hours he was all right again, the two surfmen had to go to their waists in the water to get to the Capt." In an article from February 1, 1909, we find out why he was aboard. At low water in the afternoon of January 31, Capt. Cummings with some life-savers and others boarded the vessel and saved most of the clothing and personal effects of the crew and many articles of value which were movable.

The Captain was standing in the rigging on the offshore side when something parted and he went into the surf which was breaking with violence against the vessel. Someone threw him a rope which he grasped and an attempt was made to haul him on board. He struggled to keep his hold on the rope but yelled to those on board that he couldn't hold on and would have to let go. He let go the rope and went down.

As he reappeared a second rope was thrown him, which he managed to lay hold to, but was unable to retain and he again went under the water.

Frank Carleton, Dennis Quinn and James Ward were meantime making a great effort to reach the drowning man in a boat, which was several times swept back on shore by the surf.

As Capt. Cummings lost his hold on the second rope, the sea swept him in toward the shore and the three men in the boat leaped overboard, and after a desperate struggle, reached the captain and brought him ashore.

He was given immediate attention by Capt. Stanley and the crew of the station, who put him to bed. He was completely exhausted and considerably bruised. His rescuers made haste to get into dry clothing.

The vessel stood well the pounding of the heavy seas and is apparently not much damaged, although the foremast is sprung and the hull appears to be badly strained. She has swung around broadside to the sea and now gets the full force of the surf. An attempt will be made on Monday if the sea calms down to take off the deck load of heavy lumber.

The final story comes from Francis Christopher Murphy. He wrote to Edward Rowe Snow on January 14, 1978, about Snow's recent story about his beagle and the North River. Murphy wrote, "I have a story to tell you about my dog, a St. Bernard, and the North River and the schooner "Helena". . . . I would like to go back to tell you that I live at 35 Common Street here in Scituate. I have lived here since 1920 and previously at Tichnor Place off Beaver Dam Road, that was then Willow Street. I was born there in 1896, one of six children of Mr. and Mrs. William H. Murphy. For thirty years Mr. Murphy was a member of the life Crew at the Fourth Cliff. . . . Before the gale of November, 1898, the beach patrol from the station went north to the key-post at the southerly entrance to Scituate Harbor. The night of the gale

Saint Bernard Puppy

my father had the middle patrol north. On the way he said that slabs (pine used for kindling) were flying through the air like shingles and bricks were coming from the chimneys and banging down the roofs. I remember his saying that it seemed that, and I quote,"all the devils in hell were loose that night". The next man to make the morning patrol was Marcus Barbour. He went to the north end of the Fourth Cliff but couldn't continue as the river had broken through. Previous to that there was a road from the Third Cliff to the Fourth Cliff. It would be where the mouth of the river is now.

"Now allow me to return to my dog Bruno. When the men from the station were off duty during July and August, only the keeper was at the station. My father had a carpenter putting on a dormer window on our house. One afternoon when I was talking to him, he asked me if I would like a St. Bernard puppy. Of course I said, "Yes," and asked my mother. She said, "You know we have one dog, and I don't think your father would like it." However, I took the four o'clock train to North Scituate and met the carpenter, who rode a bicycle, went to his home and picked out a puppy. On the five o'clock train a man offered me $5.00 for the puppy; I refused.

At supper time my father came in and saw a puppy on the kitchen floor. He asked, "What is that?" When I told him it was puppy, he replied, "I know, but what kind?" When I told him it was a St. Bernard, he replied, "Good Lord, he will eat us out of house and home." We kept the dog, and he was great with children.

When he was full-grown and my father was going back to the station from a day-off, he would take the dog with him. He would walk the beach, and after a few days, he would swim across the river and come home.

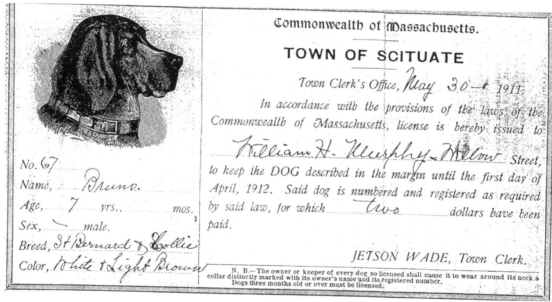

One winter night during a northeast snow storm, he walked the south patrol with the surfmen. But when the man returned, the dog didn't come into the station. The man then went to the door and heard the dog barking. He went towards him, and at the same time, the surfman on lookout at the top of the cliff came down and said a short time before he had seen a light. They then saw the "Helena" ashore. . . . A reporter from a Boston newspaper came to the station and was told about the dog first seeing the "Helena". He wrote the story, but added a falsehood saying the dog was put in the breeches buoy first to test it. Some story! However, later a man came to the station and wanted my father to take the dog to the dog show that was to be held in the Mechanics Building in Boston.

By getting permission from Superintendent Bowley in Provincetown, my father took Bruno, all expenses paid, for three or four days and told the story about the dog and the

North from Fourth Cliff

Fourth Cliff and Mouth of North River

"Helena". As you know, the "Helena" stayed on the beach and broke up. . . .

Regarding my dog Bruno, I came home on a weekend pass when I was in the service during WWI and asked about Bruno. After some hesitation, I was told he was put to sleep. I said no more.

Some additional things I have thought of:

- At times after a dry summer, the cistern at the station would go dry, and the men had to take a dory and row to Trouant's Island for their fresh water.

- As I have told you, there was a road from the Third Cliff previous to the November gale of 1898. My father told of one time when they had to work four wrecks one after the other. The property now known as the Scituate Country Club was a farm owned by Henry Welch, who belonged to the Humane Society. The keeper at the station told my father to go and ask Henry to come to the station with horses to pull the beach cart. Mr. Murphy was sent as he was the youngest member of the crew.

- Did you know that at one time there was no road up to the station from Humarock? It only went about where Hatch's Gunning Stand was. One Saturday, I was at the station when the coal for the winter was coming down from the Welch Company of Scituate Harbor. The men had to unhitch a team, and with four horses, they would pull a wagon over the beach stones with the load, unload it at the station, and go back for another load. It was a day's job, but then the men were only paid $12-$14 a week."

I enjoy your articles.

Sincerely,

Frances Christopher Murphy

Right: remains of the schooner Helena on beach at Fourth Cliff. Above: Surf boat from North Scituate Life-saving station. Top Right: Drawing of a Surfman from 1880s.

Previous page: Newspaper drawings of Helena breaking up on beach at Fourth Cliff

South from Fourth Cliff

SOME SHIPWRECKS HELPED BY FOURTH CLIFF LIFE SAVERS

- December 1, 1868. Schooner. Name unrecorded. Wrecked on Fourth Cliff beach near Charity House.

- January 9, 1886. Schooner Joel Cook. Captain Springer. Of and from Philadelphia for Boston. Wrecked on Third Cliff.

- Jan. 9, 1886. Schooner Isaac Carriten. Ashore on Humarock Beach.

- Feb. 10, 1888. Schooner Agnes R. Bacon. New York for Boston. Wrecked near the Fourth Cliff.

- June 25, 1888. Barque Chattanooga. Puerto Rico for   Boston. Wrecked at the mouth of the North River.

- Feb. 15, 1906. Steamship Devonian. Ashore at Fourth Cliff. Liverpool for Boston. Passengers and general cargo saved.

USSLSS Fourth Cliff, 1899

- May 19, 1899. Catboat Nancy Hanks. Surfmen assisted the owner of this boat which had been ashore since the great storm of last November, to move it down near the channel, where it would float at high water.

- August 4, 1899. Two young men landed near station in a small boat, as they were afraid to be out after dark. Surfmen hauled their boat up on the beach and transported them across the river, so that they could walk to their homes.

- August 7, 1899. American sloop Whip. Stranded 2 ½ miles NNW of station at 2:45 a.m. The station patrol warned her of her proximity to the beach by burning a Coston light, but the master reported that, although he saw the signal, the wind was too light for the sloop to work quick enough to clear the beach. Lifesaving crew at once launched the surfboat and boarded her, but could do nothing until the tide flooded. At the master's request the keeper pulled to Green Harbor to obtain assistance from a tug which lay at that place. As the sloop was leaking, the surfmen from Fourth Cliff Station, who had arrived at the scene, stood by during the absence of the Brant Rock crew. The surfmen returned, manned the pumps, and upon the arrival of the tug, ran a line to her. At 9 a.m. the sloop was floated and taken into Green Harbor.

- August 8, 1899. Small boat, no name. Stranded while trying to enter a cut through the beach against a strong ebb tide with a dory in tow. Surfmen floated the boat and towed it into the river, then carried the dory across the beach.

- September 27, 1899. Rowboat, no name. Capsized 1 ½ miles from the station, throwing two men into the water. They were picked up by a passing yacht and landed near the station. In the meantime the crew manned the surfboat and pulled out the boat, but the sea being too heavy to tow it in or right it, they anchored it and returned to station. Furnished dry clothing to the two rescued men. On the following, day surf men bailed out the boat and towed it ashore, returning it to the owners.

- October 7, 1899. Dory, no name. At 1:30 p.m. two men capsized in a dory while trying to cross the break in the beach about half a mile N. of the station, and were in danger of being carried seaward by the strong ebb tide which was running. Two surfmen, being close at hand with a dory and seeing the accident, pulled out and rescued the men, landing them safely across the cut.

- Oct 12, 1899. Sloop Dione. Stranded about three quarters of a mile N. of station. Surfmen went on board and ran out her anchor, but it proved to be too light. They returned to station and got a heavier anchor with which they succeeded in hauling her afloat and then took her to an anchorage in the river.

My Fanciful Trip to Hotel Humarock – 1900

Photo from Arthur Brown Collection.

From Sea View
Station to Hotel
Humarock by
barge.

Photo collection of
"W. Ray Freden"

It was a muggy, sweltering August day as I walked down Atlantic Avenue heading to South Station to catch the express train to Sea View, Marshfield. I was looking forward to spending the next two weeks at the newly refurbished Hotel Humarock in Scituate away from the smells, noise, and frenetic confusion of the city. My friend Charles Jackson from Congress Street, raved so much about his month at Humarock last year that I decided to check it out. Because of Charles's enthusiasm and my respect for his judgment, I sent for the Owner and Proprietor Fred Merrill's 1900 booklet describing the hotel and its amenities. After careful examination of the booklet, these factors: the convenience of being an hour from Boston, and whose best families from Boston were patrons, a beach five miles in length with the finest surf bathing at any time during the day, large, airy, well-furnished rooms to accommodate two hundred guests, a first class table,

Charles Jackson - from
Arthur Brown Collection

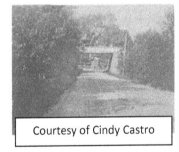

Hotel Humarock, *Humarock Beach,*

POST-OFFICE AND STATION,
SEA VIEW, MASS.

FIFTH SEASON.

Frederick Merrill, Proprietor.

PERFECT SERVICE,
COMFORT, REST,
QUIET, AND HEALTH.

OVERLOOKING A MOST CHARM-
ING VIEW OF THE BEACH AND
OCEAN.

activities including, boating, bowling, billiards, tennis, croquet, music, parties, concerts, and hops, I was convinced to try it. I contacted Mr. Merrill at his Boston office at 19 Congress Street that next Wednesday and secured a room for the first two complete weeks of August (August 5 through August 19) as well as tickets on the express to Sea View on August 5th with a return to Boston for Sunday August 19th . As the train thundered over the railroad bridge across the North River, the broad open vista of water, marsh, and various varieties of landforms numbed and overwhelmed my senses with nature's beauty. I wanted to get off the train and walk the streets and trails just to drink in the sights, sounds, and smells of nature's drafts, but the train continued on through Marshfield Hills passed the water tank and depot at East Marshfield Station, which would later be changed to the Marshfield Hills Station, rumbled across the Pleasant

Courtesy of Cindy Castro

Street Bridge before it slowed down and headed into the Sea View Station and my destination. As I gathered my baggage and exited the station, there my transport waited for me, ready to take me to the hotel. Swiftly my belongings were loaded onto the barge and we pulled out of the station and headed south along Summer Street to the Hotel Humarock. The driver, a garrulous and long-time resident of Littletown/Sea View kept up a running travelogue all the way to our objective. I did not mind it in the least as I was struck with curiosity. He began by having us observe that the Sea View Railroad Station was the largest station on the Duxbury and Cohasset railroad line, proudly pointing out its two stories that made it unique. He added that the present station replaced a one story building that had been built in 1870. Our driver asked us to observe the various corn fields that lay to the eastern side of Summer Street. Then he expanded with pride on the long and distinguished history of Sea View by stating that during the 18th and early to middle 19th centuries, sea captains, shipbuilders, industrial entrepreneurs, farmers, and merchants made their homes, ran their businesses and mills along Summer Street and Little's Creek. Pausing to take a deep breath, he continued that shipyards like White's Ferry, Halls' and Keenes' yards hummed with activity further along the North River in Sea View. He scoffed that Humarock's more recent history could not compete with that of Sea View. He concluded by emphatically stating that Sea View had a Post Office while Humarock did not, as if this detail was conclusive proof of Sea View's importance over Humarock's. As we slowly journeyed along the dusty road, he expounded upon the residents of the various homes and buildings we passed: from the Randall family home with its building for the manufacture of reed pump organs next to the stately Jedediah Little's home, and so on. As we slowly turned onto Elm Street, no dialogue was needed for scenic beauty of the open fields, barns, livestock, and fences of the Belanger property which lay to the west of Elm Street and along Ferry Hill Road spoke of their own beauty.

Summer Street Sea View

Perched on the top of a mostly treeless Holly Hill to the west of Elm Street and bounded by a long stone wall at its base, majestically sat a most beautiful country estate. Looking at our astonishment, our driver stated, "You are looking at the estate of former Governor George Emery built in 1885. He was appointed in 1875 by President Ulysses Simpson Grant as governor of the territory of Utah with full veto power. He was said to have brought financial, political, and economic stability to Utah so much so that the people of Utah named a county after him. He retired to his farm on Holly Hill in Marshfield and is presently the president of the Marshfield Agricultural Society." We proceeded down Elm Street along Ferry Hill on our east to Holly Hollow before turning left onto Sea Street and coming to the bridge to Humarock. Just before the bridge to both our left and right ran Ferry Street. This part of Ferry Street on our left ran along the base of Ferry Hill and had several large houses bordering the river, two of which were the Sea View House and the North River House. Our driver added that there were probably only three or four houses on the top of Ferry Hill at this time. As we crossed the six hundred foot Humarock

Bridge the clean, fresh wind from over the bay, struck and cooled us immediately. In stately glamour rose the Hotel Humarock with three floors of 200 rooms with wide piazzas and verandas that graced spectacular ocean and river views. I could not wait to check in, unpack, and then go exploring. We

Interior of room at Hotel Humarock

approached the hotel along Marshfield Avenue and disembarked after reaching the end of Marshfield Avenue. We exited our barge named Sea View and walked up a wide stairway to a veranda and into the lobby to check in. I found that there were wide halls, lighted by gas, rooms with electric bells, and a telephone. I was also informed that a stable was connected with the Hotel and that buckboards, surreys, traps, etc., can be obtained at moderate prices. Just like a child at Christmas I couldn't wait to begin to investigate.

After a superbly prepared dinner, I took a walk along the beach heading south to the mouth of the North river. Even though the temperature was in the upper eighties the sea breeze off the ocean felt refreshing and healthy. I recalled my waiter's comment about the area of beach in front of the hotel being part of the southern patrol route of the Surfmen from the Fourth Cliff Life-Saving station. He had explained that these stations were manned during the "active season" from 1 August to 1 June the succeeding year with the keeper on duty the whole year. Each Life-Saving station generally had two surf-boats outfitted with oars, life preservers, boat compass, drag, boat hooks, hatchet, heaving line, knife, bucket and other outfits. Other items in the station included boat carriages, two sets of breeches-buoy apparatus (including guns and accessories), carts for the transportation of the apparatus, a life-car, cork-jackets (life preservers), Coston signals, signal rockets, signal flags of International and General signal code, medicine chests with contents, patrol lanterns, barometer, thermometer, patrol clocks, the requisite furniture for housekeeping by the crew and for the help of rescued persons, fuel, oil, tools for the repair of boats and apparatus, and minor repairs to the buildings, and the necessary books and stationery. The men who made up the crews of the Service were known as Surfmen, because

Crew Fourth Cliff Life Savings Station

those on the East Coast, where the Service began, launched their boats from open beaches into the surf. Surfmen could be no older than forty-five and had to be physically fit and adept at handling an oar. A glance at the muster rolls of the Service shows that most Surfmen listed their occupations before as "fisherman" or "mariner." The number of men composing a crew was determined by the number of oars needed to pull the largest boat at the station. This meant the crews ranged from six to eight, but by the turn of the century, some stations were staffed with at least ten men. Because keepers selected the crews, regulations were enacted to prevent nepotism. Many Surfmen, like the keepers, remained at one station for long periods of time, but some moved on to other stations in order to be promoted. Surfmen were ranked by order of their experience, with Surfman Number 1 being the most experienced and second in command of a station. Fourth Cliff station had two patrol routes the southern he had already explained and a northern route over Fourth Cliff across the barrier beach and along the three cliffs to Scituate Harbor. In the areas where overlapping patrols could not be maintained, like the Fourth Cliff, the Surfmen patrolled for five miles or more. At the end of his patrol, there would be a stake with a patrol-clock key attached. The key was inserted into the patrol clock and the surfman would be able to prove that he had completed the patrol. My waiter would have continued to expound about the Life-Saving Service, but I was anxious to be outsides, so I excused myself thanking him for the information and left. I later found out he was the son of one of the Surfmen from the Brant Rock Station just across the Old Mouth in Marshfield.

On the veranda of the hotel I gazed north and south trying to decide which way to explore. The north beach area seemed to have more development then the south; I could only see two houses south of the hotel then the mouth. North seemed to be more interesting, so off I went like an explorer

Facing north from cupola of the Hotel Humarock

immersed in new sights, sounds, and scents. A wooden revetment provided me a boardwalk on which to meander and observe homes both completed and under construction. As I approached Dodge and Newport Streets along the revetment, I met another intrepid adventurer coming toward me. "Good afternoon, sir, enjoying a walk and this beautiful fresh air?" I asked.

"Indeed," he responded, "I had decided to take a constitutional to the Fourth Cliff Station to watch their daily activities, however, today being Sunday the Surfmen are off and not due back until the evening patrol. But it is a wonderful day for a stroll! Enjoy the day and the solitude," he intoned. Gazing west to Holly Hill, I had a perfect view of the pastoral Emery Mansion and the fields both lying within

Facing Holly Hill from Hotel Humarock

and without its property with livestock grazing contentedly there. Scanning behind the houses I observed that most of the homes had chicken coops either attached to the back or to the rear of the house. Privies, always essential, were unobtrusively located to the rear of the property. I decided to walk back along Central Avenue, so I walked the short length of Newport Street to Central.

Stopping here I gazed across the wide expanse of salt marsh to Little's Creek, with the North River meandering its way through them, while seeming to lovingly caress the islands called Pine, Hen, and Trouant. In the far distance northerly rose the Fourth Cliff, Third Cliff, and Colman Hills and in front of them more marsh, islands, brooks, and the North River again winding its path inland. What beauty!

Turning south, I continued south on Central Avenue until I reached Dartmouth Street, one side running east to the ocean and the other west to the river. On the west side I came to Colonel Theodore A. Dodge's house. I remember reading about Theodore Dodge, who was from Brookline, and many years ago had a house erected in Humarock not far from the Hotel Humarock. What struck me at the

The J. M. Dodge, Home, Humarock Beach, Mass.

time was that he erected this home and gave use of it to the Sisters of St. Margaret, an order connected with the Church of St. John the Evangelist of Boston, as a home for destitute children. The Sisters began taking poor children from the city into the country. They first took these children to Winthrop for two summers, then to Barnstable for a year. Dodge gave use of his new house, as well as provided a fund which partially supports the institution. The home is called, in memory of his wife Jane, "The Jane Marshall Dodge Home." Sister Adeline is in charge. The picture above shows the house, Sister and her charges.

I continued along passed Dartmouth Street and reached the intersection of Central and Marshfield Avenues. Turning right, I walked past the stables and glanced across the river at the Sea View House on Ferry Street to the right at the end of the bridge.

VACATION AT HOTEL HUMAROCK – DAY 5

I awoke this morning to the calming restrains of ocean waves breaking serenely on the shore, a bright sun brightening up my room while a refreshing sea breeze cooled it. After a healthy swim in the brisk surf, morning ablutions, and a delightful breakfast in the hotel's dining room, I set out for my day's hiking adventure.

My first stop was the USLSS Station at Fourth Cliff to observe and hopefully participate in the breeches buoy drill which was held every Thursday. For this practice with the beach apparatus and the breeches buoy, each station had to select a drill ground, prepare it by erecting a spar, called a wreck pole to represent the mast of a stranded vessel about seventy-five yards distant, then perform the exercise as if it were real. Each surfman knew his job in detail from constant practice and having committed to memory the Service Manual that detailed every procedure a surfman should know. As I finished the approximately mile and a half hike to the base of the cliff, I saw that the drill ground had been set up on the side of the cliff with the wreck pole set in the ground at the cliff's summit. Quite a crowd had gathered, particularly excited children hoping to be selected for the

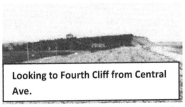
Looking to Fourth Cliff from Central Ave.

practice since women, children, and helpless people are the first to be removed from a wreck. The keeper had already selected "the victims" to be rescued. Excitement continued to build as the crowd anxiously awaited the keeper's command to begin the exercise. "Begin," bellowed Captain Stanley, and the crew sprang into action, dragging the apparatus to the drill ground where they would affect a mimic rescue by rigging the gear and taking a person ashore from the wreck pole in the breeches-buoy. Captain Stanley closely watched his watch as the drill

proceeded. As the 'victim' reached safety, a wide smile of achievement broke from his face – time was under four minutes! If one month after the opening of the active season a crew cannot accomplish the rescue within five minutes, it is considered that they have been remiss in drilling. The purpose of hastening the work of mimic rescues gives the life-savers the utmost familiarity with the apparatus and prepares them for working speedily in utter darkness and under the most trying weather conditions. No such speed was expected at an actual shipwreck when storm, surf, currents, and motion of beached crafts conspired to obstruct rescue efforts. The only goal then was to save lives in the most efficient and timely manner possible.

Breeches Buoy drill Fourth Cliff Life Saving Station Humarock

I meandered along a path along the edge of the turf, beaten hard by the life-savers' patrol. It is so near the edge that I marveled that a person can walk it on a dark night and not lose his footing. A misstep would land him sixty feet below, on the coarse gravel and stones of a particularly hard beach. From the top of the cliff at low water, I saw the boulders that lie hidden just beyond the tide line. I gazed at the new mouth, intrigued by what had occurred during the Portland Gale of 1898, barely two years ago. Then, Mother Nature had unleashed her power with use of the waters built up in the land, marshes, and rivers that lay behind the barrier beach, and like a giant excavator scooped out and disposed of the beach that had connected the Third and Fourth Cliffs for centuries; the resulting waters surged through and daily widened the opening to the ocean beyond where, for years before the old shipbuilders had asked Congress to cut an artificial point for the river and their ships. For several minutes I studied the mouth. The opening was directly at the northern end of Fourth Cliff, and at right angles with the coastline; but when entering it a person must give the cliff a wide berth

Fourth Cliff and new inlet

on account of the sunken boulders. At low tide there is about six feet of water across the river's mouth. When you are inside the mouth, I observed two channels: one to the south and one to the northwest. Westward is a small island in the marsh with a few cottages on it, and a bathing beach; and beyond rise the hills of Marshfield. From my vantage point, a more fascinating spot to which to spend a day or a week cannot be imagined. The air was pure, the scenery spectacular. The water was clear and pure and warm enough for a pleasant swim. One of the visitors standing next to me on the cliff informed me that he had summered for over the last five years at Humarock and had clammed in the flats along the old river bed and had caught flounders by just dropping a line anywhere, and sea fish directly off the bar.

I continued my hike by heading south along the hummocks along the river's edge. The scenery all along the river was particularly pleasing. The banks of the river were well wooded, and the uplands presented a diversified blend of farms with cattle and livestock grazing contentedly on its slopes, country places and wooded rises. I reached the bridge into Sea View

Ferry Street, Humarock, Seaview, Mass.

and crossed into the past. The Hotel Humarock and the newly constructed homes and cottages that made it up are the new, while Sea View with the stately homes of former ship-builders and sea captains presented the old. When I inquired of an old-timer, who contentedly sat on his front porch on Ferry Street next to the Sea View House, about the history of Sea View, he launched into a history that would have credited any historian.

"Why," he lectured, "this here site in front of my house was where White's Ferry crossed in the 17th century and where ships were built in the 18th century." He pointed south where Ferry Street continued across Marshfield Avenue and along the South River. "Down there, the Halls built vessels like whalers, brigs, schooners, and sloops that sailed all over the world. They also built famous packet boats that plied trade between Boston and the local communities along the river. Among the items traded were lumber and farm produce, and in return they brought to the valley's country stores goods that ranged from staple products to those items purchased in the China and Mediterranean trade." He continued, "One of them

Hall Brothers, Sam, brought fame to their family, but not from their North River shipyard, but from his East Boston one. But that's another even longer story." Lowering his voice like we were conspirators he added, "Sam also constructed the schooner Lapwing for none other than Daniel Webster himself! Why when Sam died in 1870, he owned 170 acres of home and meadow in Marshfield; some of which was pretty much around us. His holdings here were on

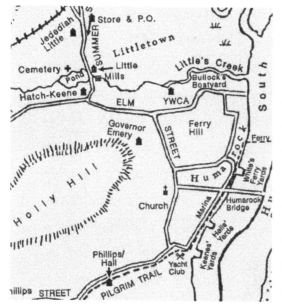

Holly Hill, and extended along Elm and Ferry Streets and included the John Phillips house at 100 Ferry Street and forty acres of farm land diagonally across from Phillips house, not bad for a local lad! Sam's daughter married George W. Emery in 1866. Emery was the governor of Utah Territory for Ulysses Simpson Grant himself. He proudly concluded, "Look behind me up on the western top of Holly Hill, see that mansion up there. Well, that was their home. Impressive ain't it!" Thanking him, I started to walk south along the river when he called out to me, "The land just south of where the Halls built ships was the site of the Keene Yards. They were busy constructing vessels before the Halls. Make sure you stop there! You may be lucky enough to find some artifacts from those ship-building days. They lived along Elm Street from Sea Street to Ferry Hill road."

I spent the rest of the day walking Ferry, Elm, and Summer Streets and attempted to

Facing Sea View from Pleasant St./Dog Lane

absorb the history I had been told while capturing in my imagination images of the past. These images included men industriously building vessels of all types in shipyards lining the river I had walked along. I also pictured men and boys from Sea View who manned these vessels built by local men

and who plied their trade to places like Boston and the various landings along the river while visiting exotic locations in the Far East and the Mediterranean. But filling my mind also were mind pictures of the families of men, women, and children and the lives they experienced in these homes lining the streets I hiked. No wonder I was mentally exhausted by the time I decided to return to the hotel late in the afternoon. To strengthen me for the return walk back

A. Stevens Store on Summer Street in Sea View
Photos pages 112-113 from W. Ray Freden Collection

to the Hotel Humarock, I stopped at A. Stevens & Son's General Store for a snack, which I greedily consumed. Invigorated, I was now ready to return, which I speedily did. Upon return I was determined to take a only a short nap, but the mental and physical activity put me out for the count.

Bridge over Pleasant St.

Courtesy of Cindy Castro

Base of Fourth Cliff – United States Life Saving Station

Hotel Humarock – Marshfield Avenue,

Humarock Lore: Fact or Fiction. You Judge!

"Truth is stranger than fiction, but it is because Fiction is obliged to stick to possibilities; Truth isn't."   *- Mark Twain*

It was a dark, cold, moonless night as a lone fisherman's, arms resting on the top rail of the bridge, languidly gazed down at the water and felt a pull on his line. He reeled his line in and eyed his catch, "Perfect," he uttered. He examined the glass bottle carefully noted the brand Hennessy Cognac. A teetotaler himself, he grinned with satisfaction because his thirsty neighbors would pay dearly for this catch and hopefully others yet to follow. Does this sound like some television Untouchables episode from the early 1960's where Elliot Ness (Robert Stack) is searching for illegal hooch making it way illegally into the United States? No, this was real life in Humarock and elsewhere in the United States from 1920 to 1933 as opponents of an extremely unpopular law matched their temperance opponents' intensity with an inventiveness of their own. "The illegal production and distribution of liquor, or bootlegging, became rampant, and the national government did not have the means or desire to try to enforce every border, lake, river, and speakeasy in America. . . . The demand for alcohol was outweighing (and out-winning) the demand for sobriety. People found clever ways to evade Prohibition agents. They carried hip flasks, hollowed canes, false books, and the like. Neither federal nor local authorities would commit the resources necessary to enforce the Volstead Act. For example, the state of Maryland refused to pass any enforcement issue. Prohibition made life in America more violent, with open rebellion against the law and organized crime: https://www.archives.gov/education/lessons/volstead-act".

DID RUM-RUNNERS USE HUMAROCK?

When I first thought about Prohibition, I thought first of bathtub gin, speakeasies, Al Capone and gangsters, and Robert Stack playing Elliot Ness. Later as my perceptions broadened and I remembered the Roaring Twenties as a time of social changes begun and attempts at social engineering that failed, and that prohibition ultimately caused more havoc to and consequences for the body politic then anyone ever imagined. Finally, I see the Great Depression as an extension of Prohibition looming like some ominous presence ready to descend upon some unsuspecting and helpless victim.

The prohibition of alcohol in the United States was one of most famous—or infamous—times in recent American history. While its intention was noble (to reduce the consumption of alcohol by eliminating businesses that manufactured, distributed, and sold it), the plan backfired.

What happened constitutionally then is a lesson to us today about trying to engineer social or constitutional change through legislation. Prohibition was enacted under the 18th Amendment to the U.S. Constitution. To this day, it is the only constitutional amendment to be repealed by another after the passage of the 21st Amendment. What was the impact of this social experiment, if any, on Humarock?

Rum-Running Probe At Humarock Beach shouts the headline of a Boston newspaper on September 1, 1925. Six members of the Humarock Beach Improvement Association appealed directly to Gov. Fuller yesterday at the State House claiming that the Scituate police have failed to correct conditions of rum-running, trespassing, and general disorderly conduct on or near Humarock Beach.

Joseph G. Bryer, president of the Humarock Beach Improvement Association, said that he appealed to the Governor because the Scituate police had failed to correct the situation. Not only has prohibition "fallen down" on the beach, but rum-runners are openly flaunting the law and others are swarming over the private property adjoining the beach and breaking trespassing laws.

The Governor arranged a conference with General Alfred Foote, commissioner of Public Safety, Capt. George Parker of the State Police Patrol, and assistant Atty. Gen. Alexander Lincoln; the conference lasted an hour. Gov. Fuller said that he would direct Gen. Foote to investigate the rum-running charges, but that trespassing issues were strictly local matters to be handled by local authorities.

In an article dated one day earlier, Scituate residents were surprised at the charges levied by the HBIA concerning rum-running. Several residents claimed these charges were the result of an earlier dispute at Humarock Beach. Authorities claimed that certain residents in the vicinity of Humarock Beach believed that they owned a section of the beach and posted No Trespassing signs where the road ended and where Selectmen had allowed parking.

About 10 days ago a sturdy fence appeared across the town road shutting down traffic from the beach and driving many Sunday visitors away. The next day the Board of Selectmen accompanied by Chief Stewart of the Scituate Police investigated, and according to authorities declared residents had no legal right to block a public way. The Selectmen ordered the fence to be taken down and hired laborers to do this work.

A small insert appeared in the October 9, 1925 paper. Arthur J. Bean of Melrose has brought suit in Superior Court against John F. Dwight of Scituate and also against Ernest Severans, Herbert G. Summers and Nathaniel Tilden, three Selectmen of the town to recover $2000 for the destruction of a fence he erected on a street in the town closing Humarock Beach. The fence was burned August 22. The incident was given publicity at the time.

Finally, in a Scituate Herald article of May, 1930 the headline reads RUM RUNNER IS  CAPTURED/ Boat With a Broken Rudder drifts ashore at Fourth Cliff with a load of liquor. According to the article, rough seas and a broken rudder led to the capture by the US Coast Guard and police during the early morning hours on Monday morning. The captured vessel had evidently taken on a load of 600 cases of liquor from a larger ship outside in the bay and was discovered late at night by the Coast Guard. The police were right on the job with the Coast Guard and all during the early hours right after midnight were watching for the landing of the vessel. The appearance of a number of empty trucks in the vicinity caused the police to get busy and all night they were following the trucks and in turn, the trucks were following the police. Off shore the boat was drifting along looking for an opening to get into the North River, or at the harbor when the propeller broke and the crew was unable to control the vessel and ashore it came as daylight shone its light. When the boat was fast aground, an attempt was made to burn the craft, but the Coast Guard and police were too quick and the vessel was seized. Some of the cases of liquor were thrown overboard to lighten the load; it didn't work. The Scituate police picked up about 85 cases of liquor and the boat load was taken in charge by the Coast Guard. Later in the forenoon the boat was gotten into deep water and was towed to Boston. This is the largest seizure which has been made on the shore in a long time.

To continue the story I quote from Ray Freden's Blog **Prohibition & Rum Running in Humarock**:

> "Illegal contraband liquor was a profitable enterprise for the water people. Boat motors were quickly converted over to more powerful and faster ones, and the insides of vessels were gutted for more space. A schoolmate, Alfred A., told me that his stepfather's lobster boat was a "rum runner." It had a big motor in it, and was quite narrow for a lobster boat.
>
> Safe unloading areas were located. Bays, harbors, rivers, creeks, and other landing spots were found. Humarock was one of these safe places—or at least more safe than other harbors. Federal funding was weak and the revenuers had to spread themselves thin.
>
> The North River mouth was the water highway out to the mother ships that were waiting three miles out to unload their contraband into smaller boats and dories. A very reliable source told me that most of the dories came from Hatch's Boat Yard and gunning stand. Others came from the North River. Most of the dories were powered by two rowers.
>
> On a good night, a row out to the "Mother Ship" and back took most of the darkened hours, depending on the weather. On occasion, unfavorable weather would delay the boatmen's return. Daylight would give them away, so they would row up into a remote creek cover their dory with marsh grass, and hunker down for the day with nothing to eat or drink! Up to 20 cases could be safely stacked in the dories, however greed and poor judgment sent many boats floundering and losing their contraband. Some of this contraband would find its way to shore, where scavengers would find liquid gold!"

Danny Clark, D.W. Clark's great-grandson and namesake, recently related a story to me about a bottle of Hennessy Cognac that is in his possession. Danny's father was

postmaster during the time of prohibition, which as we know was very unpopular with a large number of Americans. There was a knock on the Clark family's door late one night. As postmaster, Clark was the face of government on Humarock, and as such had a difficult balancing act between government agent and neighbor to many who felt that the government law was wrong. Anyway bottles of cognac had been found buried in the sand along the river or had drifted into the river. The bottle had been presented to Dan's father.

The bottle has never been opened although Danny told me that they almost opened it during the Blizzard of '78. As a long time seller of liquor, Danny showed me the trick to see if the contents were still good. He said, "You swirl the liquid around and if there are bubbles at the top then the contents are fine." He showed me and the contents are fine!

Back to Ray's story of rum runners in Humarock:

"Lookouts were needed to warn the boatmen of any danger that may come about. Lookout posts were stationed from the Sea Street Bridge to Fourth Cliff.

The lookout on the bridge was a well known local that had a non-drinking reputation, and liked to fish. His gear was tin bucket, bait, a sharp knife, a hand line, a flashlight and cigarettes. Time on was 9 to 10 pm; off was daylight, rain or not. If the boats were out, you were on. Over would go the line, baited or not. Sometimes this lookout was joined by a friend – his line would go over with a bottle of hooch tied on the end. This was to be retrieved periodically.

The hooch was unloaded at various locations. The cases were picked up by Chevy 6-cylinder panel trucks. Chevys were quieter that the Ford Model A's. Canvas snap-on signs were attached to each side with a local milk company logo.
I was told, by the same reliable source, that only once, during this guard's time on the bridge, did he have to call off a landing.

One night, just before midnight, a big black Packard with four men inside, strangers, stopped on the bridge and asked where so-and-so's cottage was. The fisherman gave them directions, and off they went. The fisherman/guard flashed a signal to the lookout on the point down river, and signal was passed on to the cliff.

That night's truck was turned around and left. No one else ever reported seeing the car or the men. No one saw them leave; no one reported using so-and-so's cottage. However, this was a subject not discussed, and questions were unthinkable.

My late friend Phil, a Sea View native, told me the following. It seems that Charlie, Phil's father, took a walk to Pine Island (at the end of Warren Avenue Marshfield). While coming back, he saw a newly tracked path in the marsh grass. Off he went to investigate. He found something that was covered over with marsh grass. A case of 11 bottles of hooch!

Even though Charlie was a teetotaler, he was not going to leave this find. He covered it back up and waited until dark. Charlie made his way back through the cedar grove to the edge of the marsh, found the case of hooch, then made it home without being seen, he hoped! He stashed the case in the cellar, where his wife would not find it, as she was death against alcohol.

Within a few days, word reached Charlie, that Wally, a heavy drinker, was on a killing rage. It seems that someone stole his property from the Island. He was telling everyone in Sea View that if he found out who stole his property, he was going to kill them!

You see, the property was never Wally's. He probably found it stashed in one of the creeks by a boatman. Charlie never uttered a word. Some of Charlie's friends enjoyed a holiday gift."

The three Photos: Courtesy of the Boston Public Library, Leslie Jones Collection

Photo of Bottle of Danny Clark's Hennessy Cognac is courtesy of the author

One humorous story and a snapshot of the prohibition era times story needed to be told. It involved the wedding of William Tecumseh Sherman (Teak) of Greenbush, Scituate, and Dama Rose Bates of Beechwood, Scituate. It took place during a blizzard on Thanksgiving Day, November 24, 1927. The full story appears in Dianne Sherman's book *Teak*. The wedding was held in the home that Teak had built for Dama on Ford Place in Greenbush. Teak had moved in a month after the builder, Aubrey Totman, had completed work on the home, but Teak slept on the living room couch until his bride could join him in the upstairs master bedroom.

The ceremony was conducted by the Reverend Allan Creelman before the brick fireplace that Alden Bates, master mason, had built for his daughter's wedding present. The happy couple were flanked by Dama's sister Myra Frye, the Matron of Honor, and cousin Fred Clapp, the Best Man.

> "They exchanged promises while family and 'the gang' stood in the living room to witness and applaud the newlyweds. All then filed into the dining-room for wedding cake, finger food, and liquid warmth.
>
> The reception was in full swing when the stories began to be told and whiskey from pocket flasks drunk. Prohibition was the law of the land, but that did not stop anyone from getting plenty of liquid refreshment from Chief of Police Bumper Bates, Dama's cousin, who had recently acquired a number of blue ribbon bottles of Canadian Club from unnamed sources. The bottles had remained stashed under bales of hay up in his hayloft. That same loft had been the recipient of many of the finest labels secreted from various ship wrecks when Bumper's grandfather had been Wreck Master for the town.
>
> Always the first on the scene of a floundering coaster, Elias James Bates could dutifully begin counting all the boxes of liquor, after eliminating the first ten, and send a written report to the ship owners. Somehow, a few boxes always managed to float away on the outgoing tide. . . . The marriage celebration lasted three days until Bumper Bates refused to bring any more Canadian Club to Greenbush. That ended the party. Callahan, Cousin Fred and Herb Frye stayed to clean up while all the others staggered home in the snow *Teak* pp. 13-15."

The complex network of trails, creeks, streets, and access to the ocean made the area around the mouth of the North River in Marshfield and Humarock an ideal landing-place for illegal bootleg liquor in the late twenties. Almost anyone with access to a power boat could travel the two sea miles to 'rum row' offshore, and even when the Coast Guard increased its surveillance, Scituate's tipplers were seldom thirsty. Hiding their liquid gold in hidden spots in the marshes or along banks where isolated homes were few and far between, bootleggers were easily able to load and to distribute their contraband in easily camouflaged trucks.

On December 5, 1933, the required number of states ratified the Twenty-first Amendment, which repealed the Eighteenth Amendment to the United States Constitution which had mandated nationwide prohibition on alcohol. With its passage, the Twenty-first Amendment the United States' attempt at social engineering ended.

Photo courtesy of W. Ray Freden collection

Hooch carrying Chevy 1930-1931

The Wilcox truck above would have been perfect for rumrunners because its engine was quieter then a Ford, and a canvas top was easily camouflaged with a symbol of a local diary. Also the isolation of some local farms and their locations on creeks/brooks, like Branch Creek in Marshfield or First Herring Brook in Scituate, with their easy access to the river by boat and nearby streets and roads proved to be a boon for those who skirted the law and a hindrance to those who enforced the law.

IS SECESSION EVER JUSTIFIED?

Town Report 1907 – TO THE INHABITANTS OF THE TOWN OF SCITUATE: Humarock Beach has a growing and desirable summer settlement. The town derives an income of about $1600 annually from that section through taxes, with a very little outlay.

The Selectmen think the residents of that locality are entitled to some improvements in their roads, therefore we recommend a small appropriation for the building of the road laid out by them.

Do you think the above might be a response to **Article 37 of the 1905 Town warrant** that was Voted? It read, "That the Selectmen be and they hereby are instructed to appear before the Committee of the Legislature on March 8th 1905 and oppose the petition to set off that part of Scituate known as Humarock to the Town of Marshfield."

In the summer of 2012 feelings were inflamed again when the town stopped the tradition of July 3rd bonfires on the beach. Some residents claimed the town handled this in a very heavy-handed manner. A meeting of over 100 Humarock residents was held at the South Humarock Civic Association's clubhouse to discuss this issue. In a Jessica Bartlett July 26, 2012, Globe article she wrote, . . . "Although there has been talk of secession by some", Langlois said

"Humarock isn't at that point yet." According to Jack Kwesell, whose son-in-law John Jacey moderated Sunday's meeting, the focus is on the July 3 issue. "The issue is the assault. We'd like to know the reason behind it," he said.

Selectmen chairman Joseph Norton said, "If we could have a calm and sensible discussion, I don't think the town has any problem" discussing an issue not in litigation.

As for the issue over the laws on bonfires, Selectman Tony Vegnani said, "I don't think they realize that bonfires are illegal . . . and if they don't agree with the law, they should go to the State House."

In conclusion, Humarock residents have sometimes historically felt ignored by town officials due in part to the separation of Humarock from the rest of the town.

HAVE YOU VISITED THE SQUARE IN HUMAROCK?

The Square,   Humarock, Mass.

In August of 1932 a visitor to Humarock purchased a postcard (pictured above) and drew an arrow on it (as I have done above). On the back was a message, the name and address of the recipient, a one cent postage stamp with George Washington's image and the dates 1732 and 1932 with the word WASHINGTON between them, and on the left the words Pub. By E.D. West Co., South Yarmouth, Cape Cod. Mass. For W.C. Clark, Humarock, Mass. The message read: Dear Mum, I am spending the day around the Cape. The arrow on the front shows you

where Norman has his Summer Store. Am on my way to see Bertha now. Love to you and all. Gladys. It was addressed to F. M. McKean, 25 Crescent St., Waltham, Mass. It was stamped Brockton, Aug. 10, 4 pm 1932.

Bob Brian visited, not only the area pictured here on the left, but owned property here and in CT as well. But he loved Humarock and its history so much that he

created a website with his postcard collection on it. The image on the previous page, left, is one those cards. "He posted the following: "This is what the center of town looked like for many years. Does anyone remember the name of the little spa on the corner where we used to get sodas and play the jukebox in 1950's? And the owner's name? I believe the A & P was next door to it. . . ?" Bob was right. From my photos the name of the spa was Ferris's, which provided Soda Fountain Service and Hot Coffee, Toasted Sandwiches, and Fried Clams. Before Ferris's the store was known as Jack's Soda Fountain circa 1940s. The sign said Faders, but the locals called

RIVERSIDE HOUSE – HUMAROCK BEACH
SEA VIEW – MASS.

it Jack's Place. It was owned by Jack Fader, who lived on Elm Street up the hill across from Ireland Road. Next to Ferris's, heading toward the beach, was the real estate office owned by the Morehardts and next to the real estate office was the A & P (see top picture next page). Across the street was Clark's General Store. If you carefully study and compare all these pictures, you can see how the square has changed over the decades.

On the Riverside House – Humarock Beach postcard on the left was written: "Aug. 12 1906 Went to Marshfield Hills Aug 10 came home Aug 13 1906." Ray Freden said it was Josselyn's Riverside House and was a store and rented rooms. Look below at the postcard. It is titled Marshfield

MARSHFIELD AVE., HUMAROCK, MASS.   7463

MARSHFIELD AVENUE, HUMAROCK BEACH, MASS.

Ave., Humarock, Mass and it shows two cars parked outside McManus Ice Cream and smaller sign *the Surf*. In Ray's days it was the Surf. Look carefully at the bottom postcard on the right you will see the Riverside House but it is now labeled FIRST ? Was this the First National that I was told was in Humarock? Look to the left of the same picture you see Dick Smith's Mobil Station a small building and his home. Then across Central Ave. you see Ferris's. The small unnamed building used to sell fireworks on the Fourth of July before WWII.

One of the oldest pictures of the Square after the destruction of the Hotel Humarock shows the Hotel Royal. Below you see construction of the stables that would become Dick Smith's Mobil Station from Marshfield.

This is Humarock's Town Square, but do you know where the Town Green was?

As Paul Harvey once said, "Now you know the rest of the story!!!" The Square, or as Mary Ellen (Keenan) Mastriani laughed, "Sqway-ah" as we all called it, as in 'I am going down to the sqway-ah,'" has undergone many changes but still continues providing current residents with a business center.

Those Were the Days My Friend At Humarock & The Square

"Through the door there came familiar laughter// I saw your face and heard you call my name// Oh my friend we're older but no wiser// For in our hearts the dreams are still the same." – Mary Hopkin

Charlie Fagan and 'The Chariot' 1927 Humarock Beach

Photo left courtesy of Mary Ellen Mastriani. Tennis was very popular in early Humarock. The Tapley family donated land to be used for people interested in playing the game. From Dick Shea's memories: ". . .Tennis was the major sport then, and the one tennis court in Humarock was the major gathering place of the athletic-minded. Every Sunday there would be doubles matches between the senior members of the Dow, Lynch, Swift, and Boynton families. I especially admire Mr. Swift, he was a small man, but so fast. . . . There was also a court up on Ferry Hill, and I knew the son of the owner and used to play there sometimes. There were wild roses growing in the nets at the ends of the court, in which the balls were always getting caught." See photo below

"Middle photo: There were three tennis courts in the 40's. My Dad used to care for them in the 40's and 50's There were two tennis courts across form 51 Carlton Road owned by Emery Laskey. The other court was behind the residence on the corner of Pollard and 110 Carlton owned by the Fretz's and the High's, the daugher was the late Nat Lommis. My Dad took care of these also." Ray Freden

Top left: Charlie Fagan (second from right) 1931 Humarock. Top right: end of Oliver Street. Middle left: Seaplane over Humarock. Bottom left: South River 1930.

All Pictures on this page courtesy of Pat (Fagan) Arnold.

Picture right: Bev, Ruth, Sheila, Kath, Marcia. August 1953

Picture left: front boat Frannie's: Frannie, Paul, Dave, Marsha. Billy's boat back: Bobbie, Carol, Jackie. August 1953

Left: Ethelyn, one of Charlie Fagan's girlfriends. 1932 Humarock.
Bottom photo: Marshfield, 1921. Possibly Kent Park area.
Photos courtesy of Pat (Fagan) Arnold

Do you remember the unexpected visitor who crashed on Humarock Beach Oct. '67?

Photos below courtesy of Pat Arnold.

Previous page: Dave, Pat, Dot, Katie, Paul.

Left: Billy Rose

Bottom photo: Dot and Carol in Dave's Mercury in the Parking Lot

All photos courtesy of Pat (Fagan) Arnold August of 1953

How many of you remember square-dancing in the parking lot on Friday evenings in the summer?

Pictures from the next two pages are courtesy of Ruth (Seaberg) Wile. Top: fun at the Square early 1950s. Bottom: 1944 where Postscript land and Revere Street eventually were.

Top: 1946
Brunswick
Street.

Middle:
1943 view
from river
of
Brunswick
Street

Bottom: Ruth in either 1942 or 1943

Ready

On Your Mark

Go

WOW!

Polar Plunge Humarock Beach 2019
Twenty Years Old This Year

Photos courtesy of W. Ray Freden. Top: Charlie Randall boat captain.

Middle: Humarock and Ferry Hill from Holly Hill with views of Belanger's Farm.

Bottom: Humarock from Ferry Hill ©1910-1911.

All Photos on this page are courtesy of W. Ray Freden.

Top: Burkett Group Seaview

Bottom: Belanger women: youngest daughter, Mom, oldest daughter

Sailing, Motor-Boating, and Naturism on the North River

Matthew Chapter 7:3 - *Why do you observe the splinter in your brother's eye and never notice the great log in your own?*

With the concept of leisure that took root in the late 19th century and that spread well into the new century, new uses of the North and South Rivers developed. In one chapter I spoke of the North River Boat Club and sailing and social activities that grew around it. As the horseless carriage and other new inventive technologies were invented, a revolution in the mode of travel took place. The invention of the gas engine made it possible to build a power boat cheap enough to be within the reach of the average person and it was only a relatively short time that these crafts zoomed up and down the rivers replacing sail boats for business and pleasure.

MOTOR BOAT ON THE RIVER

The first power boat appeared on the river in 1894 and was owned by Henry D. Smith of River street, Norwell. His twenty-six foot craft could be hired for parties and for several seasons he did just that. In fifteen short years, his single pioneer vessels had given way to a fleets of motor boats that cruised the rivers.

While Mr. Smith deserved credit as the first motor boat owner, it was Alfred L. Lincoln who deserved the credit of having a draw placed on the railroad bridge and who instituted the action that led to removing the rocks from the river bed, making it more easily navigated. With his yacht, the Unome IV, he compelled the railroad officials to put in a draw as it was too expensive to send down a crew to demolish and rebuild the bridge every time he chose to go in or out of the river, which he had done several times in the summer of 1909. He started the petition that was presented to the State Harbor and Land Commission and at the hearing he was active in seeing that a favorable showing was made before the board. In addition, he and others led the way in filing petitions and causing those petitions to be inserted in the town warrants for the Annual Town Meeting in Scituate, Norwell, Marshfield, Pembroke, and Hanover calling for appropriations to remove rocks along the river, particularly at Rocky Reach where more rocks resided thAn along the whole course of the river. A preliminary survey and appropriations were made and a contract was signed with Thomas Fitzgibbon and his steam derrick. The rocks were removed and the whole cost being $15,432.08. With these impediments removed, the number of powerboats increased each season as more new boats were added. The only downside was that the sound of the chugging of engines could be heard at any time and on Sundays and holidays, it was continuous.

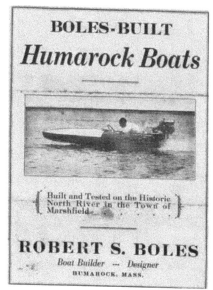

On a pleasant Sunday the open bay just inside the mouth was alive with boats, their occupants fishing, bathing, or at low tide digging clams, and other parties on the beach picnicking and having clam bakes.

Many of the boaters went out to the fishing grounds in the early morning and returned later in the day.

Some of the boatmen owned camps along the river and a few built boat-houses and house boats. Other entrepreneurs saw opportunities for associated new businesses like boatyards where powerboats could be built, repaired, and stored. For example, on the lower river from the mouth to Humarock in the early 1920s a number of boats were kept: William L. Healey built twenty-boats at Humarock and had the care of many others. A long list of people who moored their boats in this area nearly obstructed the channel. Among those named were: Luther Little, John Eames, the Thayer brothers, Royal Brown, Frank Dwight, the Hager brothers, E.H. Randall, Mr. Damon, Dr. Edw.

Dwight, Charles Randall, Victor Belanger, Ralph Hatch, Leon Hatch, Robert Boles, and Dr. Thurber. The river has seen many changes. Shipbuilding, freighting, and gundalowing had their day and have passed. Fishing and seining in the river are practically gone. Pleasure craft and summer camps reigned supreme during the twenties with power boating continuing to increase with each year that passed. Now let's look at an unusual power-boating happening.

LEISURE ON THE NORTH RIVER

What was leisure to some people certainly was not leisure for others. The first naturism groups began in France and Germany after World War I and spread rapidly in Germany to groups in opposition to Nazism because it emphasized being healthy by being in the outdoors, breathing fresh air, and exercising in the nude. As the Nazis gained power during the late twenties and into the thirties they passed legislation opposing nudity and jailed anyone found guilty of breaking the new 1933 law. In Britain in 1934 a new word appeared in the Health and Efficiency magazine naturism and it was suggested that it replace nudism. The word, however, would not be generally accepted until the 1960s. The 1930s saw the height of naked sunbathing reach its crescendo in the United Kingdom. Sunbathing magazines lamented the crackdown by Hitler and his Nazis in Germany. Ideas about liberalism, pacifism, and natural health made their way to the United States by thousands of immigrants fleeing from Germany. Many were followers of a German social movement called life reform, and migrated to the West Coast where they practiced vegetarianism, raw food diets and nudism. They lived in the mountains and slept in caves and trees. A group called The Nature Boys epitomized this way of life. One of them wrote the song Nature Boy, which was a hit for Nat King Cole in 1948. This alternative life

Two Mile section of Marshfield

style may be interesting to some, but what has it to do with Humarock and the area around Humarock? Maybe absolutely nothing, you'd respond.

When I started researching this book on Humarock, my answer would have been the same. Then a friend of mine, Jim Spinale, who had lived most of his early life in Rockland, told me an encounter he had on the North River with a group of nudists not far downriver on the Marshfield side near from where the highway (Route 3) now crosses the North River. He, his brother, and his father had been invited by his father's boss to Humarock to ride in his boat up the North River. The boat had a platform on the bow and this is where Jim and his brother reclined. As they came around the area of Two Mile, there diving off a diving board at the end of a dock were several nude children. Seated on chairs beside the dock were several adults, also nude. When their boat approached, they the adults crossed their arms and legs until they had passed. At the time I just filed the story away as an interesting one, but did not pursue it. Months had passed and during an interview with a resident of Humarock and Sea

Pat Arnold's friend Ruth

View, Pat (Fagan) Arnold, who during the early 1950s when she was around fifteen, told me the following tale: She and a group of several of her girl friends, all of whom were in their teens, crowded into their friend Ruthie's boat to leisurely meander up the North River towards Pembroke. Their excursion came to an abrupt conclusion when they came upon a group of naked people along the banks of the river where the Hatch mill is located. Startled and embarrassed they powered the boat full ahead giggling trying to figure out how they were going turn around to get home without passing this naked group. When discovered by the girls, this group simply crossed their legs and their hands and discreetly covered areas of their bodies not normally exposed in public, or if they had towels simply covered themselves with them.

With these facts I decided to see if any long-time residents, particularly whose families had been here for generations had ever heard about these naturists on the North River. I wrote to Ray Freden and called Cynthia Krusell with my inquiries. To my surprise both of them responded Oh, yes, the stories were true. Mostly everybody from that era in the immediate vicinity knew about these stories; they were well-known. Additionally anyone from this group and their relatives were long dead, so there would be no one who would be embarrassed by the story. It turned out that the people involved in this story had life stories very similar to yours and mine; stories of hurt and woundedness, or of anger and jealousy. So, were these actions deliberately far left of the accepted norms for the day, or were they experiments in a

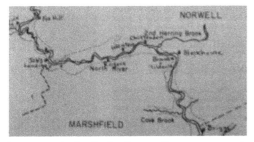

new experiential lifestyle? We will never know, however, given the divisiveness of our times a lesson may be offered. When we can somehow separate the person from what their actions were, and begin to consider what decisions we would have made in their shoes, then we may be able to move onwards and write a new story, one in which we are able to learn and grow. Cynthia related that there was a brother and sister, who did not get along, and as a result each built on their own land on the North River docks with diving boards and canoes. The brother and his wife and a few of their friends were members of a group and enjoyed swimming in the nude while the sister and her husband were not and did not agree with this lifestyle choice. The brother and his wife were very good friends of Cynthia Hagar Krusell's father and mother. She emphasized that they were very good people who ran a girl scout camp WySibo (which meant peace) that was very popular with girls from the Marshfield Hills area during the 1930s through 1950s. Girls who attended the camp, which included Cynthia, have fond memories of the camp, the campfire songfests, and the badges the girls earned. The girls loved it there. The owners of the camp also made it available to the boy scouts for winter campouts and when not needed by the girl scouts. The adult members of this group were not an in your face type of group. They were not pushy types or exhibitionists. Sometimes when boating on the North River with their adult friends, never with children, group members might disrobe and swim naked along the boat. Ray added that the couple had four adopted children; the oldest, Debbie, was his age and that he would swim there with Debbie. Always with his clothes on and Debbie was clothed as well, for she never swam nude with outsiders. Ray also said that the parents had three or four hothouses where they raised various flowers for the Boston Wholesale Market. Ray added that two of his friends would attempt to catch a glimpse of the group: one by boat and the other by airplane. When discovered, the people would discreetly drop a towel in front of themselves or as mentioned before cross their arms and legs. The reactions of four long time residents' parents varied from acceptance of people involved but not their lifestyle, to strict orders to children not to go there, with all the parents in agreement that all people have different views of how to enjoy life.

As Americans we sometimes share in a legacy of titillation, embarrassment, or uneasiness with nakedness. When we examine other peoples' actions through our culture's lens, we sometimes make judgments based upon our feelings and reactions. In doing so, we have limited the humanity of the other by not separating the person from their action. If, however, we can see the other as a real person like ourselves: human, with our brokenness, with our imperfections, and with differences in the way we view the world, we may then accept our own humanity as we accept our neighbors' humanity. This may provide us to write a new story of our life, one that allows us to learn, grow, and be more accepting of others' differences. Then by accepting our differences and that of our neighbors, we may put an end to the cycle of divisiveness that afflicts us today.

Hatch Mill, Route 3 area of the North River

MYSTERY ISLAND OFF HUMAROCK?

The following whimsical, or was it whimsical, story appeared in a February 8, 1935 issue of the Scituate Herald. Chairman of the Board of Selectmen W. Irving Lincoln, several days  prior to the story received a letter from Fannie D, Emmerick of Philadelphia who made inquiries regarding a group of people who live on an island just off the Humarock shore. The letter is as follows: "W.C.A.U. Philadelphia. Department of Records. City Government of Humarock. Eastern Massachusetts. Gentlemen: I have been informed that there is an interesting group of people living just off the shore of Humarock who have a peculiar history, but have been unsuccessful in finding out anything definite in books of record or history in the public libraries. Could you inform me specifically where I could get some detailed information about these people, in connection with a magazine article I am writing. Your cooperation would be very much appreciated. The people I refer to are, I understand, those who are living on an island-like piece of land just off the shore in rudely erected homes they have built themselves, the land having been allotted them by an ancient grant. Very truly yours, Fannie D. Emmerick, 3053 Mickle Street, Camden N.J." The unknown author of this article commented, "From the tone of the letter it would seem as though the writer had somehow or other got the impression that there is a queer race of people living off Humarock, compared perhaps with "hill billies" or something of that kind." What is your initial reaction to this? Well, withhold your judgment, and continue reading.

On February 22, 1935 a letter to the Scituate Herald by Alice Phillips Bauer of Rockland has an interesting response. It read: "To the Editor of Standard: Reading the article by Selectman Lincoln of Scituate relative to 'Life at Humarock, Mass," I would say, looking back 45 years, there were groups of people who used to spend the summer months southwest of the present mouth of North River below the last bridge, nearest the ocean. They built small houses out of seagrass and dried sea weed and some used rough boards and brick while others used tents. Fires were built over stone mounds on the beach and here the meals were cooked out in the open. Each family had a rowboat and this was the only means at this time of transportation. I have many photos of the life at this summer camp 30 or 40 years ago. Some Rockland residents may remember the time and date my father rescued J. William Beal and George A. Capel of Hanover and George Hunt of Rockland from great peril on this river and I have the silver watch and medal awarded to him by the Humane Society. Summer life at this rural resort was ideal. I personally summered 12 years there and each season more people came to join us, especially artists and novelists, as the rugged and wild life were really unique. No one ever was sick and the perfect quiet at night, only the roar of the ocean, and the boats along the shore that were anchored.

Our drinking water was taken from a boiling spring on the bank of the river. Wonderfully fresh and cold, although surrounded by salt water, and when the tide came in it covered the spring. We had to obtain the water at low tide. We would row up to it and fill stone jugs. We learned to catch lobsters under rocks, to properly cook fish on an open grate, to swim and fish and later, yes, I believe we were the first to own a motorboat on the river. We were taught how to get a motorboat out of the mouth of the North River; this was some feat around the rocks, considering the strong ocean current there.

My father built the motorboat there and had a high powered engine and named it the "Sala." My grandfather's estate borders on this river for one half a mile and I believe Dr. L. Vernon Briggs' book which he wrote on shipbuilding on North River speaks of the life there years ago. Also Elmer Turner of Pembroke has copies of old deeds of some of the old grants. Presently I am compiling some works on brick building and manufacture on the river. I believe I can give a complete story on the life at Humarock from 1890 to the present time, together with photos and write-ups. Very truly, Alice Phillips Bauer, 23 Webster St., Rockland."

Postcard and Photo of W. Irving Lincoln from Scituate Historical Society's collection.

What do you think – Fact or Fiction?

DID YOU KNOW THAT:

- On April 16, 1851, the Brig William from Cadiz to Boston was wrecked at Fourth Cliff. This was the same day that the Minot Light Lighthouse was destroyed in the Gale of 1851?

- With WWII still underway, Humarock residents were advised by the Army to take shelter in the underground rooms at the Fourth Cliff military installation as the Great Atlantic

Hurricane approached in September of 1944? Some residents took up the advice. The storm was responsible for sinking the Navy destroyer USS Warrington approximately 450 miles (720 km) east of Vero Beach, Florida, with a loss of 248 sailors. The hurricane was one of the most powerful to traverse the Eastern Seaboard, reaching Category 4 when it encountered Warrington, and producing hurricane force winds over a diameter of 600 miles (970 km). The hurricane also produced waves in excess of 70 feet (21 m) in height. In addition to Warrington, the Coast Guard cutters CGC Bedloe (WSC-128) and CGC Jackson (WSC-142) both capsized and sank off Cape Hatteras. The hurricane also claimed the 136-foot (41 m) minesweeper USS YMS-409 which foundered and sank with all 33 on board lost. Further north, it also claimed the lightship Vineyard Sound (LV-73), which was sunk with the loss of all 12 aboard. It also drove SS Thomas Tracy aground in Rehoboth Beach, Delaware. I thought I would end this section with an article from a newspaper on September 16, 1944 titled 'Hurricane Lesson'. It stated that this storm, almost as powerful as the one in 1938, did not cause the loss of life as its predecessor did because the great majority of New Englanders learned the lessons from the first, which is to get under cover and stay there. The experience recalls the classic story of the child who, years after the French Revolution, asked his grandfather: "And what did you do in the Reign of Terror, grandfather?" "Well, I lived through the d-----d thing!" the old man exclaimed. An alert Weather Bureau, Public officers, Federal and State, city and town agencies of all kinds, the Coast Guard, and the Red Cross all played their roles admirably.

- On February 15, 1906 the Steamship Devonian came ashore near Fourth Cliff. It was bound for Boston from Liverpool. Passengers and general cargo were saved. A Boston Globe headline for February

16, 1906 broadcast that: STRANDED DEVONIAN FLOATED - Big Steamship Lies Over Night Off Quarantine Station. Ashore 15 Hours in Dangerous Position Off Third Cliff at Scituate. The article goes on to say that the ship was 10 miles off course, the weather was bad, and the night dark. It was also storming and like many other vessels had lost her course. Life Savers from the Fourth Cliff station and the Mass Humane Society crew from Third Cliff quickly arrived at the scene, but the captain of the Devonian wanted to wait until light because the ship was afloat from the bridge to the stern. Matthew Hoar, surfman from Fourth Cliff under Captain Fred Stanley's direction had heroically climbed on board the Devonian and had conversed with the Captain informing him about the conditions of the land he was stuck on. As daylight approached, so did the crowd of onlookers. Two hundred curious and sympathetic townspeople had gathered by late morning, and by the time she was afloat, the number was over three hundred. With high tide coming at a little after four pm, the tug Patience began pulling the Devonian at 3:29 pm. With very little effort the Patience pulled her from Third Cliff. Captain Stanley's succinct words said it all, "Well, she's off all right. Come on boys!" And they started back to their station to get a little sleep.

U. S. Life Saving Station, Humarock, Beach, Mass.

THE MYSTERY OF THE WRECK ON HANOVER FLATS

Who doesn't like a good mystery? Right. Thank you, Ray Freden and Edward Rowe Snow for solving one mystery for me – the location of Hanover Flats and for providing most of the

This was where the SC-241 was/is - Hanover Flats

information contained here. In searching through Scituate's town meeting records during the 1740's for information about Fourth Cliff, I kept running across references to ownership and possession of the Hanover Flats. Since I wasn't interested in Hanover, just Humarock, I skimmed over these records, shame on me. Later, I recalled older residents asking me what I knew about the mystery of the wreck atop the marsh at Hanover Flats. Was it a rum runner that had been trapped and destroyed under heavy gunfire during the violence of Prohibition and the Roaring Twenties? Another version opined was that it actually was a very successful rum chaser that, after its career had ended and during a terrible gale, went ashore on the Flats. Yet another version was that it was really a submarine chaser that had been converted into a rum runner during prohibition and operated in the Marshfield – Scituate area very successfully for years, during which time the smugglers buried lots of cases of liquor at various places in the marsh. As Ray Freden wrote, the advocates of this last view would take you out to the marsh and show you the various hiding places. Edward Rowe Snow wrote about these stories and regaled people who lived during the 1940s in New England with similar tales. Many people who

Here is Dorothy Snow Bicknell on remains of the SC-41 Subchaser. c. 1955. Taken from E. R. Snow's book.

clammed the area passed the wreck's ribs and some planks which seemed to lend credence to the stories. Hanover Flats is the marsh that is between Hen or Tilden's Island and the foot of Fourth Cliff. When Ray Freden's father arrived in Sea View in 1927, he worked for Charlie Clark of Clark's Store. The wreck was there before he arrived and people who lived there came in for groceries during the summer, but he could not recall their names nor where they were from. Ray remembers dories tied up to the stern, a large box-like structure in the middle, and a tall flagpole near the center.

In a 1967 Edward Rowe Snow article about the SC 241, a much more plausible and accurate story appeared. "A total of 447 SCs were built. The New York Launch and Engine Company at Morris Heights, New York built the SC 241 in 1918. Commissioned April 8, 1918, and captained by Ensign Robert L. Mills, she was 110 feet long, beam

14 feet 9 inches, and a draft of 5 feet 8 inches. Her top speed was a theoretical 18 knots, but in reality 14 to 16 knots was more likely. She was powered by three 220 HP gasoline engines, with three props, a gas tank capacity of 2400 gallons, with a 1000 nautical mile cruising radius. They were rugged and available in large numbers at the time. The subchaser (SC) was designed for offshore patrols and anti submarine warfare. Her armament included a three inch gun, two 30 caliber machine guns, and one Y gun.

The SC 241 left New London, CT, on May 13, 1918, after being outfitted with submarine detectors and wireless telephones. She arrived in Halifax, Nova Scotia, five days later. On July

11, 1918 while in the company of SC247, she sighted a U-boat on her starboard in thick fog. Springing into action, she pursued the U-boat and when less than 35 yards away fired depth charges from her Y gun. One charge landed 10 feet in front of the periscope and followed a few seconds later by a powerful explosion. Was the U-boat actually destroyed? Was it ever identified? It is not known.

After the war, the SC 241 was struck from the naval registry and sold for scrap. She was stripped of her armament, engines, and all hardware. Sometime later she was sold to John F.

Smith, towed by tug to the South River, where she was anchored. During a November storm in 1925 she was torn from her mooring and left stranded on the Hanover Flats. The Smith family dug a trench in the marsh and the vessel was settled

into the south side of the flats. The family added five rooms, a rear porch, and a southerly facing stern landing area. For years the family enjoyed their summer home. The enjoyment included clam digging contests testing which individual could dig the most clams. Dorothy Smith Johnson remembers local fishermen paying her one dollar a bushel. John Smith retired and eventually sold the subchaser. During WWII the ravages of time and torched by vandals around 1943, she burned to her waterline as fire companies watched helplessly from Central Avenue. No one was ever charged with arson. Untruthful stories told by Humarock kids

who claimed to have boarded the vessel in the early spring or fall when she was deserted and claimed to have seen skeletons inside added fuel to the mystery over time." Janet Fairbanks from Scituate and whose family vacationed in Humarock loaned me some old family photos from the 1930s in Humarock, and low and behold there was a photo of the old subchaser/vacation home on the marsh.

If you ever take a boat ride along the South River as night descends, let your imagination take over and picture in your mind's eye the shadow of light dimly flickering through the wreck's windows as it sits atop the marsh. Turn to the ocean and listen to the card games and smell the cigars emanating from Hatch's boatyard you slowly motor past. Picture in your mind

hunters huddled in gunning stands patiently awaiting the arrival of migratory birds lured to the marshes and flats by Leon Hatch's tame geese. Then as you approach the base of Fourth Cliff from the river with a ghostlike fog shrouding all, you can conjure images of surfmen starting or completing their patrols along well worn-paths with heightened senses straining to see or hear danger. Or maybe your imagination is more in the line of the mystery of rum-runners or of haunted, scary tales told around campfires. (The above aerial photograph of Hatch's boatyard and gunning stand is courtesy of Bob Graci.)

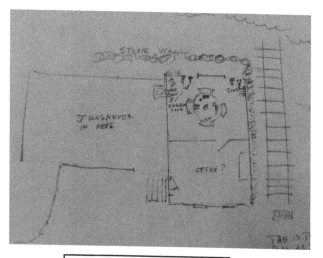

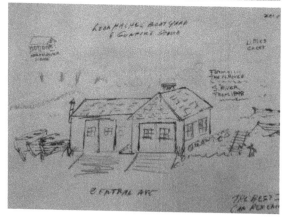

Sketches of Hatch's Boatyard and Gunning Stand and SC 241 by W. Ray Freden from his collection

Previous page: Dolly Snow Bicknell and her father Edward Rowe snow canoeing by skeletal remains of subchaser (1959). Janet Fairbanks family picture of subchaser with room additions (1937).

HATCH'S BOATYARD AND GUNNING STAND

I first came across Hatch's gunning stand when Dave Ball and I were researching our book about the Portland Gale of 1898. We had found that hunting in the marshes along the North and South Rivers was an extremely popular leisure activity for many during the late nineteenth century and well into the twentieth

century. Family gunning stands were found particularly in an area around the New Harbor Marshes. The Henderson Brothers of Norwell's stand was located just northwest of Trouant's Island while the Clapp Brothers of Greenbush's stand rested at the base of Snake Hill across from the old mouth of the North River. A third gunning stand Hatch's was

situated in Humarock on the west side of Central Avenue fronting the North River approximately where Seaview Avenue intersected it. A fourth gunning stand rested on the South end of Hen Island. In 1898 it was one of the only buildings on this section of Central Avenue on the river while on the ocean side was the USLSS station at Fourth Cliff at the southern base of the cliff. As you have seen from the previous article's aerial view of it, by the 1940s there was little left to indicate where or what it had been used for. We had also uncovered several harrowing and tragic first-hand accounts of what happened to hunters trapped in their stands by the horrific gale. The harrowing accounts left us of the Clapp Brothers

and the life-savers from Fourth Cliff spoke of bravery and heroism that I have spoken about in other parts of this book. Keeper Stanley's report for November 28, 1898, summarized the aftermath, "Spent the day in clearing away the wreckage about the premises and looking for any bodies that might come ashore." Since the publication of our book, I have come to find out

Hunting near Peregrine White farm

that Hatch's gunning stand was a lot more than just a gunning stand.

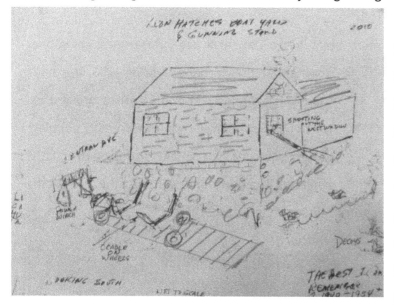

It was also a boatyard for the fixing and repairing of boats with rails that led down into the river for their launching. It was in later years a place where beach shanties could be rented and cars parked. Later owners even charged local teenagers a fee to walk across their land to the boys' boats drawn up on the shore of the now South River. The name of Leon Hatch became associated with the boatyard and gunning stand during the decades of the 20s through the forties, but who was he? He appears in two newspaper articles, one from 1925 the other from 1926, one reference in a

Selectmen's meeting in 1927, two interviews, and his obituary; not a lot to try and summarize about a man.

In the 1925 news article, Captain Leon Hatch of the Humarock Beach Gun Club took Capt. Ernest O. Haines of Roslindale and his son on his 15 foot dory Jonah fishing. Using a light cod line for six hours they didn't even have a nibble. It looked as if the dory's name would prove prophetic. Then a strike and for an hour they fought to bring in the catch. Finally they used a light gaff to bring the fish near the boat. Hatch saved the day by thrusting his arm into the fish's gills and dragging it on board. They caught a 400 pound halibut 6 feet 6 inches long. A picture accompanies the article. Could it be Hatch's Boatyard? The answer from Ray Freden was, "Looking at it logically, there

One of Leon Hatch's tame ducks doing his thing. Courtesy of Janet Fairbanks.

Hatch, the building did have a window in front and on the side. Any boats moored were on that North side of the building, deepest water, there is a launching ramp beside a building looking like that, That corner room looked like an office in that section 25 years later, I walked thru it. I don't think Leon would be hanging out anywhere else, and had the right place to hang a 6'6'' fish! That fish could been hung on that L. side corner & taken from the front of the building." An intriguing article, the next year in September was concerned with Leon's flock of 108 tamed geese. The article begins with an explanation of how hunters used wooden bird decoys during the hunting season to lure a passing flock of wild fowl into range of their guns by having them stiffly ride the waves in front of their gunning stands. But with the upcoming hunting season nearly upon him, Leon Hatch of Humarock, MA., came up with a novel approach to salt marsh hunting, he used his trained flock of 108 sleek and handsomely marked black and grey birds, which, not long ago, were as wild as the birds of passage they now decoy so unfailingly. The article then explained the process on how the tamed birds are used. As soon as the wild geese are spotted, the tamed females, who were kept ready on the roof of the garage behind the stand, were allowed gracefully to fly out to lure their country strangers to their own destruction. When the upcountry visitors have landed to sate their curiosity, there is a sharp crack and the trained flock hurried back to their rooftop retreat. Their nervous country cousins beat it up river minus several of their plump and edible members of their company. Hatch took no chances that his valuable live decoys became targets themselves by having attached a tangling throng to the leg of each decoy and by first having chosen the birds to be targeted by the hunters who belong to his club that used the shack. His valuable flock has required ten years of care, training, and work. Several problems were overcome from disease to ulcers and airborne germs. Hatch pointed with pride to a huge, pink-footed, pink-billed gander, a great Northern laughing goose, so-called because of his laugh-like hiss made when angry; "He is the king of the coop!" Hatch concluded the article by stating that he gave his tamed group perfect liberty and they have been seen flying miles up the river, but once hunting season is open things change. He sorted them out, marked them according to the year of their birth by having placed rings on their feet; he has also penned them up. His final point is that only his older, thoroughly trained, and mated birds were used as decoys while the younger generation dozed through autumn awaiting their turns. I also found in the Scituate Selectmen's meetings for June 2, 1927 that Leon Hatch was issued a Sunday license for , 5-pd. and a Tonic license, 1-pd. Hatch also spoke at the meeting of the condition of Central Avenue - three or four bad holes, the worse by Crosby's. Mr. Hatch thought five or six loads of patching material would put the road in fair shape. The matter was referred to Archie L. Mitchell, Highway Surveyor. Mr. Hatch additionally spoke concerning the sale of lobsters by a Marshfield man, also that an ice cream truck was doing business at Humarock. The board advised seeing the Chief of Police. Finally he spoke of the care of the clam flats and the increasing of mussels on the flats. Mr. Hatch offered his services, free of charge, to take care of the flats. In two interviews a woman was mentioned as living with Hatch, one person thought they were married, and the other said no and that her name was Lemira Davidson. She continued operating the shacks on the beach, parking, and collection of fees for walking across the property. The final item uncovered was an article dated November 26, 1953 which read: Hatch – Formerly of Scituate and Kingston, November 25, Leon Hatch, aged 68 years. Funeral service at the Shepherd Funeral Home, Pembroke Centre, on Friday, November 27, at 2 p.m. Interment in Fern Hill Cemetery, Hanson.

Calling hours are to be omitted. I leave you with these few facts about Leon. May he rest in peace.

Successful hunt in Sea View area. Charlie Randall
c. 1910. Courtesy of W. Ray Freden collection.

WHERE HAVE YOU GONE JOE DIMAGGIO; WERE YOU EVER IN HUMAROCK?

The answer is maybe. I am going to use my two sources: Mary Ellen (Keenan) Mastriani and Patricia (Fagan) Arnold both presently live in Marshfield, and both of whose families had cottages on Humarock. Mary Ellen presently lives with her husband Joe on Smoke Hill Road in Center Marshfield emailed me that her "Two grandmothers: one and her husband, my mother's parents, lived at 52 Central Ave, between Manchester & Lowell where I lived right after I was born -- - my father's mother lived on Newton St on the seawall." Pat presently lives on Holly Road and her father, Charlie Fagan, had a home on Oliver Street in Humarock. It was built in 1919 with an addition added sometime later during 1930s. Ironically, Pat's Humarock home was next to Mary Ellen's grand-parents home on Newton St. I had heard a few times since I moved to Sea View in 1973 that Marilyn Monroe and Joe D. had visited Humarock, but I

Pat's house top originally built in 1919; bottom addition added sometime in the 1930s

hadn't lent too much credence to it until I talked to Mary Ellen and Pat. You judge their two stories. Mary Ellen wrote, "I was very happy that we were able to make your lecture. . . . Our house is/was right next to the tennis courts you referenced last night, 54 Central Ave, and I learned to play tennis because we could run over morning, noon or afternoon and get up a game. I was trying to gin up the name of the family that owned the courts and you came up with it -- Tapley I believe was the family. . . . One summer, a neighbor on the seawall, Buddy Noel and family, rented a HORSE! and stabled it there at the courts. I never rode it but many did, on the beach. And the horse survived. The Noel family was related to the actor Jack Lemmon (Mr. Bud Noel and Jack were cousins) and I remember seeing him walking the seawall when he visited. . . . My grandmother, Gertrude H. Keenan, rented at least one season to Dom DiMaggio. Legend says there were sightings of Joe DiMaggio and Marilyn Monroe in Humarock. I can't confirm but . .. who knows. My grandmother's house was on Newton, one of the "twin houses" on the seawall, the one with the red trim." Pat lived right next to Newton Street on Oliver Street. Sometime during the fifities, not exactly sure when but she remembers the day like it was yesterday; rumor had it that Joe and Marilyn were coming to the cottage that Dom had rented next to Pat's home. Pat said that there have never been more people who visited her that day. When her parents came home they wanted to know why all the commotion. When told of who might come, they nodded with resignation and calmly went in the house and went about their business. No, Joe and Marilyn didn't show up that day. But more rumors surfaced as they were purportedly seen in Marshfield. But nothing ever verified.

Pat's friend Doris in front of The Surf during the 1950s

An interesting side story is that Pat's father Charlie's friend was the actor Sterling Hayden. Sterling was planning a trip to Papeete in Tahiti and wanted Charlie to go with him. Charlie reluctantly couldn't go because he was getting married. Most people my age remember both Jack Lemmon and Sterling Hayden but younger folks may not, but Sterling Hayden wrote two acclaimed books The Wanderer and The Voyage as well as leading a storied life during WWII. With Humarock as a destination for two Hollywood actors and celebrities, it is possible that word about Humarock may have spread to these different circles. Who knows for sure?

Base of the sea wall with children playing around it on Oliver Street

Top picture: courtesy of Pat Arnold. Hayden's map of the voyage to Tahiti. Bottom photo from author's collection - Hunters near Rexhame Beach, Marshfield.

Boats and More:

In Vernon Briggs' epic study of shipbuilding on the North River were listed the many shipyards that lined the North River from the Hanover Yards just south of the river's source to the Marshfield yards which were very close to its mouth; Briggs noted these yards and ships also included those from Scituate Harbor. Briggs noted that over one thousand twenty-five

Launching of Helen M. Foster from Chittenden Yard

vessels were constructed from 1650 to the 1870s. The last being the Helen Foster launched in June of 1871. During the late 17th through the early to middle 19th centuries, North River shipbuilders, shipyards, and vessels were known all over the world. But as the years passed and the demand for larger, faster vessels increased, the skilled shipwrights of the North River Valley moved to new shipbuilding centers. With the passage of time, the old yards became deserted and there were few people living who knew their locations or their stories. Decades passed and much history was forgotten.

Then in 1919 a group of men who were strongly interested in the North River formed an association whose purpose was to mark the shipyards locations along its banks. The problem was that few people knew the exact location of the different yards. Luther Little of Sea View became the president of the North River Historical association with Hugh Bancroft of Boston, vice president; J.S. Hathaway of Brookline, secretary and treasurer. The association's executive committee was composed of Alfred Lincoln of Weymouth, Roger Dix of Scituate, and Edmund Sylvester of Hanover. Funds were raised and ten

Plaque for Roger's Shipyards

tablets, mounted on heavy concrete posts, were placed at ten of the principal yards where in locations they could be easily seen by occupants of boats passing up or down the river. Today, a cruise along the banks of the North and South Rivers will yield these markers ravaged by the weather and time, now going on one hundred years. The intention of the association was to mark other yards at a later time, but this did not occur. One of these markers is located at

White's Ferry just across from the Bridgwaye Inn. Its marker stated, "More than fifty-nine vessels of 16 to 400 tons were built here," this probably doesn't mean much of anything to a stranger reading it today. How different would be the stranger's perception if he/she only knew that some of the vessels built here were well known and had intriguing tales associated with them: The Columbia, first to carry the American Flag around the world and the first to explore the Columbia River in Oregon and have it named after her; The Beaver, one of the Boston Tea Party ships, or the Maria, which sailed for over ninety years and visited almost every major port in the world.

Finally, their interest would be piqued to learn about one of the most notorious, goriest

crimes in American history, involving hatchet murders, stabbings, shootings, and a shipboard lynching that occurred on a whaler from Nantucket. The vessel was the Globe. In 2002 two books were written about its fatal voyage and Samuel Comstock, who in 1824 led a mutiny while in the Marshall Islands. He was later murdered by his fellow mutineers. Two survivors lived for twenty-two months, half-prisoners and half-adoptees of the natives until they were rescued by a landing party for the U.S. schooner Dolphin. How's

that for adventure!

So did this legacy end with the launching of the Helen M. Foster in 1871? Not really; what about Bob Boles-built Humarock Babies or the Roger Crawford-crafted

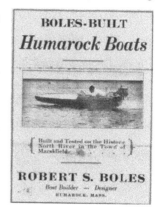

Swampscott dory, Melonseed skiff, or the Gunning dory? How about Ron Brown and his family's Tidewatch sailboats? These are stories that need to be told. What about the businesses that repaired the boats? Research on the Carver Taylor shipyard revealed that most of its business was in the repair of vessels at its yard just east of Little's Bridge. There is a much bigger story here including Hatch's, Townes, Sims, and others.

Let's begin with Boles-Built Humarock Boats. Bob S. Boles designed, built, and tested his boats on the historic North River in the same building that Roger Crawford today builds his boats.

From BOLES-BUILT HUMAROCK BOATS brochure PAGE 4.

In his brochure, Boles has three Hull designs for prospective buyers to choose from. One design is Humarock Baby Hulls, a second is for Humarette Hulls, and the third style for Humarock Outboard Runabouts. Besides listing the class, length, beam, weight (approx.), and price and information about the Humarock Baby Hulls, he states,

> Humarock Baby Hulls are extremely fast, as their records show, but they have always been noted for their turning ability, comparative ease of riding, and ability to stay whole and in shape in spite of rough usage. These qualities are not obtained by accident. Much careful thought and experience gained from extensive testing has gone into them. The original type of bottom and hull, modified to meet increased speed and other factors, has proven as successful as in the earlier boats. Each year brings improvements, and these hulls will be faster and better handling boats than ever in 1934.

> With the increase of speed and power, the value of thoroughly strong construction becomes of much greater importance. A few dollars saved on first cost is an expensive saving if the hull breaks up or changes shape in the first

rough water race. Genuine strength comes only from careful planning and individual building by experienced workmen. Humarock Baby . . .racing hulls are built by workmen with years of boat building experience; men who follow racing and take nearly as much interest in the success of the boats as do the drivers themselves.

Photo care of George and Ruth Wile at the Antique Boat Museum in Clayton, NY

To prove his point, Boles had three photos of Clinton R. Ferguson. One towing three well-cared-for Humarock Hulls at the end of the 1933 season; another showing him as National Amateur Champion, Class A, Division I. (He also broke the Class C, Division I record in August); and a table full of trophies won by Ferguson in 1933.

SOME OF TROPHIES WON BY CLINTON R. FERGUSON IN 1933

In an article written by Peter Crowley it was stated, "The accomplishments of Clint Ferguson would be extraordinary in ANY decade or era of outboard racing. They are perhaps more outstanding when you consider that they took place during the highly competitive and difficult times of the 1930's. Racing in this era required thousands of miles of travel on roads before there were highways and in cars before they were reliable. These racers were the "dare devils" in little hydroplanes, which were built before the age of plywood. The name Clint Ferguson became a household name during the 1930's, in a time when outboard races were covered in every major newspaper across the country. He was able to acquire the right mechanic, gathered the best equipment available and blazed a trail through the pre-war era of outboard racing like few other drivers. His driving skill was legendary. Clint's accomplishments came as the result of his strong desire to succeed, his considerable effort and his unmatched talent. Clint drove with the intention to win races. His driving style was characterized by excellent starts on the inside lane and his ability to get every ounce of speed out of his various raceboats. His speed and

Bob Boles and friend on Ferry Street

his extraordinary driving skills can be illustrated by his ability to win 10 national championships and 14 speed records in only 8 seasons of racing."

Kudos to Robert Boles, for his creativity in design, workmanship, and testing of his creation *Humarock Baby*, and Clinton R. Ferguson, for his skill, achievement, and performance as he broke records throughout the 1930s.

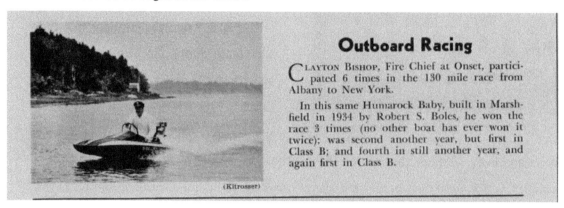

Outboard Racing

Clayton Bishop, Fire Chief at Onset, participated 6 times in the 130 mile race from Albany to New York.

In this same Humarock Baby, built in Marshfield in 1934 by Robert S. Boles, he won the race 3 times (no other boat has ever won it twice); was second another year, but first in Class B; and fourth in still another year, and again first in Class B.

(Kitrosser)

Another man blessed with a creative spirit, knowledge, and skill, Ron Brown, also had a vision of running a small boatbuilding operation, Tidewatch Yachts Inc., in Marshfield in the early 1970s. Christina Brown's childhood home on Preston Terrace served as the company's headquarters. Her late father, Ron Brown, made his living as an architect, but "his first love was yacht architecture," she said. "He had a real job, and that's how he financed this side business." The business was truly a family affair: Her father designed and built the boats, her uncle, J. David Lukos, served as president of the company, and her grandfather, the late J.B. Lukos, also worked on the boats.

Chris Brown's father had sketched out blueprints for a ketch sailboat, dubbed the Tidewatch 39, and began building a prototype in 1970. Her father, uncle, and grandfather spent months cutting, fitting, and assembling each piece of the sailboat inside a nearby barn, not far from Preston Terrace. And in January 1971, the first Tidewatch sailboat rolled out of the barn. The prototype was named Windwatch. In February 1971 the family sailed the vessel around Biscayne Bay off the coast of Florida, and then sailed all the way home, following the Intracoastal Waterway.

After the successful maiden voyage of Windwatch, Brown built three more Tidewatch sailboats in the same mold. And one by one, the four sailboats were sold.

As the years went by, Brown and her family often wondered what happened to them.

In October of 2007, she received an unexpected answer in the form of an email sent by her friend, Mike Donahue. Mike's message contained a link to an advertisement that Donahue had stumbled across on a boating website. It was a Tidewatch sailboat. And it was for sale.

The Tidewatch sailboat in the ad was owned by a radiologist in Maine, who had purchased it 15 years ago and named it Fuzzy Image. The following weekend, Brown, her husband, Michael Bell, her uncle, Dave Lukos, her brother, Matthew Brown, her 11-year-old niece, Mara Brown, and Donahue climbed into a van and drove 150 miles to Yarmouth, Maine, to check out the vessel, mainly for nostalgia's sake.

"We really thought she'd be a wreck," she said.

Captain Chris Brown, her husband Mike Bell, and Mike Donahue with the cap on the Tidewatch.

But as it turned out, the boat was in good shape. "We recognized it immediately," she said. Upon closer inspection, Brown and her relatives confirmed that it was the fourth and final Tidewatch sailboat, which had been launched in 1974.

As their entourage toured the boat, the memories came rushing back. The ceiling of the main cabin provided 6 feet, 5 inches of head room. (Ron Brown was more than 6 feet tall, and he designed the boat to accommodate his height.)

"It was exhilarating and very much felt like deja vu," said Brown. "It was kind of like I stepped back in time. I hadn't been aboard one of these boats in 35 years. It was a trip down memory lane. It was a weird feeling for all of us. My brother, uncle, and I had all been on the original boats. That was a thrill for all of us. My husband, he had heard stories and seen pictures. He was blown away, too."

The Tidewatch sailboat had been out of the water for two years.

It needed some work, but overall, it was in good condition.

Chris, her husband Mike Bell, Mike Donahue and his wife Mi Sun, came up with the money to buy the vessel. After transporting it back to the South Shore, the first order of business was to rename it from Fuzzy Image to Windwatch, in honor of its sister boat.

After months of work with many people pitching in to help bring her back to her original glory, she was ready to be launched, which occurred in late August of 2008. On Sept. 6, Windwatch made its competitive debut in the 18th annual Great Chase Race, hosted by the Hull Yacht Club. Windwatch and its five-person crew - Brown, Bell, Donahue, Lukos, and Dietenhofer - finished in 68th place out of 94 boats.

Some dreams really do come true.

Roger in a Melonseed on the North River. Courtesy of Roger Crawford - photo by Ray Freden

Roger Crawford comes from a family of craftsmen who settled in Milton, MA, from Nova Scotia in the early twentieth century. These forefathers instilled in Roger not just a skill and passion for their craftsmanship, but their tools as well. In a building whose walls have witnessed the creativity, vision, and design of many styles of boats and boat-builders, as well as an area rich in maritime history, as over 1000 ships made their way past by this very building on to a wider world. Roger has joined this brotherhood of builders by displaying his passion, skill, and enthusiasm for his creations: the Swampscott Dory, the Melonseed Sailing Skiff, and the Gunning Dory and for the repair of other vessels like Racing Sculls. Like all work, there are slow times and when the slow times arrive, Roger has plenty to keep busy. Racing kayaks from boating clubs and individuals take a beating during their seasons. Roger receives truck loads of kayaks needing his skills to bring them back to peak condition.

Roger and his assistant John Dietenhofer have crafted vessels different from those made by the Halls, Whites, and Keenes from a different time but in the same general location. One of the most interesting things he remembered concerned the railroad rails for launching and

storing boats next to his building. Roger was told that the rails were from the old Quincy railroad, the first built in this country. He even has a railroad nail from it. Is it from that time? Roger with a smile says, "That's what I was told, but is it the truth? Who knows?" Maybe some future archaeologist will dig up the rails and answer our query. Roger has blended this love of things past, the skill and craftsmanship of 19th century workers, with modern technology to produce unusually elegant vessels that surely would have pleased the Sea View's past builders, like the Halls, Whites, and Keenes. He used fiberglass to construct replicas of eighteenth and nineteenth century boats used for fishing and hunting. The Swampscott dory replicated a 16-foot craft for fishing off the beach while the 13' 8" Melonseed skiff, a sleek, fast, seaworthy craft, recreated a vessel used along the middle Atlantic coastal states for duck hunting. Roger's knowledge of dories is encyclopedic. I sent him some pictures Ray Freden, a friend of both ours, had sent me of Charles Randall and his dories circa early 1900s. Roger sent me a thank you for the pictures and this, "I looked at the photos and find them fascinating. I believe that the Randall's boat as shown in two images is a Toppan motor dory made in Boston around or just after the turn of the century by the Toppan Boat Company in Boston. They built perhaps hundreds of those dories in several sizes from perhaps 18 – 25'. This knowledge and attention to detail separates workers from craftsmen."

Adorning the walls of his shop are his family's tools, constant reminders of their legacy to him and his gratefulness to them. These tools however, are more than historic ornaments to Roger. He will reach for his grandfather Dugas' bevel square or his father Walter's ball peen hammer or an old carpenter's folded ruler before utilizing much more modern versions.

Roger, a still slim and fit septuagenarian, is the owner of Crawford Boat Building. His sterling reputation for building finely manufactured crafts is international in scope. "The most important thing that goes into each boat is passion," he says. "Without passion and enthusiasm, you can't get the results we strive for in everything we do." His repair shop is the longest area business on record, but like all historical thinkers, he remembered those who came before him, not just artisans either. Roger traced for me those before him who repaired crafts like Duke Townes, or designed new and faster hulls like Bob Boles, or those who danced in these buildings during the 1920s. Roger is a firm believer in the preservation of history, before the stories and those who remember them are lost. The building he has spent the last 43 years working in was very well constructed as he points out, showing and explaining its strengths, but he also is cognizant of the ravages of time on old structures and the need for repair before the decline is irreversible. He also opined a reflection that extends this thought. He has been working in his shop for over forty years, but people, especially during the summer, will stop in, shocked to find that they have passed by these doors, for in some cases, twenty

years and never realized he was there building these fine crafts. He said for, most people today everything in life is like fast food: quickly delivered, but has no noticed taste, no quality, and little healthfulness.

Sue Scheible in an article for the Patriot Ledger July, 2018, wrote,

He [Roger] grew up in Milton, a 1962 graduate of Milton High School, and after studying business at Burdett College in Boston, he became a competitive surfer and owned a chain of surfing shops on the East Coast.

While helping a friend repair boats, he was drawn into boat building, starting with dories. In 1987, a customer brought in a beat-up Melonseed skiff found abandoned under a pile of leaves. The original Melonseed was a 19th-century work boat used in duck hunting in the Delaware and Chesapeake bays. It could handle open, rough seas. The designer is not known, but Campbell [Crawford] was intrigued by its lines and took on the job of reshaping the hull.

When he tested that boat in the South River near his shop, he was surprised by how well it rowed as water flowed past the hull in a variety of conditions. When he sailed it on Scituate Harbor in mid-winter, he wrote in his blog, "To my astonishment the boat was remarkably well behaved as I sailed near a fleet of frostbiters that were capsizing all afternoon."

Hooked, he took a cast of the boat and began making Melonseeds along with the Swampscott dories. Soon he switched over to Melonseeds only because they sold so well. Customers raved about how easy they are to handle.

The lines of the skiff have been described as "a symphony of curves" in one magazine review, and the Melonseed is a leader in the day-sailer category. Crawford has sold the skiff from Norway to Israel to the Bahamas. . . . In the shop, he works with Oliver Berry, 26, of Plymouth, who started as an apprentice more than five years ago. Longtime associate, John Dietenhofer of Hejira Wood Works in Duxbury, is now a subcontractor.

The Melonseed has a fiberglass hull and deck, made by the true hand lay-up method. Crawford runs his hand over the richly varnished surfaces on a finished boat and points out the teak woodwork and bronze hardware.

"Lining up every detail adds enormously to the satisfaction of building each boat as perfectly as possible," he says.

A point of pride: From a quarter to a third of Melonseed owners are women.

"No other boat manufacturer has ever had that ratio of men to women ownership, and some of the women sail circles around the men, too," he says.

One of those is Carolyn Sones of Humarock, who still has the fifth Crawford Melonseed made in 1989.

"I wanted a sailboat I could handle myself, not a dory, and I have enjoyed this for almost 30 years," Sones said at the June regatta. "I can throw it on the trailer, put it in and out (of the water) by myself."

For Roger Crawford, the memories of his early sailing days are special. "I don't think

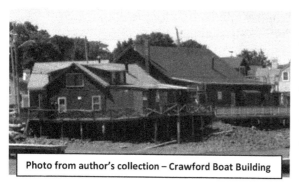

Photo from author's collection – Crawford Boat Building

sailing is ever more fun than when you are just discovering it," he said. "That first magic moment when you try something and feel you have a hang for it. You can lose that easily if the boat is too big. This boat makes you feel like you are 14 all over again."

One final point that Roger made that I wholeheartedly agree with is that gratefulness is the most important thing in life. This is seen in his use of the tools passed on to him. He pointed to two of the T-squares hanging on the wall. One he bought twenty years ago and the other passed on to him from his grandfather. His grandfather's is the better tool by far. But gratefulness isn't just about tools, it has to do with the people who have helped us to be better people. Roger has a friend from kindergarten who has to deal daily with life-threatening health issues, but who is always grateful for every minute

of every day. His gratefulness is contagious, even, as Roger says when he, Roger, starts to moan or groan about his life. His friend snaps him out of his negativity by saying, "Get over yourself, look at all the things you should be grateful for." His pointing out the gratefulness that surrounds us all; we should all have friends like that.

Thank you, Roger, for allowing us to see the world we once did when we were young and to discover again the happiness and joy of doing what we love no matter what our field of endeavor was. And thank you for displaying the fine craftsmanship that is in the finest tradition of Sea View shipbuilders and your example of gratefulness to those who shared their time and talents with you.

The above picture in on Ferry Street just before it intersects with Sea Street. The second picture is a postcard circa 1930s from Ferry Street where the Bridgwaye Inn is today. The third picture is a postcard circa the 1930s of Ferry street just up the road from the previous two pictures. The house on the right in the middle of the picture is the Carlton house (Compare with the photo below).

Corner of Sea and Ferry Streets. looking south. Humarock Beach, Mass

Intersection of Sea Street and Ferry Street during the 1940s.

A VIEW OF THE RIVER, HUMAROCK BEACH, MASS.

The Carlton house shows a small gable on the N.W.end, See house center middle right of picture. The Carlton house today now has an ell on the N.E. end.

The river still has the same bend. The separated strip on the L. side in Humarock was definitely there up to the 70s, but only a mussel bed seen at low tide. Finally it was dredged up, the last of it by Jerry Miller for his dock or dock to be. That long pier between Berry Ave & Harvard Street had to do with its removal also.

Parking Issues in Humarock

Parking at Humarock since my arrival in 1973 has always posed challenges, but I had no idea that the issue was one that stretched back to the 1920s and continued through the 30s

and well into the 40s. As I tried to get as complete a picture as I could, I was stymied by the fact that two Town records' books, that contained crucial minutes during this critical time, were missing and had been for years. However, documentary evidence of what was enclosed in those Selectmen's Meetings records existed in file cards created by WPA workers. When workers attached to the WPA, one of FDR's depression era projects, came to Scituate during the depression, they inventoried and catalogued the Town's records and also prepared, on index-sized cards, summaries of the issues and in what books the records could be found. Besides the fact that the parking issue was a long-standing one, several other facts emerged, or at least they did for me. One was that a leading role was played by the Humarock Beach Improvement Association and other groups who established a presence there, as well as individuals who were committed to the improvement of Humarock, whether by giving to the town land for parking, recreation, or land for a town green, or by giving land to the government for national interests, and in many other ways, always for the betterment of their community. A second was that members of the Humarock community were on both sides of the issues, which in some cases LED to confrontation with town officials. A third impressive fact was the speed at which Humarock grew, developed, and changed. Finally, as much as things change, it is amazing to me how they remain the same. The enjoyment of spending a summer vacation in Scituate, whether it was at the Hotel Humarock, a cottage nestled along the river, or in an ocean front home, has not changed for either adults or children over the decades. Yes, the bathing suits have changed, revealing much more, the homes have grown larger and streets more densely developed, the stores of many varieties have given us many more choices, and businesses have grown being but reflections of their times. But the memories of life in Humarock for almost 120 years have been stored away in the minds and hearts of the many residents and visitors who have gratefully called Humarock home.

Please read and follow the issues, personalities, and results of the Humarock's parking issue.

Bk C-17 p. 141. Selectmen's book February 26, 1916. Regular meeting of the Board this day. All present. Orders #ed 321 to 359 included were drawn Hearing on petition of Ashton W. Sherman in behalf of the Humarock Beach Improvement Association, in regard to the laying out as a town way of a part of North River Avenue. Voted to lay out the same as a Town way. The Selectmen by Jetson Wade, Clerk.

Humarock Improvement Association **S-106 p. 85** July 28, 1923. Protected against giving Sunday License to Leon Hatch. Complained about condition of Humarock Bridge.

Humarock Beach Improvement Association – **S-106 p. 96**. September 13, 1923. To furnish two parking stations at Humarock.

Humarock Beach Improvement Association – **S-106 p. 97**. September 20, 1923. Accepted parking regulations as voted September 13, 1923.

p. 47. May 26, 1927 . . . The Humarock Beach Improvement Association willing to cooperate with the Selectmen. Mr. Tilden suggested placing of two large signs at the corners of South River Road and Central Avenue, "Dead end, no parking." Owners will take care of the 'no trespassing" signs.

p. 138 Selectman's Meeting 1928. Humarock Parking. Finally in a 1928 Selectmen's meeting over a request by a committee from the HBIA to hear their suggestions for traffic and parking regulation at Marshfield Ave., Central Ave., and North River Avenue, as the committee (Mr. Brier, Dr. Keenan, Mr. Brown)was opposed to the conditions as they were on July 15th; and wished to have the plan which was in operation on Sunday July 8th to be put in force. The Association volunteered to have additional parking spaces for residents of Marshfield and Scituate but did object to throwing open that community to great crowds from the nearby towns and cities. They added that there were not adequate accommodations to take care of thousands of visitors. Two men were in opposition Mr. Morehardt, claiming his living depended on crowds coming to beach and he had an $8000.00 investment to maintain, and a Mr. Rooney; they wanted the regulations as of July 15th continued. The Board asked that the two parties submit statements in writing before the next Board meeting. Mr. Brier from HBIA asked that the regulations of last season be applicable to next Sunday July 22nd. Meeting adjourned. Matter taken under advisement. . . . The Board decided to leave the enforcement of the regulations at Humarock in the hands of the Chief of Police (Litchfield)for Sunday July 22nd. The Board was unanimously in favor of the printed regulations being in force at Glades Road Sunday. Mr. Lincoln wishing to call attention of the Board to the fact that he was still in favor of the regulations being the same as last years. At the suggestion of the Town Counsel, Mr. Marr, the following vote was passed: "To authorize the Chief of Police to make traffic regulations not in conflict with those published by the Board on July 13, 1928 or with other town or state laws, and to instruct the Chief to propose for publication by the Board, any additional or changed rules for regulation of vehicular traffic where publication with a penalty for violations is deemed adiviable for their enforcement." William G. Smith

p. 68. Selectmen's Meeting June 27, 1929. A hearing on the parking regulations at Humarock Beach was given by the Board and suggestions from Mr. Brier, Dr. Keenan, Mr. Morehardt and Chief Litchfield were received. Mr. Charles Langille of the Marshfield Board of Trade called and expressed his views to the Board. The matter is taken under advisement and the members of the Board with Surveyor Mitchell.

S-109 p. 74. November 12, 1931. The weekly meeting of the Selectmen was held this afternoon. All members were present. A warrant for $8903.26 was signed. Town Counsel Marr conferred with the Board regarding acceptance of the deed of lots at Humarock Beach for municipal purposes. Certain restrictions in the deed relative to the type of building that might be contructed thereon, its distance of set back from the street and a requirement to keep the property free of rubbish were considered and deemed reasonable. In as much as the article authorizing the acquisition of this property provided for 'taking' the property (Article 33 of the Annual Town Meeting of 1931) Mr. Marr was of the opinion that it might be wise to ask the Town at the next annual Town Meeting to ratify the action of the Board if they decided to accept the property under a deed. Although the article does not stipulate that it shall be taken by eminent domain proceedings and may be construed to authorize taken by purchase, it was felt wise to ask the Town to ratify the Board's action if taken by a deed. The Board felt it unwise to take by eminent domain as the grantors might not agree to the purchase price of $900.00 and in event of a suit, might cost the Town much in excess of the appropriation. The Board voted to accept the deed and to ask ratification by the Town at the next annual meeting. James W. Turner, Clerk.

p. 163 March 28, 1940 Regular Meeting of the Board of Selectmen [Scituate]. All members present. Records of previous meeting read and approved. Considerable time was taken up with discussion of providing a water service at Fourth Cliff, the land formerly owned by Tapley being purchased by the Schusenmeyer Brothers. It is thought advisable at this time to cooperate with the owners at interest and secure a W.P.A. project to provide the service. The tentative agreement is as follows: The Schusenmeyer Brothers. will contribute $3000.00, the Navy Department $3000.00, and the town $4000.00 for sponsor funds.

p. 167. April 25, 1940. Voted to grant to Caesar Urbani and Michael Lumenti a license for open air parking to be operative at land leased from Smalley at Humarock as described in lease. Adjourned at 6 pm. Sunday license to Caesar Urbani and Michael Lumenti to be operative at their parking lot at Humarock. James W. Turner, Clerk.

> **PARKING ISSUES – 1946. Read on to see the issue, personalities, and resolution.**

Silver Sands Realty Co.

Developers of Silver Sands at Humarock Beach
~~120 Concord Street Room 15~~
467 Union Ave., **Framingham Mass**

TEL. FRAMINGHAM 4931

GENERAL LETTER   Jan. 25, 1942

To the Property Owners at New Humarock Beach, Scituate, Mass.:

At the request of a group of property owners at New Humarock Beach, I have prepared a petition to the Selectmen of the Town
of Scituate requesting that they refuse a parking permit for this
coming season to the parking space directly adjoining Humarock Beach
at the south end, their reasons being that with Humarock Beach now
substantially built up and the town enjoying a substantial income
through taxation, that the owners should have relief from the heavy
and fast traffic that goes through the main road each weekend. This
they claim endangers the children at play and gives them no degree
of privacy which as taxpayers they may expect to enjoy. Also, that
the people patronizing the parking space do not stay within the
bounds of the parking space but migrate down the private beach which
is reserved for the owners at New Humarock. It is not only this
using of the beach that annoys the property owners but the fact that
cans, papers, and broken bottles generously litter the beach after
such a weekend and this too adds to the confusion and danger of the
property owners using the beach. All these statements are contained
in the petition to the Selectmen.

Inasmuch as it is impossible for any one group to undertake
the job of getting signatures on this petition, this office is making
up a list of approximately fifty owners and sending it together with
this letter and the petition to the party at the top of the list and
request that each petitioner, as he receives these three instruments,
will sign the petition and forward this letter, the list of property
owners, and the petition to the owners immediately below his or her
name, who will in turn forward it again to the next party below his
or her name.

It is without doubt going to take considerable time to get
the petition signed and back to the office and we can only hope that
each one will immediately upon receiving this petition sign the petition and forward all papers to the next party, otherwise we will fail
to have it in the hands of the selectmen prior to their spring meeting.
Naturally this is being circulated for the benefit of the property
owners, but should you have objections to signing the petition, kindly
cooperate with your neighbors by forwarding it at once to the party
next in line.

Very truly yours,

William E. Roblenmeyer

SILVER SANDS REALTY Co.

WES

179

C. L. MOREHARDT

CONTRACTOR

JOBBING OF ALL KINDS

To the Board of
Selectmen

HUMAROCK, MASS., Jan. 30 1946

My Dear Mr Shea, Mr James, Mr Lincoln:

We own around 9 acres of land at the south end of Humarock Beach We would like to have the zoning lifted on this land.

We want to park cars and trailers, put up bath lockers, cottages and a stand.

There is almost 700 ft. Beach frontage in this parcel, we would do every thing in our power to keep our patrons on this frontage.

If we can get the zoning lifted and a parking permit, we will gladly allow parking space on Marshfield ave.

We would like to put a real estate office in this Marshfield ave. space.

yours Respectfully
Hazel M. Morehardt and
Carl L. Morehardt

Recd Jan 31~46

180

THE HERMAN NELSON CORPORATION

CABLE ADDRESS: HERNELCO BENTLEYS CODE

GENERAL OFFICES · MOLINE, ILLINOIS

THIS LETTER IS FROM OUR
SPRINGFIELD BRANCH OFFICE
25 HARRISON AVENUE
SPRINGFIELD, MASS.
TELEPHONE 3-3322

February 20, 1946

Board of Selectmen
Scituate, Mass.

Gentlemen: Outdoor Parking Permits

It is my understanding that you are to take up at your meeting on February 21st, Thursday, the question as to the granting of parking permits at Humarock Beach for the coming summer season.

As a property owner and a taxpayer I want to be recorded in opposition to any such permit being granted.

When I was in the market to purchase a summer home I traveled up and down the Coast from the State of Maine to the tip of Cape Cod and finally decided to purchase the property at Humarock Beach. The beaches at Scituate, including Humarock, have a good name, no matter where one travels and are recommended as ideal places for a man with a family to invest his money because the rights of a taxpayer are guarded by the laws of the town. During the last two years you have granted a permit to an individual and on Sundays and holidays he operates, not a public parking place, but a public nuisance. He himself is not in any way interested in the betterment of the real estate nor is he interested in seeing that the standard of living is maintained by people who are sufficiently interested to invest their money in property at Humarock Beach. The Board of Selectmen could have seen what the owners are subject to if they had taken upon themselves to spend a few hours at Humarock Beach on any Sunday or holiday. As early as nine o'clock in the morning people in droves come on to the beach from the public parking place and from then until dusk and sometimes after that, property owners are forced to sit on their porches and watch some very degrading situations such as having liquor buried in the sand, using the beach for their toilet, and having their children watch some of the most degrading, low, vile tactics that can be carried on by people under the influence of liquor.

If your Board again sees fit, despite of the opposition of the people who pay taxes and help maintain the Town of Scituate, and grants the outdoor parking permits, then it is possible of course for property owners to sell their investments to the likes of the individuals who use the beach during the time stated above. I do not believe that it is the intention of your honorable Board to tolerate such conditions unless it is your desire to turn lovely Humarock Beach into another Revere Beach.

I trust that the Board of Selectmen will see to it that the rights of the taxpayers are protected and that the petitioner for such a permit

THE HERMAN NELSON CORPORATION MANUFACTURES HEATING, VENTILATING AND AIR CONDITIONING EQUIPMENT is requested to withdraw his application so that Humarock Beach can remain just what it was founded for - a residential beach for people who are sufficiently interested in the welfare of the Town of Scituate to purchase property so that their families can be provided with the privileges that go with such investments.

The gentleman who operated the outdoor parking area last year was very uncooperative with the property owners. The sanitation requirements of the State of Massachusetts are a matter of law and should be lived up to. The law provides that certain toilet facilities shall be provided for each person and I believe that if you will check the law you will find that the operator of the parking area failed to live up to the law in this respect.

As I have pointed out before, if it is your intention to allow Humarock Beach to become another Revere Beach then you will show this to be your opinion if you allow the parking permit. However, if you feel that the rights of the property owners, the protection of their families and the betterment of the Town of Scituate is your intention you will not allow a parking permit to be granted.

I trust that your honorable Board will give this matter very serious consideration and weigh your decision because your decision affects the many taxpayers and their rights of Humarock Beach against an individual who has no interest in the beach other than the monetary gain which he derives from such ventures as outdoor parking.

Thanking you, I am

Very truly yours,

J. E. Carey
for Grace F. Carey

Hearing re petition from Humarock summer citizens protesting public parking in Humarock held Selectmen's Office February 21, 1946 at 2:00 p.m.

Chairman Shea read petition and then letters received protesting the public parking.

Fifteen citizens present.

Mr. Hathaway spoke against the parking, said the transients did not contribut anything to the Town.

Mr. Dow spoke representing Mr. Cheever who was unable to attend. Read a letter the Board of Selectmen had already received from Mr. Carey protesting. Mr. Dow said that represented the feelings of the Humarock Beach Association. Chairman Shea then asked him to repeat the story he had told him on a previous visit regarding an incident that happened on the beach last summer. Chairman Shea asked him if the police knew about it and he answered they were aware of it. (Indecent exposure by shell-shocked veteran)

Chairman Shea asked Chief Stewart if he had any record of it and he answered they did not.

Chairman Shea then had those present and were against the parking to sign their names.

Mr. Morehardt said the Carey letter was not taken as it was written. When asked about toilets Mr. Morehardt said they had toilets now. And referring to the beach incident said the War Veteran did not come from a car parked in his space but was visiting a resident. Referred to two other spaces that had no licenses. (Smiths and Clarks).

Mr. Urbanie was asked to speak and said he had had his parking space in 1930, before zoning went into effect. Also he has a Lord's Day and Common Victualers license. Up until three years ago the nearest house was 3/4 mile away. and about 200 houses have been built around him since that time. Says he never has had a complaint about the parking space.

Mrs. Smith answered Mr. Morehardt's accusation about parking without license, says the parking is for business only and there is no sign saying parking. Mrs. Clark stated they had not had parking since the law regarding toilets came in.

Chairman Shea asked Chief Stewart to give his views on the public parking at Humarock and he said he was always against all parking at Humarock. Also he had never heard any complaints about the parking, but he still has the same views as he always had, that Humarock is residential entirely. Stated the town owned parking space was patronized more by Marshfield residents than by Scituate.

Chief Cole stated the Marshfield Ave. parking space a danger to the community. Protests against it as a menance.

Chairman Shea asked Mr. Urbani if he would be hit very bad if parking was baned and Mr. Urbani answered he would be.

Mr. Matterson spoke against public parking but also stated they couldn't be blamed for all things. Thought if there were a parking lot in South Humarock only with police protection that would eliminate alot of trouble.

Mr. Flannigan asked why have public parking in Humarock at all, thought the beach would be a lot better off.

Mr. Hathaway though the Selectmen should entertain the idea of only one parking space.

Chairman Shea asked for a vote. Only two in favor of one lot and three against. Others wouldn't vote for one and against the other.

Chairman Shea explained that in order to get help from the State for repairs and possibly a new bridge at Humarock the beach could not be called private or kept private as the State does not give aid to private beaches.

Mr. Morehardt says his space can only take about 35 cars and that would not make much more of a crowd on the beach.

Mr & Mrs A. W. Matheson,

Mr & Mrs F. D. Flanigan

Dr. & Mrs. Arthur O'Burns

Mr. & Mrs John J. Carroll

Mr & Mrs Clifford W. Dow Jr

Mr & Mrs. A. H. Hathaway

O. P Schultz 90 Brunswick. (Phone)

Yes.

Carl Morehart 1930)
Ubani 1930) originated

Rebutial

Mrs Richard Smith

Mr Clark

no. yes.
3 - 2.

Chief Stewart

vote So. forking
Space only

against forking

Chief Cole
against morehart.

Recd Feb 28 - 46

May 6, 1946

Copy to Mr. Cody

Mr. Walter G. Cheever
234 Slade St.
Belmont, Mass.

Dear Mr. Cheever:

In answer to an application dated
April 30, 1946 from Hazel M. Morehardt seeking
a renewal of her parking permit on lot at 79
Marshfield Ave., please be advised the Selectmen
at a meeting held May 2, 1946 voted to deny her
a parking permit at above location.

Yours very truly,

DHS:HLD

Dennis H. Shea
Chairman, Board of Selectmen

186

Late 19th & Early 20th Century – Humarock News

The late 19th century was a time of great change in the United States. The Civil War had ushered in the Age of Industrialization. With industries now located in one area, the need for both skilled and

Photos on this page from author's collection

unskilled labor became critical. This culminated with an exodus of people both from U.S. farms and from countries abroad who poured into America's cities with the hope for a new and better life. During this whole process new technological inventions were changing life in ways never before imagined like the telephone, phonograph, and the skyscraper. Our country was in the midst of changing from a rural nation that relied

on agriculture for more than half its population, to one whose industries perched in cities became world leaders by the end of the century and into the early 20th century. Transportation systems were also evolving from dependence on the horse and sail to steam-powered vehicles both used on land and the

sea. Railroads paved the way but change heralded the emergence of the United States as a nation and a force to be reckoned with. All of these things contributed to what I call the democratization of America. By the late 19th century, the average working American began to share in a new concept – LEISURE! Now average

Americans could do the things the rich did, just not to their scale. As the middle class grew, so, too, did opportunities for them to enjoy things like the rides offered at hotels along the shore, boating along

rivers and bays, or taking a train to vacation for a day, week, or season at some mountain or beach resort.

Newspapers, looking to sell papers, would have sections dedicated to people and announcing who, what, when, and where individuals were staying. Many news services did this and are a great source of information. Let us examine some of these pieces of history as they pertain to Humarock during this period from the late 19th through the early 20th centuries.

- July, 1884. Arrivals at the Hotel Humarock included families from Rutland and Bennington, VT, Omaha, Nebraska, Toronto, Canada, Philadelphia, PA, and Buffalo, NY. Also were many from towns and cities of Massachusetts: like Plymouth, Worcester, Arlington, Newton, Milton, and Boston to name just a few. Two family names from Boston drew my attention: C. E. Jackson and wife and Mr. and Mrs. John W Leatherbee.

- August, 1886. Before giving a long list of names, the article titled Humarock Beach announced that Richard J. Walsh, a probation officer from Boston, and his family and the family of Frank M. Wells, superintendent of the streets, Boston, are also at the hotel. Mr. and Mrs. W.N. Carpenter of Chicago have discarded their single wheels and now ride a tandem. Finally, the article noted that there was a pretty children's party Wednesday evening. The march was led by Miss Louise S. Jackson of Fitchburg and Alfred S. Brown-Hamlin of Jamaica Plain. Before a long list of people and their towns was a weather report: The storm Wednesday night gave a heavy swell Thursday, and the surf bathing was the best of the season.

- July, 1889. Following is a list of arrivals at the Hotel Humarock, Seaview. Like the entry above, it contained a long list of names. The ones that struck my attention were: again the Jacksons but this time with Lucy Jackson. Also included were H.W. Wadleigh and wife. A surveyor with this name surveyed the first development of

Photo courtesy of Arthur Brown

Humarock for the Fourth Cliff Land Company in 1882. I wonder if he liked the area so much that he came back with his wife for a vacation. The list of names was twice as long as the one from 1884. Was this indicative of Humarock's attraction?

- August, 1896. Humarock Beach. Before the Hotel Humarock's long list of people and the towns or cities where they resided, came these two new pieces of information: The Rogers family, who have a cottage over the river, will return to Worcester, Saturday (I wonder if this Rogers family was related to the one that stayed at Hotel Humarock in earlier times?). Thursday evening a progressive whist party was given at Hotel Humarock. Prizes were taken by Mrs. Hamblin of Jamaica Plain, Mrs. Ulman of Chestnut Hill, Mr. Armington of Providence and Mr. Dow of Woburn.

- Aug, 1900. Many new arrivals at this place from Boston and vicinity. New arrivals included people from Troy, NY, Baltimore MD, and New York City as well as towns and cities of MA.

- July, 1909. At Humarock beach, one of popular sections of Scituate's beach line, the following are located with their families: a list is then provided. My attention was again attracted to two names: Charles Jackson of Boston and James Leatherbee of Braintree. By 1909 the Jackson family was in their home opposite the Hotel Humarock's location. Later, the Leatherbees would buy a house lot and build upon it.

Photos on this page and next page from author's collection

- September, 1909. Two men were rescued by the Fourth Cliff Life-Saving station crew led by Capt. Frederick Stanley after their boat had capsized just outside the mouth of the river. The crew's boat was a difficult rescue because the seas were too rough to launch the rescue boat on the ocean. It had to be towed by a powerboat after being launched on the river side. After a hard battle with the waves, the crew rescued the two men, who by the time of the rescue, had given up hope of survival. To show how rough the waves were, the powerboat was unable to get back into the river and had to anchor off Humarock Beach.

- September, 1917. Fire Loss $30,000 at Humarock Beach. Ten Cottages Destroyed by Fire At South Shore Resort. The fire started at a cottage owned by Mrs. Nellie Winslow of Boston at about 7:30 at night. The wind caused it to quickly spread to adjoining structures on both sides of the house. Because the beach is south of the mouth of the North River it is inaccessible. Engines were forced to go through Seaview. The fire was subdued by 11 o'clock. Mrs. Winslow and a Mr. James Moore both lost two cottages. All ten cottages were insured. This fire was the most spectacular event in this section in years. It was estimated that 1500 vehicles visited the site and more than 300 people walked to view the damage.

- July, 1925. Yesterday, with the thermometer registering 96 degrees, throngs sought the beach. At Humarock Beach it is estimated 10,000 passed the day, most of whom were from inland towns. Traffic over the State highway was the heaviest of the season and efficiently handled by the police, with no accidents reported.

- September, 1928. Humarock Water Protests Heard. A hearing was held to address the protests of Humarock residents regarding the quality and service of the Humarock Beach Water Company. Joseph Brazier told the board that the district is without hydrant protection and that the pressure is so low that if he used water on his first floor, the water on the second floor is shut off. He said there were many times during the summer when the water was unfit for drinking or laundry use. A representative of the Water Company contended that the petition had not been properly drawn. Later he withdrew this objection. The president of the company, A. A. Wilder, told the commission he had received no complaints as to the quality of the water. He said the company twice a year submits samples to the State Board of Health and he said that it has always been approved. He said that in regard to the pressure, the company was prepared to make any improvements within reason. It was suggested that the commission send an inspector to study the situation in the district.

- November 22, 1929. Humarock. Mrs. Sophia Frohn passed away at her home at Humarock on Sunday November 17, aged 70 years 7 months. Mrs. Frohn was a native of Germany and made her home here the past seven years. She leaves her son, Frank Frohn, well-known manager of the former Sea View  House at Humarock, and three daughters. Burial was in St. Mary's cemetery, Scituate.

- February 14, 1930. New Water Supply for Humarock Beach.

- April, 18, 1930. Humarock. Magee's store has opened for the season. . . . R. S. Boles received two carloads of outboard motor craft a few days ago. He already disposed of a number of new boats for the season. He is very busy at his boat house getting ready for the coming season.

- May 16, 1930. D.W. Clark Dead at Humarock. Passing of Well Known Resident Monday Morning in His 78th Year ---Was Former Postmaster.

- May 30, 1930. Humarock. Big Boat Show at Humarock. In addition to his boat house at Humarock he has leased the former big dance hall next door and is showing some of the finest boats ever seen in this section of the country.

- August 8, 1930.The Humarock Outboard Racing Association will hold a series of races next Sunday afternoon. R. C. Boles of this place took part in the

11½ FOOT RUNABOUT WITH C MOTOR
Note freedom from spray and running angle

STERN VIEW
Showing bevelled chines and cockpit arrangement

outboard races at New Bedford and came out the winner.

- July, 1931. Humarock's Blind Hero Building Own Cottage on the bank of the South River. George Martin Damon, Now 17, Rescued Drowning Woman When He Was 12.

- February, 1932. Fire destroyed the bungalow camp of J. Frank Dwight at Humarock Beach. The camp was situated near the former mouth of the North River at the Marshfield line in the remote eastern section and the two companies of fire apparatus responding to an alarm from Box 29 had an eight-mile run to reach the scene. Hampered by the deep sand of the beach road and lack of hydrant service, they were delayed in reaching the camp. High winds fanned the flames with the results that the fire consumed the structure.

- November, 1932. Scituate. Town Meeting Authorizes Bond Issue. The town treasurer was authorized to issue bonds to the amount of $37,500. Ten Thousand will go for the purchase of the now private Humarock Beach water supply and $6000 for improvements at the Greenbush pumping station. The remaining $21,500 will be devoted to relief of the unemployed and the installation of a new hydrant and consumers' service at Humarock.

- January 26, 1942. General Letter to Property Owners at New Humarock Beach, Scituate, MA. At the request of a group of property owners at New Humarock Beach, I have prepared a petition to the Selectmen of the Town of Scituate requesting that they refuse a parking permit for this coming season to the parking space directly adjoining Humarock Beach at the South end, their reasons being that with Humarock Beach now substantially built up and the town enjoying a substantial income through taxation, the owners should have relief from the heavy and fast traffic that goes through the main road each weekend. This they claim endangers the children at play and gives them no degree of privacy which as taxpayers they may expect to enjoy. Also, that the people patronizing the parking space do not stay within the bounds of the parking

space but migrate down the private beach which is reserved for the owners at New Humarock. It's not only this using of the beach that annoys the property owners but the fact that cans, paper, and broken bottles generously litter the beach after such a weekend and this too adds to the confusion and the danger of the property owners using the beach. This was the substance of the letter. It was signed William E. Schlusemeyer, Silver Sands Realty Co.

- August, 1943. Navy Blimp Leads Rescuers to 3 Off Scituate; 4th Drowns. The four men had left Humarock Beach to go fishing about 5 o'clock and their dory capsized. The men had clung to the overturned boat for several hours when they were sighted by the blimp, which had been on a routine mission. The blimp dropped a smoke bomb which attracted the attention of mackerel seiner, the *Providenza*, captained by Salvatore Firicano of Boston's North End. The vessel was brought to the spot about four miles off of Humarock in time to save three of the four men. The fourth man had become exhausted and sank from sight just before the *Providenza's* arrival.

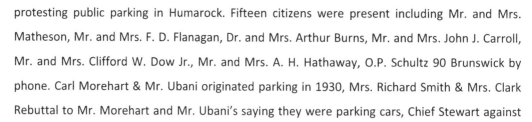

- February 21, 1946 hearing at 2 p.m. in Selectmen's office regarding a petition from Humarock summer citizens protesting public parking in Humarock. Fifteen citizens were present including Mr. and Mrs. Matheson, Mr. and Mrs. F. D. Flanagan, Dr. and Mrs. Arthur Burns, Mr. and Mrs. John J. Carroll, Mr. and Mrs. Clifford W. Dow Jr., Mr. and Mrs. A. H. Hathaway, O.P. Schultz 90 Brunswick by phone. Carl Morehart & Mr. Ubani originated parking in 1930, Mrs. Richard Smith & Mrs. Clark Rebuttal to Mr. Morehart and Mr. Ubani's saying they were parking cars, Chief Stewart against parking, Chief Cole against Morehart. Vote on South parking space only: No: 3- Yes:2. Isn't parking still an ongoing issue?

A Day with the Jacksons

To understand this next story you need to understand where the Jackson/Brown house was. Above with the black arrows pointing to the fence in front and back part of a house is Brown house. The arrow in the front is pointing out a wooden revetment, almost like a boardwalk before Portland Gale of November, 1898. The black arrow in the rear is pointing to the chicken coop while the main house is in between the arrows. Arthur Brown told me that the house in 1898 had a porch on the second floor out front, but other than that the house is the same today as then.

The owner of the house in the 1930's was Charles Jackson and in his grand-daughter's words "was a bit of a ham!" Charles was an artist of some renown and a very well-respected organ musician. If you closely examine his picture the truth of grand-daughter's words are evident. Jackson's background as an artist and musician lent credibility to his dramatic, artistic nature. Arthur Brown related to me that he has become very friendly with the Jackson's grand-daughter who is now in her eighties. The story, pictures, and her remembrances have helped him understand and have empathy for those who lived in this very house before his family.

As the story unfolds, we meet the main characters in our drama. Charles (above) his daughter Florence Elizabeth Jackson Daniels (below right), and his grand-daughter Joyce (in front of her mother) about three years of age in this picture. The location is in front of the chicken coop. According to my memory of the story, it was near the end of the season and Jackson's daughter and grand-daughter had treated the chickens as pets, especially the one that was left. Jackson went out, gathered the chicken and in front of his daughter and grand-daughter twisted its neck killing it. He then began preparing the slaughtered chicken for supper. His daughter and grand-daughter were horrified by the violence and death of their pet and spent the rest of the day in tears. Finally when supper was prepared and ready to eat, the waterworks of crying began all over again. Nor could they consume the chicken..

Photos on this page courtesy of Arthur Brown

194

Humarock: Military History

The Armed Forces that used the Fourth Cliff from the 1920's to the present were: the Navy, the Army, and the Air Force. Each use will be discussed in this chapter.

The history of a military presence in Humarock is traced back to 1910 when the Army Corps of Engineers made a partial survey of the area. The purpose was a master plan for an inland waterway from Narragansett Bay through the Taunton River, then by canal to theNorth River and finally to Boston. With the termination of the master plan, the survey was never finished.

Shortly after the end of World War I a United States Navy Radio Compass Station (Radio Direction Finding Station) existed at Fourth Cliff and was maintained until the opening of World War II. The station began operation circa 1920 and was staffed on January 1, 1921. The Real Estate Office of the Air Force validated the date of December 5, 1921, as the first recorded Real Estate Deed of Ownership of the site.

At this time the only structures on Fourth Cliff were a Coast Guard shed (whose purpose was maintenance of boats and life-saving equipment), not constantly manned during the 1920's and a private summer residence of an individual who bought the old Coast Guard Station from the Federal Government.

During the early 1920's the Navy site consisted of: A Radio Compass Station, a generator shed (used to recharge batteries), and a building for quarters. The site was operated by a crew of four enlisted Navy personnel. The RDF was a small structure about eight feet square with the coils wrapped about and within, on a rectangular frame. A wire mesh screen separated the frame from the operator for safety. The antenna was mounted in the middle of the coil and the

operator sat within this structure. The total acreage of the site was 2.56 acres and had 8 buildings. All of this fenced Naval area was bounded by Central Avenue to Division of Naval Installation; North and South Cliff Road to Atlantic Ocean mean high water and mean low water marks.

The installation was relocated by August of 1942 for a line of sight easement for a fire control structure built by the U.S. Army Coast Artillery.

One interesting story occurred during the 1920's regarding Myron Nunley. One evening while Nunley was on duty, a severe electrical storm developed and then broke over the site. A lightning bolt struck the antenna, ricocheted within the shed amongst the coils, bounced off and travelled through the earphones the man was wearing and terminated in the telephone box nearby. The remainder of the crew hearing the commotion and observing the brilliant flash, ran to the shed atop the hill and found Mr. Nunley dazed, unhurt, and very thankful.

As the Navy men inspected the shed they found the lightning had disintegrated the metal tacks that held the wire screening to the coils and the wooden frame!

Mr. Nunley served at the station for one and half years. After service in the Navy, he married a former Marshfield girl and still resided in Marshfield as of the winter of 1969.

This station was one of three that the Navy operated in this area. The other two were at Cape Ann, Mass. And Cape Cod, Mass. They operated on a system that a vessel would emit an electronic beam on a given frequency. In turn the Radio Compass Stations would, by means of triangulation, transmit their location to the vessel. The "electronic fixing" was done within the vessel requiring plotting the information. The system could work in reverse, if all of the stations were in communication and the ship's signal was emitted for a given length of time.

Silver Sands Development (1942)

Silver Sands became the second development on Humarock. Early in 1940 William E. Schlusemeyer headed an organization that developed the land on and around Fourth Cliff. It was named Silver Sands. In its advertisements it claimed to have successfully developed other New England resort colonies, among them two in Massachusetts (at Westford and Hamilton-Wenham) and one in Cumberland, Rhode Island. They opened their sales office around the beginning of May, 1940, and claimed in an ad from May 11, 1940, to a sales record that exceeded their expectations. The following is from their ads in South Shore newspapers:

"Silver Sands is located at Scituate's attractive Fourth Cliff, commanding an ideal view of the ocean and the South Shore coastline. In addition to the fine sandy beach which is over a mile long, this colony also fronts on the North River, providing a selection of waterfront lots sheltered from the ocean. The development is so laid out that cooling breezes are assured from practically every quarter to dispel summer's heat. . . . In subdividing the property, every effort has been made to plan a colony which will harmonize with the natural beauty of the landscape. Restrictions are being maintained to insure a community which will be among the finest on the South Shore. . . .

In commenting on his latest resort, Mr. Schlusemeyer commented, "The eager approval which visitors at Silver Sands have expressed, not alone of the development and its surroundings, but also of the prices, is a certain indication that this community will be completely developed in a very short time." The subdivision was divided into lots ranging from 5000 to 10,000 square feet; prices for the lots begin at $250 and could be purchased on convenient terms. Modern Cape Cod-style cottages were available starting at $995, with a down payment as low as $125. By June, 1940, the Silver Sands Realty Company claimed that 35 cottages had been completed or were under construction, and that upwards of $80,000 worth of sites had been sold to an enthusiastic public.

By July, 1940, the claims were that 80% of the desirable tract had been sold; that 50 summer cottages of Cape Cod design had been completed and occupied, while 14 more homes were under construction. Improved roads, water, electricity and telephone service have been installed. The final enticement was that a model Cape Cod home was open for inspection for prospective buyers.

In August of 1940 developers claimed that the number of cottages being built was up to 70 and that demand for lots was increasing. As further inducement to buy, the ads stressed several points: first, was that from a family standpoint, the sense of safety and security that prevails in Humarock. Except for stormy days, the action of the tide was gentle and gradual. The beach stretched out into the ocean on a broad even floor, which insured the safety of little folks who cannot swim. Second, the South River had a varied diversion for home owners, such as motor boats of the larger type, outboard motor boats, canoes and rowboats. The river is also well adapted for sailboats of the smaller type. Third, the fishing was exceptionally fine with many varieties that any fisherman would drive for miles to hook. A famous midnight sport is eeling from the Humarock low bridge when the moon is right and the tide is approaching high. The fourth selling point was the development's accessibility to Boston. With a choice of many fine state roads less then an hour from the scorching heat of the city, many a tired businessman escaped to a cool and delightful Silver Sands Shangri-la.

By Labor Day of 1940, the developers stated that in the last 11 months more than 250 families have purchased property at Silver Sands, and because of this demand for housing here in Humarock, they had decided to continue building at the same popular prices.

With the original tract on Fourth Cliff developed in a little over a year (145 cottages), the

developers purchased all the remaining property at Humarock Beach and the building continued. This was called Tract II or New Humarock Beach, Scituate.

As May of 1941 began, forty new homes were either completed or were under construction at New Humarock Beach.

The developers of Silver Sands and New Humarock Beach controlled approximately five miles of property which fronted the water: three miles facing the ocean and two miles facing the river. Over eight miles of roads and streets had been completed and an equal amount of water pipes and wires were installed. The New Humarock Beach continued to offer the same advantages

that the Silver Sands development had: safety, recreational activities, an incomparable landscape, a sweep of cool ocean and river breezes, and the most important aspect, moderate prices. The one drawback was that the new development was not located on land as elevated as Silver Sands.

As Labor Day approached in late August of 1941, things continued to look bright for New Humarock Beach development as more than 400 families had enjoyed Silver Sands and New Humarock beach that summer.

Then came December 7, 1941, and everything changed, not just Humarock, but the whole world. We were now engaged in World War II. War led to rationing, women replacing men in the workforce, and the Army takeover of many acres on the strategic Fourth Cliff.

Government Takes Fourth Cliff Land

Continued from the First Page

haggling over selling prices. A real estate expert appraised the cottages in the new development, and by Federal Court action the United States Government came into immediate possession, without depositing any money in the courts for payment of claims. Awards to the owners will be adjusted later.

Announced by Brandon

Announcement of the seizure of the Fourth Cliff properties was made yesterday in Boston by United States Atty. Edmund J. Brandon. He acted by direction of Secretary of War Stimson.

Federal Judge Charles E. Wyzanski approved the papers for the taking.

Although the government now owns the tiny estates, town leaders expressed the opinon that all the Summer residents would be given plenty of time to remove furniture and equipment.

According to officials, the houses will be razed to make way for the new base, and the clearance will be accomplished "in a short time."

The area taken by the government includes the Navy radio station and compass base, and it is expected that these buildings will be maintained when the new installations are made.

The development on Fourth Cliff was sponsored by a Framingham real estate man a year ago, and the houses were occupied last Summer for the first time.

Despite the war clouds on the Atlantic horizon, the Selectmen are conducting a campaign to maintain confidence in seashore relaxation along the town's fine beaches, and a circular letter sent to all Summer colonists informs that Scituate's beaches will be in full operation this Summer.

By the early 1941, the area of Fourth Cliff was the scene of many government surveys. One such team visited the site for three days during mid-February. On the second day of operations, an Army staff-car rushed to the site and the officers viewed the survey team and the windswept land area. The Colonel in command of the expedition waved his arm, encompassing the entire area and said in a most authoritative manner, "All of this has to go.........!" With that the staff-car sped off leaving the perplexed engineers alone again.

Within a short period, however, unknown to the engineers and the residents of Humarock, the acquisition of the land and area began its legal proceedings under the code name, "Silver Sands".

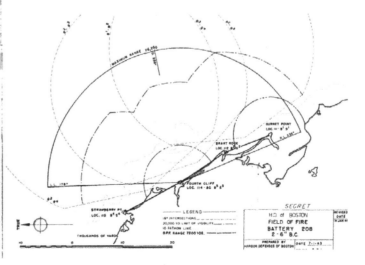

With the bombing of Pearl Harbor, the United States had entered the war on the side of the Allies. The need to strengthen our defenses and gird for war became of paramount importance. As part of the defense of Boston Harbor, a plan was developed that stretched a protective net from Nahant to Duxbury. Later as needs changed, the plan was modified, so for example, one battery of 16-inch guns due to be located in Marshfield was cancelled when the threat of an enemy surface naval attack on Boston Harbor was deemed unlikely. Included in this plan selected sites were chosen from north of Boston to the Gurnet along the south coast. Sites consisted of an early radar, fire control towers, and/or artillery batteries.

At the northern end of Humarock lay the Fourth Cliff Military Reservation, which during the war received several new assets: a battery of two modern 6-inch guns (Battery 208), plus two fire control towers, a 5-story tower right at the northern tip of the reservation, and a 3-story "tower-in-a-house" further south on the peninsula. At over 50 acres, the Fourth Cliff Reservation was larger than several other areas in the Boston defenses which were formerly designated as "forts." It had been used by the Navy as a communications site prior to the war, and was acquired by the Army in 1942. After the war, it was assigned to the Air Force and used for communications and radar experiments, and later assumed its present role as a vacation spot for military personnel and their families. Marshfield was also the location of a WWII-era SCR-296 fire control radar, built atop Holly Hill (about 4000 ft. west of the beachfront in

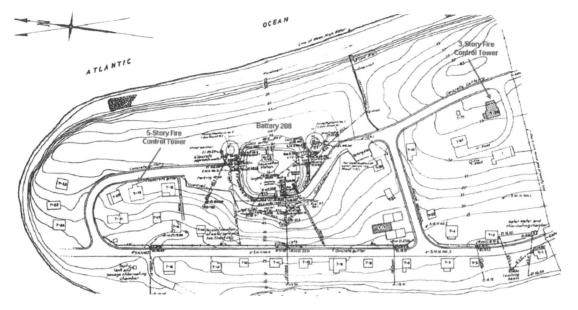

Humarock). With its antenna atop a 100-foot steel tower, this radar provided target detection and fire control data for the guns of Battery 208 at Fourth Cliff,

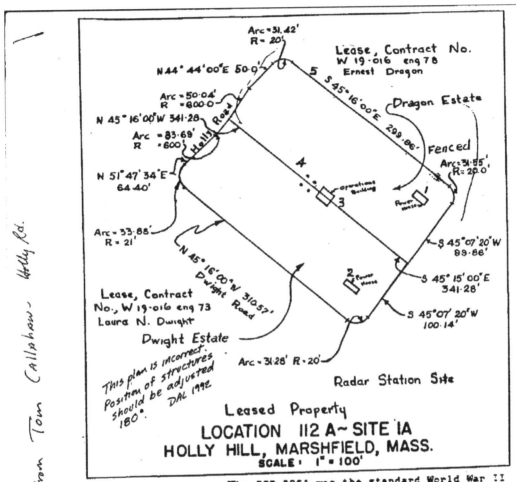

Arc =31.42'
R = 20'

Lease, Contract No.
W 19-016 eng 78
Ernest Dragon

N 44° 44'00"E 50.9'

S 45° 16'00"E 299.86'

Dragon Estate

Arc = 50.04'
R = 800.0'

N 45° 16'00"W 341.28'

Arc = 83.69'
R = 600'

Fenced

Arc=31.55'
R=20.0'

N 51° 47'34"E
64.40'

Operations Building

Power House

Arc = 33.88'
R = 21'

S 45°07'20"W
99.86'

N 45° 16'00"N 310.57'
Dwight Road

Power House

S 45° 15'00"E
341.28'

Lease, Contract
No., W 19-016 eng 73
Laura N. Dwight

S 45°07'20"W
100.14'

Dwight Estate

This plan is incorrect.
Position of structures
should be adjusted
180°. DAL 1992

Arc = 31.28' R = 20'

Radar Station Site

Leased Property
LOCATION 112 A~ SITE IA
HOLLY HILL, MARSHFIELD, MASS.
SCALE: 1" = 100'

The SCR 296A was the standard World War II fire control radar utilized by the U.S. Coast Artillery for engaging surface targets. It was authorized for issue to all modern batteries of 6" and larger on a basis of one set per battery. This set was basically identical to the navy Mark III. or FC, set utilized on ships. The function of the Radar was, during periods of poor visibility, to provide the range and azimuth of the target vessel to the plotting room of the battery. In addition it could be used to provide such data to additional batteries as required or to give spotting corrections to other batteries if advantageously sited.

Experience with the set showed that the antenna became less effective, due to decreased maximum range, at heights below 100 feet above sea level and created too much "dead zone" at heights above 500 feet.

To provide for this height requirement the obvious answer was to utilize natural heights such as hills, bluffs etc. However, at many sites on the Atlantic and Caribbean U.S. coasts, no such sites were available. For these low-lying sites a prefabricated steel tower was issued with the set.

and was one of nine such radars in the Boston system. Today the property where the tower was positioned is owned by Tom and Mary Callahan, who provided me with copies of the plans for this unit. Remains of the tower can still be seen on their property. Ray Freden was present and actually saw the underground cables for the tower when utility company workers dug up Ireland Road and inadvertently exposed these cables.

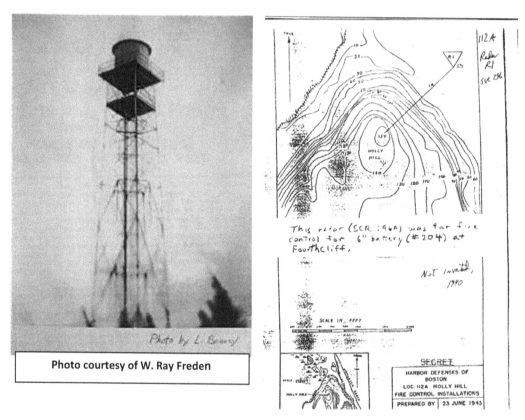

Photo courtesy of W. Ray Freden

The range of Gun Battery Number 208 to be installed on the Fourth Cliff is a tactical Battery #02, 6-inch, modernized emplacement with shielded carriage system. Construction

commenced 09 September 1942 (Ref: harbor Defense Annex: 'A'); 10 September 1942 (Ref: A52-87 National Records Centre, WDC). Scheduled completion Date: 01 October 1943. Estimated Completion Date: 01 June 1943.(**Photo Courtesy of Coast Defense Study Group.**)

This gun battery in Humarock was to have a combination of three one- and two-bedroom recreational lodging facilities (painted in pastel colors for camouflage) and a false

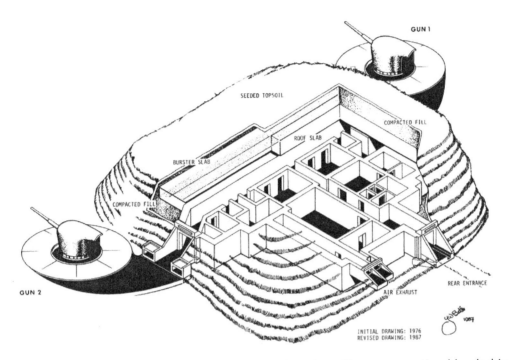

road over the command center. This was done so that the military reservation blended in with surroundings. One battery of two 6-inch guns was built here, on shielded barbette carriages with a magazine and fire control bunker between them. It was interesting to note that the concrete work was completed by a local construction company, Rugani Construction of Marshfield and when completed became one of the most unique and deadly coastal fortifications in New England.

All of the barracks and structures were under the guise of existing Humarock beach cottages and homes. As noted above, the completed units were painted bright pastel colors and the Gun Battery was concealed by a mock road and a great deal of shrubbery which remains and flourishes today. The two six-inch guns, mounted in turrets: similar to Naval units, were guided by radar that was constructed on 'Holly Hill' and connected to the guns by underground wire that ran under the river to the Fourth Cliff. The entire underground structure, composed of reinforced concrete many feet thick, was bomb and gas-proof and contained its own power plant, plotting, spotting and radio rooms in addition to ammunition and powder storage areas. The range of this battery was an estimated fifteen miles. The code number for this battery was Battery No. 208. Oh, I forgot to tell you, they even had a chemical decontamination room – very primitive when compared to what we have today, yet very modern for them.

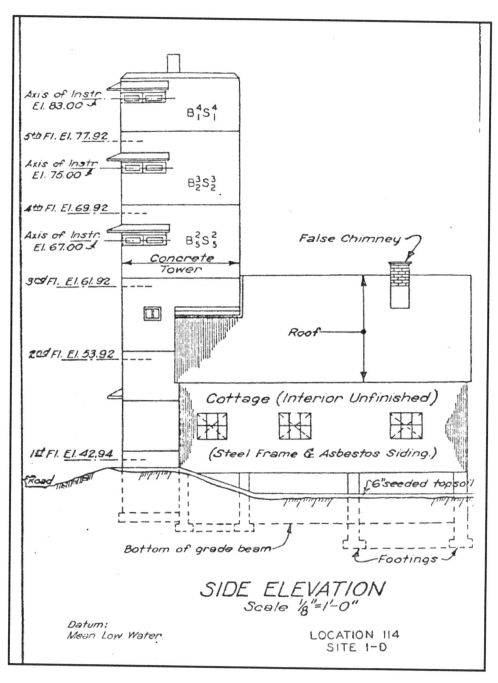

SIDE ELEVATION
Scale ⅛"=1'-0"

Datum:
Mean Low Water.

LOCATION 114
SITE 1-D

The observation tower, now utilized by NCOIC, was constructed of reinforced concrete and camouflaged with a wooden shell and false front.

The site was extremely important for the southern strategic defense of Boston Harbor. Searchlights were mounted on the beach areas, machine-gun nests were established and manned, anti-aircraft weapons were emplaced and beach patrols were created by elements of the Army garrison in conjunction with Coast Guard and canine patrols. Remains of barbed wire may be found to this date in the sand and in the water of the Coast Artillery site.

With the successful termination of WWII, the site was relieved of its armament and garrison and put on caretaker status.

On the 2 February 1948 Fourth Cliff was designated as an Air Force Field Station and on 15 March the US Air Force Cambridge Research Laboratory acquired the site for experiments.

The casement of Battery 208 was used for power and communication for the projects. New construction sprang-up near the northern gun pad of the casement. The construction of powerful antennae termed the 'Billboard' due to its configuration, and became well recognized

as a landmark. The 'Billboard' was utilized for electronic scanning operations and for checking electronic scanning with a fixed array.

During the early 1950's two steel towers or 'Yagii' antennaes were constructed to operate separately or in conjunction with the 'Billboard' antennae for radio propagation or

scatter-communications and air-to-ground communications. Final applications were DEW and BMEW defenses (part of our early radar warning detection system of Soviet Ballistic Missile launches). During 1966 the two 'Yagii' antennaes were dismantled and during the later part of 1971, the 'Billboard' antennae was removed. The site looks much as it did during WWII minus the armament.

Today this area is an exclusive vac-ation area owned and operated by Hanscom Air Force Base in Bedford, MA, and is a vacation spot for military personnel and

their guests. "They come home from Bosnia, 15break and that makes it interesting for us because we get some first-hand information about the situations oversees," said Roger Kent, manager, of the Fourth Cliff Family Recreation Area, a 56- acre parcel at the tip of Fourth Cliff, overlooking Humarock Beach and the mouth of the North River, called the New Inlet. With beautiful vistas, and gorgeous

Photo care of Pat Arnold.

sunrises and sunsets, this military haven provides R-and-R that is second to none. Please take a photo journey through parts of the Recreation Area you would never be able to observe and experience.

Top: 5 story observation tower. Next five photos through the doorway and down a corridor leading to WWII machinery.

On the final page of this section are two photos: one an underground workroom and the other one reason why this area is not open to the public.

Below one of the 6 inch gun mount platforms that has been converted to a covered picnic area.

Above: scenic view from top of Fourth Cliff. Below 3 story Fire Control Tower

Top: 5 story Fire Control Tower from outside. Below: Inside on fifth floor looking toward Scituate Harbor

DANGER

SOME MATERIALS IN THIS
BUILDING
CONTAIN ASBESTOS FIBERS
AVOID CREATING DUST
POTENTIAL CANCER/LUNG
DISEASE HAZARD

Humarock's Memorable Storms

I have seen many storms in my life. Most storms have caught me by surprise, so I had to learn very quickly to look further and understand that I am not capable of controlling the weather, to exercise the art of patience and to respect the fury of nature.   -Paulo Coelho

My first memories of terrible storms occurred when I lived in the Pinehurst section of the town of Billerica during the 1950s. Hurricanes Carol, Edna, and Diane descended on the Bay State like fierce lions. In late August of 1954, Hurricane Carol became the most powerful hurricane

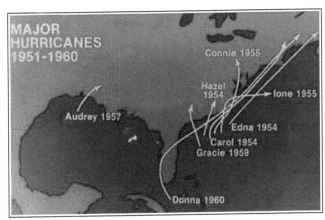

to strike Massachusetts since the Great New England Hurricane of 1938. Hurricane Carol caused widespread destruction along Southern New England shores. It was the costliest natural disaster in U.S. history until Hurricane Diane surpassed it 1955.[1] Hurricane Diane also arrived in southern New England in late August 1955, this time inundating New England with devastating floods. Prior to Diane's arrival, Hurricane Connie had saturated land with rainfall and prepared the way for Diane's severe floods. My memories as a nine and ten-year-old may be jaded by time and a brain strewn with 70+ years of accumulated experiences. I remember being terrified by the sights and sounds of Carol's fierce winds. I watched as a 'huge' pine tree fell in my neighbor's yard and worried about two huge pines in my yard that swayed dangerously in the gale. I also remembered going outside with my family as the eye of the hurricane passed; it was a very eerie sensation. We then hurried back inside as the storm's winds returned. I would only learn about storm surges when I moved to Marshfield almost twenty years later. But in the 1950's, flooding to me meant biking down to the Shawsheen River to see how far the banks had overflowed. I remembered seeing pictures of the flooding in Providence, Rhode Island, and

---

[1] The 1954 hurricane season was remarkable in that New England and the Mid-Atlantic States were struck by three destructive hurricanes (Carol, Edna and Hazel). Having 3 hurricanes make landfall in one year is astonishing when you contemplate that 5 to 10 hurricanes of this magnitude are predicted in a century.

New Bedford, MA, and listened as my father talked about the damage to his family members' property in the New Bedford area. Besides hurricanes, the only other storms I experienced were the Nor'easters of winter, and as a school age kid this meant – snow - no school - and sledding down Pinehurst Avenue. Twenty plus years later, Nor'easters, storm surge, and flood zones took on a new and intense importance. The only other storm that my family talked about was the Portland Gale of 1898 because of the role my great-grandfather Hogan played during it. I will focus on that below.

I would draw attention to four storms in relation to Humarock: three I have experienced and one that is part of my family's history. The storm that is part and parcel of my family's history was the Portland Gale of 1898. Ever since I was a toddler, family members told me stories of the sea and of my great-grandfather, Michael Francis Hogan and the steamer Portland. Mesmerized in my youth by these tales, both of heroism and of tragedy, my interest again was piqued, when on a historic tour of the Cudworth Barn in 1973 at my new teaching assignment in Scituate MA, I was shown the doors and life-preservers from the Steamer Portland. The curiosity to find answers to questions that were raised that day over forty-five years ago led to my involvement in local history. During these many years of living in an area where history and stories of the sea are common place and stretch back to the beginning of American history, it has been my pleasure to delve into this rich past while experiencing what men and women from the past had also experienced. This convergence of the past and present led to Dave Ball's and my researching, writing, and publishing a book: *Warnings Ignored: The Story of the Portland Gale of 1898*. The Portland Gale, as well as two storms in the 20th century and one this past January, have impacted Scituate, particularly Humarock, Marshfield, as well as the whole coastal South Shore in myriad intended and unintended ways. Please sit back, stoke up the fire, relax, and listen as storms and the history of Humarock blend and unfold.

THE PORTLAND GALE OF 1898

"It sounded as if all the hounds of hell were loose that night!" Surfman William Murphy.

For Humarock, the storm of November 26 – 27, 1898, was devastating. Not only was Humarock physically changed, with a new inlet between Third and Fourth Cliffs created and the Old Mouth eventually closed, **(this part of the story is told in depth in a later chapter)** but Humarock and the whole North River valley were impacted physically, economically, and socially as well.

In the early 1890's young people living in the Scituate, Norwell, and Marshfield area on the North River became interested in sailing, row-boating, and canoeing. As summer people began to flock to these towns, they also took up interest in these sports. A meeting was held on September 4, 1893, for all interested parties with the result that the North River Boat Club was organized. Several committees were formed with the tasks of finding a suitable piece of land and arranging fundraising activities to procure funds for a building. During the winter, entertainments and dances raised a substantial fund of money. A piece of land adjoining the town landing at Union Bridge was leased and a club house built. The building was dedicated

June 18, 1894, with speaking, boat racing, tub races, fireworks and dancing in the evening. During the next several years minstrel shows, dances and entertainments were given in the winter and in the summer races and dances were held at the Club House; so much so that the social life of the villages in the area centered around these activities of the club. During the summer months on a Sunday afternoon people watched boats maneuver, and other people in the evening assemblies, with the building and town landing decorated with Japanese lanterns and red fire, listened while "White's" orchestra played the popular tunes of those days. The young folks from miles around looked forward to these events. In 1895 the club was incorporated. Then the awful days of November 26-27, 1898, came. North River Boat Club member John Burton Henderson, his brother Fred Henderson, Albert C. Tilden, and George Ford, all closely associated with the club, lost their lives when their camp was overturned and washed away by raging flood waters, with the result that all four drowned. The records of the McNamara-Sparrell Funeral Homes in Norwell captured the tremendous impact the storm had on the local citizenry. After the storm a few meetings of the club were held but no social activities. With a new mouth to

the North River the boathouse floor was flooded at every tide. Members of the club decided in September of 1899 to sell the boathouse at public auction. It was sold to Walter Osbourne and

moved to his place on Winter Street where it can still be recognized. On September 16, 1899, members of the North River Boat Club voted that their organization be dissolved. The North River Boat Club was thus ended, in existence for only six years, yet another victim of the Portland Gale.

THE BLIZZARD OF 1978

Storms do strange things: they destroy natural boundaries and human life and, in the wake of danger, they build a sense of community and sharing related directly to the number of inches on the ground. Two inches and people still snarl at each other, 2 feet and all men are brothers.

-Mike Barnicle, Boston Globe

For me the Blizzard of 1978 was a seminal event in my life, something that was etched forever in my memory. I can still hear the sounds of that storm: Star Wars-like laser blasts resonating around me as I walked across the street to close a neighbor's front door blasted open by the winds; blows that shook the house as large chunks of ice driven by ferocious winds slammed into North- and East-facing walls while we huddled around the fireplace struggling to absorb some heat and security while the howling maelstrom engendered fear; and finally the eerie sound of water pouring into the crawl space under the house like a broken pipe as the tide surrounded our fragile oasis.

In the years that followed, survivors, buoyed by false impression that we had stood up to the worst that Mother Nature could throw at us, responded about the storm with trite statements that masked feelings of false humility and fear that lay just beneath their surface bluster. Statements like: "...There is nothing in New England that brings the community together quite like really bad weather," "How big's the storm?" or "Did you hear the weather report?" "Are they closing the schools?" After the storm's

Quarterdeck Blizzard of '78 Scituate, Ma

passage, it became part of our mythology. Later it turned out to be a prominent part of the local legacy and a testament to the tenacity of those of us who survived the Blizzard.

". . . As New Englanders headed off to work and school on Monday morning, a few snowflakes had begun to fall around 10 AM, it was a peaceful scene on the ground. But up above things were spinning wildly out of control. By 1:00 PM, the snow began falling at an alarming rate --- up to two inches an hour in some places. As the snow began to accumulate, commuters all over New England began to size up their drive home, calculating when they should hit the road. In state capitol buildings in Boston, Hartford and Providence, government employees were freed for home and soon a slow and steady early rush hour began to build up on the highways. All the while, the snow kept falling, harder and harder. . . . As late afternoon set in, the conditions on the roads began to worsen. . . . As cars and trucks began to slip and slide, accidents further snarled traffic. For drivers stuck on area highways, a fear factor began to set in. What may have begun as a fun, winter adventure was beginning to get downright scary. As traffic stopped and the blizzard kept on coming, drivers were now trapped in their cars with few options left. The wind began to howl upwards of 70 miles per hour in the Boston area . . . As nightfall came, the anxiety level around New England varied greatly, depending on where you were and what shelter you had. As the winds picked up and the snow kept falling, government officials were beginning to see that they had a major emergency on their hands. . . . While inner New

England had some serious snowfall on their hands, cities like Hull, Revere and Scituate had something approaching a hurricane. Winds topped 100 miles per hour along the coast and waves began lashing the shore, sometimes ripping off doors and roofs while making a mockery of local seawalls. . . . As New England woke to the morning of February 7th, not much had changed in the forecast. Snow continued to come down at an incredible rate as explosive winds pushed what had already fallen into mammoth-sized drifts.

Tales were later told all over New England of heroic acts that saved lives. Scituate assistant harbormaster Elmer Pooler was such a hero. Early in the storm he climbed onto an army cargo truck and helped rescue families from Lighthouse Point as enormous waves washed over the vehicle and ice blocks flew at him from the river.

Later a Coast Guard rescue boat got tangled in some mooring lines and lost its way. Up against the sea wall and rocks behind T.K. O'Malley's, Pooler headed back out into the storm again. Eventually each of the crew members would literally jump out of the boat and into Pooler's rescuing arms. . . .

Despite these horrific headlines that the storm produced and the 166 arrests due to looting in the area, many New Englanders found ways to come together and help one another during the Blizzard of '78. Many would remember it as a time when neighbors helped neighbors and a special community spirit emerged. . . .

Finally, after a record 33 hours of continuous snowfall, the skies cleared over New England. It was now time to begin the biggest dig-out since the great snowstorm of 1888. And in coastal communities it was time to survey the wreckage and try to put lives back together (after a helicopter tour of the South Shore, Dukakis called the sight "Simply awesome") (Blizzardof78.org)."

Scituate Historical Society's photo a few days after the storm

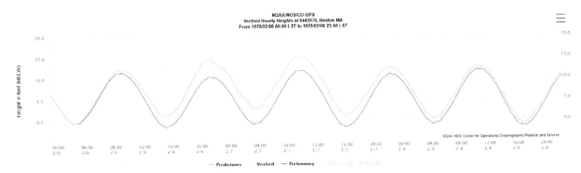

The statistics were staggering: 27.1 inches of snow in Boston (40 inches in parts of Rhode Island), 99 deaths, 4,500 injuries, 350 federal troops, $520 million dollars in damages, and 3,000 cars and 500 trucks abandoned on just an 8-mile stretch of Route 128.

In my reflections on the storm I would stress two conclusions: first, that if you challenge Mother Nature, you do so at your own peril, and secondly, that in the worst situations imaginable, humanity, in most cases, gratefully steps up, helps out, and reflects through community action the golden rule.

Having been dismissed early from school, I had stopped at Stedman's to pick up a few items. Getting into my car I noticed an ominous feel to sky and weather. After arriving home, we began to take precautions for bad weather by bringing in more wood for the fireplace, digging out flashlights and batteries, and filling containers with water. Public service calls were made informing us that shelters were being set up at the high school for those in need. I called my neighbors Rita and Bob Payne with the question "Should we evacuate?" Since my family and I had lived here a little over 5 years and nothing like this had ever happened before, I was worried. A year earlier after having read up about storms in coastal areas, storm surge, and flooding, I had purchased flood insurance. Now I turned to people who had endured many storms over years since moving here in the sixties, Bob and Rita Payne. Note: that in 1978 most of our street (Ridge Road) was composed largely of summer homes while our end of the street had only four or five year round residents. Bob and Rita said they had never left their home in the many years here and were not going to now. My wife's friend, Pat Large, two houses down from us had lost her husband at sea and with two small children was going to high ground and stay at a friend's house. We could go with her if we wanted. My wife and I decided we would stay put. As the evening progressed with the wind howling like some caged beast and snow at white-out conditions, I began to rethink my decision. During the height of the storm, my neighbor's front storm door blew open and was being blasted to and fro in the fierce gale. Fearful that the storm door would shear open and come right through my picture window, I dressed up and prepared to go and close it. As I got to the middle of the road, I glanced down the street – the tide had already breached the road. Looking up the street toward the Corrigan's house, the tide had filled in their property with the house looking like an island in the middle of a sea. I secured the Butler's door and retreated to my house. The wind, cold, snow, and ice were fierce. As stated before hearing noises like laser blasts from Star Wars movies, I realized it was the wind noisily passing through the wires supporting the telephone posts. Safely back inside my house, I told my wife that we were the highest spot on the road and that most of the road was under water. As dark descended and the wind kept up its fierce symphony while hurling ice chunks against the house, I worried about our safety. With power out and the only source of heat the fire place and the gas stove, we dragged two mattresses out of the bedroom and set them up in the living room. Then we tacked up a blanket blocking the hallway and attempted to keep the heat contained to a small area. Meanwhile I struggled to keep a fire going in the fireplace, and awaited dawn with trepidation.

Dawn arrived and the town worked feverishly to rescue people and repair areas breached by the storm waters. As a large front loader machine made its way down Ridge Road followed by DPW truck, we decided to take the town's advice and evacuate. I will never forget that ride as this huge front-end loader with its blade down pushed the tidewater aside and we huddled in the truck right behind it, gazing at the destruction first on Ridge Road then down Bayberry – finally arriving at the top of the Ferry Hill at the Walton's house. After spending a cold and miserable night with three families clustered together, I decided to walk home. Over two feet of snow had fallen, but the roads were fairly clear and the walk easy. My first task was to bring in more wood and get the fireplace going. In short order this was done. A friend from Holly Hill, Paul Sheehan walked his giant snowblower down to my house. Paul managed to clear a path to the house and a path to the wood. I opened the hood of my car hoping to get it started, but to no avail. Snow had been blown and joined with the salt air to have filled solid the whole engine block compartment. We left the hood up and hoped the sun would eventually melt the mess. With no power and no sign of power to come soon, we used our ingenuity by making a refrigerator of snow just outside our front door. Into this we placed the food from our refrigerator. With our gas stove and oven working, we able to prepare meals. With contributions from all the neighbors, meals were shared and a strong sense of community developed. Before a National Guard station was set up on our street, we were able to walk over the Julian Street Bridge. The damage in Humarock was incredible. House that looked fine from the river side when viewed from the ocean side looked like some giant had taken a knife and

sliced the front off. An amazing thing was that our phones kept working. I remember talking to Brad Dooley and he commented, "I watched waves breaking thirty feet over the tops of chimneys in Humarock." I remember an interview with a Humarock resident. When asked about what he lost, his response was, "I lost my car, my house and belongings, I even lost  the ground my house was on." I was very lucky. The damage I sustained was minor compared to the destruction I witnessed in Humarock. The government established low- interest loans to those homeowners who had sustained damage, and with such a loan I was able to repair the damage the house had sustained. But other friends of mine were not so lucky. The McCormick sisters' home on Surfside Drive was totally destroyed. Mushquashacut Pond looked like a disaster zone strewn with human detritus. A lot of homes that had been around for years and years were destroyed. Poorly-built and low-to-the-ground homes were unable to withstand the ravages of a series of 15-foot tides, strong and high wave action, and being smashed and pummeled by rocks. At the height of the storm on the first night, tragedy was sure to follow. Dave Ball related to me that first night he was asked if he wanted to be evacuated. "No," he replied, "for conditions were far too dangerous." His words would be prophetic.

Blizzard of '78 photos courtesy of: Scituate Historical Society, Pat Arnold, W. Ray Freden, Bob Branca.

Columbia picture from the author's collection. - Page 226

Tragedy came to the Sandhills section of Scituate. Two Sandhills residents Amy Lanzikos and Edward Hart were lost when a huge wave capsized the rescue boat they were in and valiant efforts to save Amy and Edward failed. Ironically another tragedy occurred at exactly the same spot eighty years earlier during the Portland Gale of 1898. As the storm intensified and fearing for their lives. Mr. Joseph Wilbur and his wife attempted to leave their Sandhills cottage for safety at Jonathan Hatch's home. Mr. Wilbur and a friend carried his wife; twice they were knocked from their feet. A huge wave swept the three of them into Scituate Harbor where Mrs. Wilbur tragically drowned after she had been torn from the grasp of her husband. Her body washed up and was found on Front Street. Had they remained in the cottage at Sand Hills, they would have all perished, for the house was totally destroyed.

● Copter Flies Like A Stork

SCITUATE — OK, storks don't bring babies, but helicopters do bring pregnant women — sometimes.

A case in point: yesterday WBZ Weatherman Joe Green, responding to a call for aid, plucked Mrs. Jean Jones from her isolated and inaccessible home on Fourth Cliff in the Humarock section, and deposited her gently at the emergency storm center at Scituate High School.

Mrs. Jones' due date had come and gone and she was reported to be in labor with no way to get out of her home because storm debris had closed off nearby Central Avenue to every kind of vehicular traffic.

Joe Green first landed the helicopter at a nearby nursing home, where he picked up Firefighter Robert Snow for the trip to Humarock.

They delivered the expectant mother to the high school instead of the hospital because her labor pains had subsided by the time help arrived, according to Fire Chief Walter Stewart.

1991 STORM SECTION TO PRESENT

Linda Greenlaw: [*warning Billy over the radio*] Billy? Get outta there! Come about! Let it- let it carry you out of there! What the hell are you doing? Billy! For Christ sake! You're steaming into a bomb! Turn around for Christ sake! Billy, can ya hear me? You're headed right for the middle of the monster! Billy?... [*starts crying*] [From the Perfect Storm]

There are certain words, like the blizzard of '78, when mentioned, elicit a visceral reaction in people. For me, such a reaction is triggered when the No Name Storm, also called the Halloween Storm and the Perfect Storm arises in a conversation. Immediate images of sea-foam coursing down the road from Ocean Drive across River Street, and down Julian Street to the bridge, tidal waters pouring into my yard almost surrounding my house, and fierce wind-driven rain are etched in my memory. Because with the destruction of the Blizzard of '78, storms both winter and summer were no longer cavalierly taken by New Englanders and particularly South Shore residents.

For many people, mention of the Perfect Storm recalled pictures of actors George Clooney and Mark Wahlberg fighting to save the Andrea Gail in the movie The Perfect Storm or of having read Sebastian Junger's book of the same title, but for those of us living in and around Humarock, Scituate, and Marshfield more devastating images are remembered.

On October 30, 1991, the so-called "perfect storm" hit the North Atlantic producing remarkably large waves along the New England and Canadian coasts. On October 27, Hurricane Grace formed near Bermuda and moved north toward the coast of the southeastern United States. Two days later, Grace continued to move north, where it encountered a massive low pressure system moving south from Canada. The clash of systems over the Atlantic Ocean caused 40-to-80-foot waves on October 30—unconfirmed reports put the waves at more than 100 feet in some locations. This massive surf caused

228

extensive coastal flooding, particularly in Massachusetts. The storm continued to churn in the Atlantic on October 31; it was nicknamed the "Halloween storm." It came ashore on November 2 along the Nova Scotia coast, then, as it moved northeast over the Gulf Stream waters, it made a highly unusual transition into a hurricane. The National Hurricane Center made the decision not to name the storm for fear it would alarm and confuse local residents. It was only the eighth hurricane not given a name since the naming of hurricanes began in 1950.

Along the Massachusetts coastline, the storm produced about 30-foot wave heights just offshore, which fashioned an additional 3- to 4-foot tidal surge on top of a 10 ft high tide. In Boston, the highest tide was 14.3 ft (4.4 m),[5] which was only 1 ft (30 cm) lower than the record from the blizzard of 1978.[1] High waves on top of the storm tide reached about 30 ft (9.1 m). The storm produced heavy rainfall in southeastern Massachusetts, peaking at 5.5 inches (140 mm).[5] Coastal floods closed several roads, forcing hundreds of people to evacuate. In addition to the high tides, the storm produced strong winds; Chatham recorded a gust of 78 mph (126 km/h). Damage was worst from Cape Ann in northeastern Massachusetts to Nantucket, with over 100 homes destroyed or severely damaged at Marshfield, North Beach, and Brant Point. There were two injuries in the state, although there were no fatalities. Across Massachusetts, damage totaled in the hundreds of millions of dollars[1] (1991 Perfect Storm, Wikipedia free encyclopedia)."

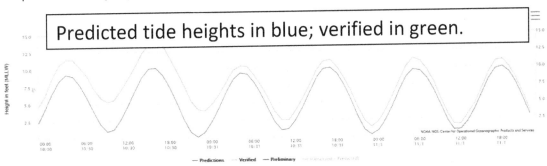

Predicted tide heights in blue; verified in green.

Above are the plotted tide heights. See that on October 30, 1991 the tides almost reached those of the Blizzard of 1978. I watched helplessly as the tide stopped about a foot from my backdoor, not quite the three inches in 1978 at the same location. Look carefully at the tide heights that follow. They are for the nor'easter (Bomb Cyclone) that struck the South Shore on January 4th 2018. The tide heights in Boston were 15 feet compared to 15.1 feet during the

Blizzard of '78. The reason why destruction was not worse here in Marshfield and Scituate is that wave heights at sea were only 15 feet high compared to 30 feet high during the Blizzard of '78.

BOMB CYCLONE NOR'EASTER OF JANUARY 4. 2018

Satellite photo of Bomb Cyclone hitting East Coast

Bottom Photo: Turner Road Scituate

Above Photo by Peter Noyes taken from Cliff Road, Humarock

Bottom Photo taken by Jean Shea, Ridge Road, Marshfield near the Julian Street Bridge.

HALLOWEEN STORM OR GALE OF 1991, NO NAME STORM OF 1991, OR THE PERFECT STORM 1991

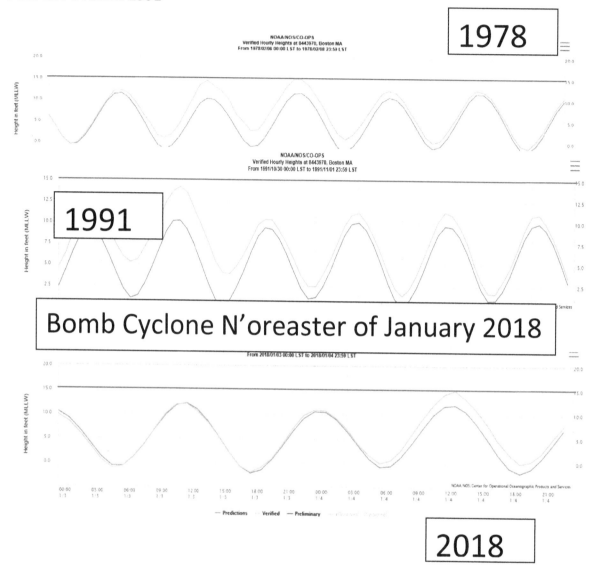

Blue is predicted tide height Green is verified

Examine carefully the above tide height charts for Boston. Remember Blue is the predicted tide height and Green is the verified tide heights and Red is a 15 foot tide. The Blizzard of '78 had the highest tide followed by Bomb Cyclone, and then the Halloween Storm. From watching and experiencing those tides from my own yard that was the conclusion. What saved us last January was that the wave heights at sea were 15 feet high compared with 30 feet high during the Blizzard of '78.

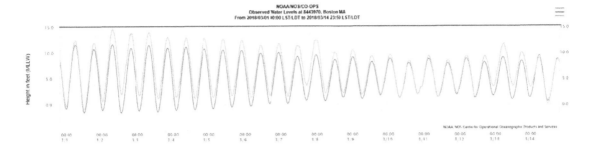

Now compare all of this to the March 2018 Noreasters. What do you see? Clearly to me, a layman, the pattern seems to have been getting worse. Hundred-year storms seem to be increasing in frequency with time between them getting shorter. Is this the result of climate change, an aberration in the weather pattern, or some other reason? I don't claim to know the answer, but the evidence seems clear from experts who do that, because the earth is warming up, there is more melting of the ice caps with a resulting increase in the ocean height. Hopefully, all of us in the Humarock area have joined the Scituate Coastal Coalition and are educating ourselves to the risks the future seems to hold.

Atlantic Drive/Central Ave/ 4th cliff area Humarock by Bob Branca

One final observation of the No Name Storm of 1991, my family raised all things up off the floor. We put important papers and documents and expensive electronics upstairs on the second floor. We did not evacuate. A point of trivia to those who love trivia: if it had been named – its name would have been Henri which was the next name on the 1991 list after Grace.

So concludes my recollections of three memorable storms that have impacted my life and my family's lives.

FEMA/Marilee Caliendo photo of 1991 No Name storm damage Town Way, Scituate.

Atlantic Drive/Central Ave./4th cliff area Humarock by Bob Branca

These First of two photos (top) is Mann Hill Road in Scituate one week before the Blizzard of 1978 The second photo (below) is taken one week later.

Sea View's Gentleman Farmers

"It is the duty of a gentleman to know how to ride, to shoot, to fence, to box, to swim, to row and to dance. He should be graceful. If attacked by ruffians, a man should be able to defend himself, and also to defend women from their insults."
Rules of Etiquette and Home Culture. 1886

As a visitor left Sea View railroad station by barge heading to Humarock via Summer, Elm, and Sea streets, he/she was struck by the activity, homes, and scenic farms that bordered

Stock pond on Belanger's Farm, Sea View

these ways. Hills, cleared of trees, were dotted with livestock grazing in their fields while stone walls served as fences along Elm Street and constructed fences bordered Ferry Hill Road. Roosting at the top of Holly Grove was the mansion of ex-Governor of the Utah Territory George W. Emery while nestled along Little's Creek was Belangerville, which was the area along the southern edge of Elm Street and Ferry Hill Road, that encompassed Victor Belanger's farm with its main house barns, boathouse and out-buildings. These gentleman farmers occupied a stratified

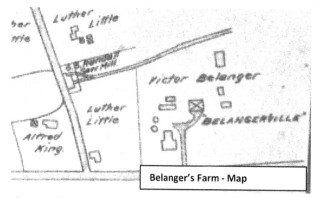

Belanger's Farm - Map

position in American society. A gentleman farmer was defined as a man whose wealth or income from other sources permits him to farm for pleasure rather than for basic income. George Emery and Victor Belanger would join with the financier and copper king Thomas W. Lawson in winning awards for breeding their livestock at the Marshfield Agricultural and Horticultural Society's Fair.

The entrance to Victor Belanger's farm was from Elm Street. As you turned into the driveway on your right was an enormous beech tree whose diameter was four feet at the base.

Proceeding down the driveway the massive main house was on your left while at the split in the driveway, a right would take you to the barn. The left would lead into a large parking area with four outbuildings on your left. The larger rectangular- shaped building housed the poultry. After the large barn and to its left, was the manmade pond called the Sea Brook Stock Farm on postcards from that era. In these postcards cattle can be seen grazing; these cattle being the prize winners from the Marshfield Fair. The driveway continued to the boathouse, which Ray Freden states is located incorrectly on the plan. It was located closer to Little's Creek bank. There was also a pump house and two other outbuildings that were not identified. According to Ray's dad, the Belangers liked to entertain. Men in formal black suits and women in gowns arrived to these soirees in big black Packards or big, black limousines. Victor Belanger died in 1907. During Prohibition, rumrunners liked the isolation and location of the Belanger Farm. Isolated from other homes and located on Little's Creek, it was easy for a boat to come up the creek unobserved and drop off its contraband. There it was loaded into Chevrolet trucks, favored by rumrunners because of their silent engines. Then snap on signs labeled Hood's Milk would be attached to the sides of the trucks and off the trucks would go. If discovered by anyone on shore, the illegal alcohol would be stored in the marsh in specially prepared holes and covered with marsh grass to be picked up at a later time.

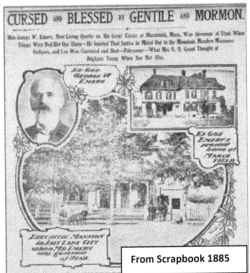

From Scrapbook 1885

Ex-Governor George W. Emery was appointed territorial governor of Utah by President U.S. Grant in 1875. In 1881 George W. Emery purchased 170 acres on Hatch's Hill (later called Holly Hill) and in 1882 an adjoining piece of land with a house. In 1885 George built a new house to the rear of the old house, previously the home of Samuel and Huldah Hall who were his wife's parents. (This new house burned in the 1930s.) In a scrapbook of newspaper clippings, one dated May 6, 1885 read, "Gov. Emery to erect an elegant residence on the rear of the site of his present one. The old house will be removed." He added to his property through additional purchases, his homestead land totaling 335 acres. As mentioned before, his wife Marcia predeceased him January 9, 1898. They had one child, Frank, who died in 1913 at the age of 47. His resume was lengthy: lawyer and member of the Boston Law firm of Benjamin Butler – appointed by President U.S. Grant as Supervisor of Internal Revenue (federal tax collector) for the former confederate states 1870 to 1874 – briefly a judge in Nashville, Tennessee – appointed by Grant as the eleventh governor of Utah Territory 1875 to 1880 who moved to Marshfield at the end of this term in 1880. He listed as his occupation in 1900 'capitalist'. In the tax evaluation of 1898, George's personal estate was: horse, two carriages, 6 horses, 10 cows, 3 carriages, and

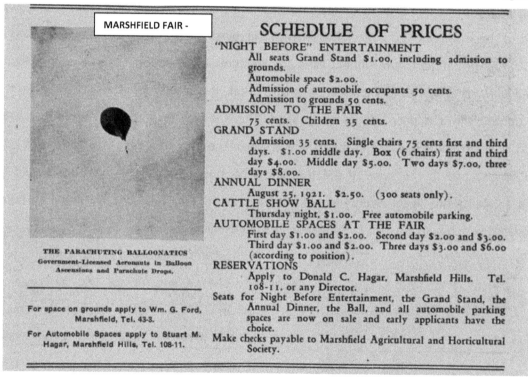

MARSHFIELD FAIR -

THE PARACHUTING BALLOONATICS
Government-Licensed Aeronauts in Balloon
Ascensions and Parachute Drops.

For space on grounds apply to Wm. G. Ford, Marshfield, Tel. 43-3.

For Automobile Spaces apply to Stuart M. Hagar, Marshfield Hills, Tel. 108-11.

SCHEDULE OF PRICES

"NIGHT BEFORE" ENTERTAINMENT
All seats Grand Stand $1.00, including admission to grounds.
Automobile space $2.00.
Admission of automobile occupants 50 cents.
Admission to grounds 50 cents.

ADMISSION TO THE FAIR
75 cents. Children 35 cents.

GRAND STAND
Admission 35 cents. Single chairs 75 cents first and third days. $1.00 middle day. Box (6 chairs) first and third day $4.00. Middle day $5.00. Two days $7.00, three days $8.00.

ANNUAL DINNER
August 25, 1921. $2.50. (300 seats only).

CATTLE SHOW BALL
Thursday night, $1.00. Free automobile parking.

AUTOMOBILE SPACES AT THE FAIR
First day $1.00 and $2.00. Second day $2.00 and $3.00. Third day $1.00 and $2.00. Three days $3.00 and $6.00 (according to position).

RESERVATIONS
Apply to Donald C. Hagar, Marshfield Hills. Tel. 108-11, or any Director.
Seats for Night Before Entertainment, the Grand Stand, the Annual Dinner, the Ball, and all automobile parking spaces are now on sale and early applicants have the choice.
Make checks payable to Marshfield Agricultural and Horticultural Society.

furniture. His real estate holdings included a house 15,000 Hall house 1400, G. Sherman house 200, Phillips house 550, stable 400, stable and tool house 350, barn and shed 750, ice house 60, beach house 10, windmill and tower 50, C. Little land 1 acre 150, N. Keene land 2 and ½ acres 150, P. house lot ½ acre 50, land east of road 17 acres 850, pasture 5 acres 100, mowing west of road 8 acres 400, new house lot 3 acres 300, home meadow 36 acres 360, B.G. meadow 3 and ½ acres 50, salt meadow 4 and ½ acres 40, pasture 106 acres 1270, woodland 70 acres 1000, beach land 10 acres 30, Hatch Hill land 164 acres 2000, Keene pasture 42 and ½ acres 825, G.S.

house lot 50, Sherman meadow 6 acres 60, Phillips meadow and beach 7 acres 100. For his times he was a very wealthy man.

Living quietly on his estate in Marshfield, Massachusetts, on a hill commanding a wide view of Massachusetts Bay, he was interviewed about his time in Utah. He talked about meting out justice to outlaws there. He recalled inviting President Grant to visit, which he did. He also told of his introducing President Grant and Mrs. Grant to Brigham Young. Mrs. Grant when asked by Emery, later, what she thought of Young, her response was, "He is one of the most entertaining men I have ever met." Later Emery would discuss his diplomatic visits in Utah by the Emperor of Brazil Don Pedro, and the Prime Minister of Canada and his wife. They came on two or three different occasions while the Prime Minister of Australia came once, as he was returning from a trip from England and was returning home. Governor Emery was also very busy with family after returning home to Massachusetts. At a Wednesday, September 9, 1896 family meeting at the Hotel Nantasket with seventy family members present, he was elected to executive committee of the Emery Family. They then determined that the next family meeting would be held the last week of next June at the Emery Farm in West Newburyport. Amazingly with his resume being what it was, other members of the family were better known and gave

Emery Mansion

the addresses at these convocations. Emery was chosen President of the Marshfield Agricultural and Horticultural Society on November 19, 1889 and re-elected in 1890. September 11, 1890 was Governor's Day at the Marshfield Fair and attendance was large. Gov. Brackett and a large contingent of Massachusetts' political leaders arrived on the 11:30 a.m. train from Boston, and was met by the president, George W. Emery, and escorted to the grounds and there a procession was formed and marched to the hall, where the annual dinner was partaken of. Addresses were made by President Emery, Governor Brackett, and Prof. N.S. Shaler of the State board of agriculture. The Governor and his staff spent the afternoon by visiting the various departments and witnessing the track events. In 1891 President Emery called to order the third and last in a series of farmers' institutes held at Agricultural Hall on March 11, 1891. He then introduced the main speaker ex-Representative Henry A. Turner of Norwell, who spoke upon "Both Sides of Farming." Later at the same meeting after a discussion about poultry farming, the Hon. William R. Sessions, secretary of the board of Agriculture, spoke upon "Massachusetts Farming," dwelling particularly on dairy farming. A later 1895 article with ex-Gov. Emery related that for 15 years following his time as governor of Utah, that every year he returned to Utah to check on their material and educational progress, which he found to have been wonderful. The Emery mansion passed from his family to the Dwights and finally to the Parkers during the 1940s. In 1946 the Parker family was bankrupt and the family walked away from the house. A friend of Ray's brother broke into the abandoned house. Inside he found it to be fully furnished with food still in the pantry. He also found a great amount of girl scout equipment and a coin collection. All of this he left behind. In the mansion's garage were three cars: a big

Packard sedan, a Jaguar convertible, and an expensive American vehicle. Ray Freden remembered two of the girls, who were driven by the family's chauffeur to and from Thayer and Derby Academies. Ray was told there may have been a third girl or possibly a boy rounding out the family, but he searched and was never able to find what happened to them. On July 10, 1909, Ex-Gov George W. Emery died at Marshfield, Mass.

By the 1905 Fair the reigns of leadership were passed to Thomas W. Lawson as he was elected President of the Marshfield Agricultural and Horticultural Society.

In the 1906 Fair, which opened on Wednesday, August 22nd and would last for three days, the farmers' attention was captured in the forenoon of the first day by contests in the big oval by all kinds of work horse contests. During the afternoon, among the most notable cattle was a large consignment from the magnificent stock farm of Victor J. Belanger of Sea View which took prizes in several classes. Other prize-winning cattle were those from the

Dreamwold Farm of President Thomas W. Lawson of the organization. Lawson's hand and the hands of other gentleman farmers could be seen in this Fair. Lawson would be presiding over the dinner, his first since becoming president. It was also mentioned that the 1906 fair was just like an old time cattle show from half a century ago, thanks again to Lawson who had the fair buildings and grounds overhauled at his expense.

In 1921 Lawson was President Emeritus of the Marshfield Agricultural and Horticultural Society. In October of 1922, the property and buildings of Dreamwold were put up for sale by

Photo previous page: Thomas Lawson. Above: Part of Thomas W. Lawson's Dreamwold estate, Scituate, MA

Trustees Horace T. Fogg and William A. Burton. In the last days of his life Lawson was confined to his bed with diabetes in the Nest, as his estate was being sold. One of his friends and a

trustee came to him with $550 in cash that had been found. With that money Lawson had a phone line installed by his bed and played the market. Six weeks later he had amassed $40,000 which he promptly gave his children. He died within days. With the end of World War I and Lawson's death, the days of the gentleman farmer would be numbered. With Emery's death his mansion and farm was sold to a Mr. Dwight from Auburndale; when he lost his fortune in the Crash of

Ferry Hill Development, Marshfield, MA

1929 Holly Hill began to be divided up and developed.

Previously Ferry Hill would be surveyed with plots covering that hill and eventually Belangerville would follow suit. One more gentleman farmer and his large farm was constructed atop Deer Hill, the Seager Farm. David C. Seager from Boston made his first purchase of land in Marshfield in 1898, later purchasing additional properties. This land was located on a hill, soon to be known as Seager Hill, off of Pleasant Street and Summer Street. He established a working farm here which included horses, pigs, sheep, cows, a bull, fowl and a mushroom cellar. David employed a farm manager from Scotland and several farm laborers from Italy who lived on the farm. At the time the Seager Farm was accessed by two gravel roads: one going up at Deer Hill and the other down with a stone gutter (**see photo below**) that crossed Sea View Station property.

Coming down Deerhill Lane

David C. Seager was born at Syracuse, New York, and was a resident of Boston by 1893.

Main House Seager Farm

In 1900 his occupation was listed as manager of real estate and by 1903 he was living in Marshfield loaning relatively large sums of money to many individuals in the form of mortgages. He was also a cranberry grower for twenty years, owning many bogs in several times. He was also the Secretary of the Massachusetts Board of Agriculture from 1917 to 1921. He died in Boston on February 12, 1939 age 69 and unmarried. He was survived by nephews and nieces. In 1943 his nephew, Theodore Seager acquired 12 acres of the farm with the house. The remainder of the Seager Farm was sold by the executor of David's estate over the next several years.

Other farms, not as extensive as these three, graced Sea View, one of which was a farm with peach trees and grazing, fenced sheep along the borders of Pleasant Street and Summer Street while others grew tomatoes and corn.

On Pudding Hill Lane was the Seeley Farm owned by Augustus and Sarah Seeley. In the 1907 Valuation of Personal and Real Estate their total estate was valued at more than the Seager Farm was at that time. It, too, had horses, cows, fowl, hen house, pigeon house, stable, barn and houses and 42 acres of land. See pictures of the Seeley Farm on the next pages.

They are all gone now, but their legacies and memories remain.

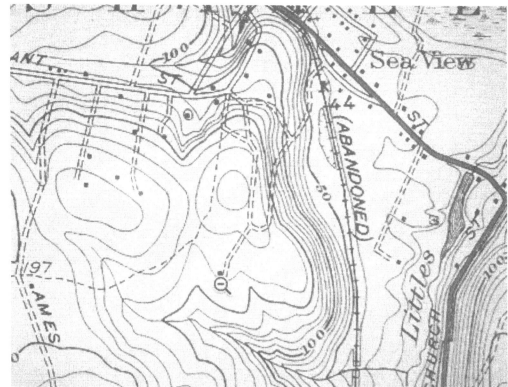

See Cursor on map – location of Seager Farm on Deer Hill; dotted lines indicate gravel roads.

244

Seeley Farm on Pudding Hill Lane.

The farm was located on Elm Street and Ferry Hill Road (house is now #334 Elm Street). Victor W. Belanger was born in Canada and immigrated to the United States in 1879. While living in Worcester, Massachusetts, in 1881 he founded the newspaper "Le Courrier de Worcester" with his brother Louis Belanger. He became a United States citizen in 1889 and was an inventor with numerous patents held by the New Era Spinning Company in which he owned a controlling interest. In 1900 he listed his occupation as "capitalist", and in 1910 listed his occupation as 'farmer."

Victor made his first purchase of property, land and buildings, on Elm Street in 1899. During the next six years he continued to add adjoining land along Elm Street and Ferry Hill Road where he established a working farm of 21 acres. There were open fields planted with crops, a pond, an orchard, a greenhouse, barns and other outbuildings, horses, cows, a bull, hens and ducks. The cows and bull were a herd of Jersey stock which Victor exhibited at the Marshfield Fair where he and his animals received several awards.

He was certainly a gentleman farmer. He employed a farm manager from Sweden, who lived on the farm, and farm laborers.

Victor died at Elm Street on August 12, 1916, at the age of 59. After his death the farm was owned by his widow Mary, who sold part of the land, and their two daughters, Angelique and Victorine. Mary passed in 1938 and the daughters sold Sea Brook Farm in 1942.

St. Theresa's Chapel – Sea View

A group of men living in the Humarock/Sea View area wanted to build a church on May 17, 1925, when Saint Theresa, "The Little Flower of Jesus," was canonized. Among this group

Summer Street, Sea View – Donovan home 101 Summer St. on left.

were: Henry Hanley, Thomas Donovan, Louis Vachon, Thomas Dolan and William P. Brennan. With the blessings of Father Patrick Buckley, the pastor of St. Mary's Church, Scituate, they each donated one hundred dollars and set to work to fulfill their dream.

With a small Catholic community composed of not more than 35 summertime and year-round St. Mary's parishioners, they attended mass often in the home of Katherine Donovan at 101 Summer Street in Sea View and sometimes in the ell of her house where pews and an altar were installed. The Donovan home was formerly the George Pecker residence located next door to his shoe factory. Mary Louise Randall from Marshfield also was instrumental in building up the congregation.

Dr. Edwin Dwight, himself not a Catholic, and the only resident on Holly Hill having purchased the mansion and lands of Governor George Emery in the early 1920s, was approached by our zealous group and agreed to donate land for the church. He had one stipulation, however, and that was that the Church be in keeping with the surroundings.

"By 1927, their dreams had flowered. Appropriately, since their church embodied the budding faith of the founders, Father Buckley choose Saint Theresa as patroness. But the lovely hillside stone and wood structure had not been built without much 'joyful effort' as one witness put it. There had been continuous bridge parties, endless sales and auctions, a gala dance every year, and the great generosity of St. Mary's

parishioners. When Father Richard James Cushing blessed the church in August, 1927, after preaching on St. Theresa's beautiful life, Father Buckley was able to boast: 'It's paid for.'

As St. Theresa's had answered the needs of an original handful, there were in the 1940s even more demands of a growing flock, now nearly 300. When Msgr. Edmund Moran was appointed first pastor in Marshfield, daily and Sunday Masses, devotions and novenas were expanded at St. Theresa's.

Interior looking forward to Altar

Except for 1955, when the church was used year round, St. Theresa's has remained a sort of 'sub parish' of St. Christine's. One need only attend to find the same spiritual bond of founders in the faithful of today. Especially is this so in men like Thomas Dolan of Roslindale

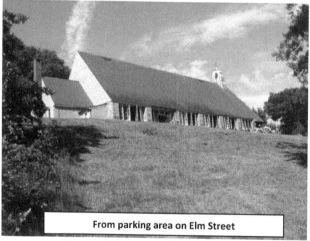

From parking area on Elm Street

whose years of willing work have not gone unappreciated. Many recall the penny and cake sales he helped run with Father Flynn from the porch of Old St. Christine's rectory. And there are others . . . the scores of Jesuits, particularly Rev. Edward J. Welsh, S.J. of Fairfield Prep, Connecticut, who with others of his Order have helped for most of the 23-year tenure of Father Flynn. These indeed are the blossoms of the 'Little Flower'. . . . The original idea for a new parish in Marshfield in 1946 was to convert the summer mission chapel of St. Theresa's in Sea View to a fulltime parish; however,

SCHEDULE OF MASSES (1970)

St. Christine's
Sunday: 7, 8:30, 10:30, 12 noon
Saturday: 5 p.m.
Daily: 7:30 a.m.

●

St. Theresa's
Sunday: 8, 9:30, 11 (Folk Mass)
Saturday: 7 p.m.
Daily: 8:30 a.m.

Father Moran felt this location simply was not adequate. Thus he pushed for a more centrally located building, St. Christine's (from the 25th Anniversary Oct. 18, 1970 booklet).

Now another twenty-three years have passed since the 25th anniversary celebration and the 50th Golden Jubilee and with it more changes and challenges for the faith community at St. Christine's and St. Theresa's. The baton of leadership has been passed from Father Francis A. Regan to Father Thomas Walsh and recently to administrator Rev. Stephen M. Boyle. May the next seventy-three years be as fruitful to St. Christine's and St. Theresa's as the first seventy-three were.

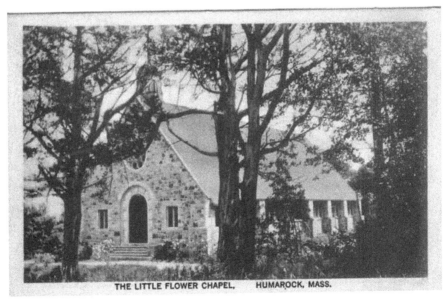

THE LITTLE FLOWER CHAPEL, HUMAROCK, MASS.

View of Chapel from Elm Street

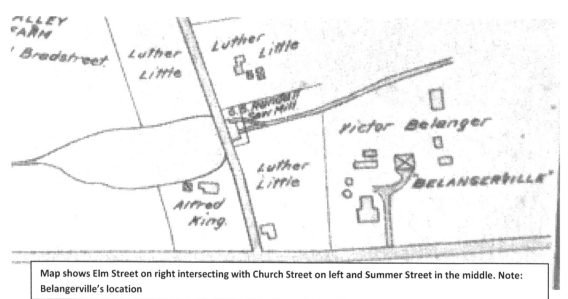

Map shows Elm Street on right intersecting with Church Street on left and Summer Street in the middle. Note: Belangerville's location

Photo of Elm Street with Belanger's driveway on left courtesy of W. Ray Freden collection.

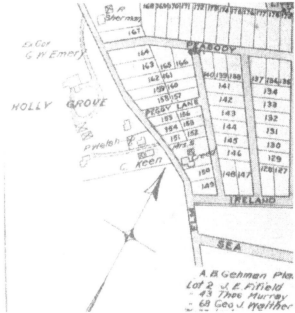

The two black and white postcards pages 1 and 3 are courtesy of the Scituate Historical Society.

Photos from pages 2 and 4 were taken by the author.

Map to left shows location of Gov. Emery Mansion of Elm Street at Holly Grove.

Looking E. on Elm St with # 250 Elm St. res. at Ferry Hill Rd. Randall photo. From W. Ray Freden collection.

Some Reflections

"Life can only be understood backwards; but it must be lived forwards." - **Soren Kierkegaard**

I began this book with the intention to tell Humarock's story because of having spent more than thirty-four years as a teacher of history in Scituate as well as a resident who had settled just across the river from Humarock. But as I have researched and interviewed more and more people in the area of Humarock, I have come to the realization that Humarock's history cannot be told or understood unless you study it in relation to Sea View's history and the history of the railroad that brought the agents of change to the South Shore in the late 1800s. The relationship between these two villages is symbiotic and as time has passed the relationship has also changed, not always to the benefit of Sea View. Now with the passage of over one hundred and thirty years, most of the residents who knew the difference and saw the changes happening are mostly gone. Newcomers, like myself, arrived and perceived that what we saw and experienced was the way it had always been.

Change inevitably brings uneasiness to those steeped in tradition as something new challenges, then coexists with, and finally seemingly surpasses something older, more culturally-rich and diverse, more settled, and whose roots stretch back to the very beginnings of our country's history. This anxiety eventually gives way to resentment as previous

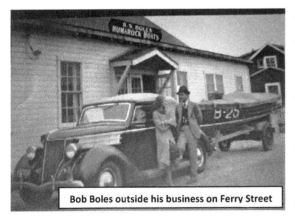
Bob Boles outside his business on Ferry Street

achievements, work, and culture are either forgotten, overlooked, or subverted by the new. Is it any wonder that long time residents of Sea View would challenge ideas that present Humarock was labeled on the Sea View side of the North or South River? Would it surprise you that a Sea View resident for generations is irritated when they see a postcard labeled Hotel Humarock, Seaview, or a business in Sea View has a name that marks it location as Humarock? Now that I have become aware of the history of Sea View, it does not surprise me in the least. The real reason explained to me for the diminishment of Sea View was the closing of the Sea View Post office after 1926. With Humarock having its own Post Office, the change in perception between the two villages became blurred over time and only realized by those who truly knew their history.

Let us begin by an examination of the Railroad station in Littletown/Sea View which played a huge role in the economic development of both villages. Littletown, or Sea View, was a

The first Sea View RR station with Thomas Stevens/ Langelle's residence Right & Alonzo Steven's residence to its Right

The second Sea View Railroad station

developed village and had been since Thomas Little began to farm there in 1650. The Little family's influence in East Marshfield and Sea View grew over the centuries as they built ships, manned those ships, built factories and businesses of all types, became merchants with shops along Summer Street, ran schools, opened tea houses, and of course, farmed the land. With the arrival of the railroad in 1870, Littletown/Sea View would become a hub of traffic and activity for the summer crowd heading to enjoy the beach and amenities of the Hotel Humarock and the Ferry Hill area. The railroad would be an economic boon to the area of Sea View and Humarock, so much so that its first station would be obsolete within a few years and the largest station on the railroad line composed of two floors replaced it. This association with the railroad also necessitated a change in name because there already existed a Littleton depot in another part of Massachusetts. This conclusion was only a guess on long time Sea View resident's Ray Freden's part but on August 20, 1873, the depot's name was changed from Littletown Station to Sea View Station.

The first Hotel Humarock was completed for the season of 1882 and had been opened

Hotel Humarock on Marshfield Avenue, Humarock, viewed from Ferry Street, Marshfield.

only for three weeks when disaster occurred. A fire started in a defective flue and the hotel burned to the ground. But rising Phoenix-like from the ashes, a new and better Hotel Humarock was ready for the 1883 season. With a capacity of 200 rooms, the hotel provided accommodations to an increasingly receptive public for the next eighteen years until fire again destroyed this well known destination. Prior to the opening of the Hotel Humarock to summer residents, there were visitors to the Humarock area. Some of these visitors were particularly interested in just absorbing the peace, solitude, and quiet of living on a peninsula that had a cliff overlooking marshes laden with all manner of natural wonders. Others were more interested in the gunning stands located along a river that meandered through both islands and marshes. Many types of people flocked to the Fourth Cliff House located on the Fourth Cliff in Humarock. William O. Merritt was the proprietor and the boarding house was only three miles from the Sea View Station and could be rented for the very reasonable rate of between a one dollar and one dollar fifty cents per day or seven to ten dollars a week. Capacity was for fourteen, so you did not want to delay your summer stay by procrastination in reserving your room.

As America entered the new century (20th), demand for rooms at the Fourth Cliff House, the Hotel Humarock, the Colman Heights Cottage and Boarding House, Riverside Cottage, and Sea View House, increased. Rooms at these residences were particularly in demand for visitors to Sea View and Humarock; they were only one short hour by express train from Boston, and finally because of their proximity to the Sea View Railroad station.

With arrival at Sea View, a barge or carriage picked up visitors and a scenic country ride along rustic country roads ensued. Bordered by neighboring fields of livestock,

Elm Steet facing east toward Ferry Hill

fields of crops, and gorgeous sea scenes, visitors welcomed a peace, stillness, and serenity that calmed nerves stressed by the hustle and bustle induced by city living. From the top of Ferry Hill and Holly Hill unbroken vistas of ocean, marsh, and river were a tonic to senses overwhelmed by the toxic noise, smells, and pollution of the city. The easy pace of country life led many to look for an opportunity to purchase land in this area so that this sense of tranquility could be permanent. Wealthy patrons glimpsed the mansion of former Utah Governor Emery commanding and controlling the top Holly Hill, as well as the farm, fields, livestock, and crops of the Victor Belanger farm conveniently settled on Little's Creek and along Ferry Hill Road as desired places for summer residences. The ship captains' homes lining the border of Elm Street added an elegance and time-honored tradition while the mills perched on Keene's pond and the factories located along Summer Street demonstrated an industriousness and work ethic that was to be envied.

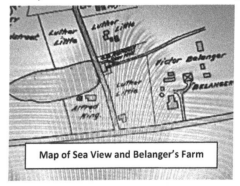

Map of Sea View and Belanger's Farm

From the Old Colony Railroad printed in 1881 Chapter on The South Shore was written, ". . . Scituate, Marshfield and Duxbury are divided into numerous villages and hamlets, 'strung along' the shore, as it were, and presenting at every point the peculiar New England characteristics, with so many qualities inherent to the 'good Old Colony times," and descended from the same. ". . . this locality partakes to a remarkable degree of the advantages and facilities for seashore 'summering' afforded by the region of which it forms a part, and holds some of these excellences in high development. The coasts are an alternation of sand-beach and rock-masses; of slightly curving surf-line, extending sometimes for miles, and broken, indented barriers, marking bold incursions inland of the restless water and the inroads for centuries of angry waves, which have diminished in their unceasing action alike the rugged rocks and the towering cliffs of sand. The billows of the ocean find no check as they roll upon these shores, save in the northern portions, where terrific ledges of iron-grey rocks stand off-shore as natural breakwaters to take the first shock of the elements. . . . City denizens some time since found out the natural attractions of the South Shore as a watering-place, and of late years the summer visitation in all parts here has been of rapid and widely extended growth. The health-giving breezes, the unrivalled facilities afforded for bay-fishing, the peaceful quiet and restful influences of all its neighborhoods, and the entire absence of conventionalities or conditions which require the sojourner to continue irksome society customs or relations, render the section much sought after by wanderers from every part of the country, and present opportunities and inducements for a prolonged indulgence in the dolce far niente, irresistible especially by city representatives or travellers from inland homes. Here may come women and children with an absolute certainty of revelling in natural delights which are at the same time safely and profitably experienced; and the extraordinary vanishing of all cares and anxieties is a peculiarity of once observable to every traveler under roof or tent-fly during summer on the South Shore."

With the destruction of the Hotel Humarock in 1901, Fred Merrill owner and proprietor

Hotel Royal and Sea Street, Humarock, Seaview, Mass.

subdivided his 120,000 square feet of land into sixteen lots. Two of these lots were purchased

Looking west at Holly Hill with the Emery Mansion on top. Ferry Hill is to the right. Ferry St. is along river.

and the Hotel Royal was built and the development of Humarock and Ferry Hill would begin. The development of the Emery Mansion began after the death of Emery in 1909 when his estate was purchased by Mr. Edwin Dwight of Auburndale, MA. during the early 1920s. Dwight

FERRY HILL
TOWN OF MARSHFIELD

lost the mansion with the Crash of economy in 1929 and died in 1931. As Cynthia Krusell in her excellent history of Marshfield wrote that at the time of his death, horses and cows were still grazing on Holly Hill.

During the early 1900s through the early 1920s development in Sea View and Humarock increased rapidly. "On the L. side below Holly Grove, the bottom house shown was the Charles Keen home built in the mid 1700s. The P. Welsh house was also old. The cape on the corner of Ferry Hill Road was J.B. Guelpo and the cape on the left was P. Sherman, the Black's in my

[Ray Freden's] day. The Sea View owned by a Mrs. Delano, and a Mrs. Josselyn, same Josselyn that owned the Riverside House in Humarock, and the North River House on Ferry Street."

Sea View House Burned down: Bridgwaye is near this location now

The railroad boom ended and the last train left Marshfield in September of 1939. The Sea View Station would eventually be closed and then sold to the Freden family during the 1940s. Ray Freden and his father would take down the station saving all the wood and nails (Ray said he missed a few that carpenters found when hit by their saws) during 1943-1945. Ray's dad would build their family Cape Cod style home on the site of the station at 53 Station Street Marshfield today. The following are pictures of the station from Ray's collection.

Sea View Station looking East. Stevens/ Doane/ Lambert house on Right # 35 Station St.-Alonso Stevens house on Left with garage & outbuildings, 189 Summer St. A rare photo courtesy of the Langille family.

Looking South about 1943, Showing the Elm trees. Charles Langille's 1938 humpback Ford on Left [Wife's car] and the Sea View railroad station on the right.

Taken by my Dad about 1943, while tearing the inside apart.

Sea View Station sign Taken by Ray Freden's Dad

Here is my Dad on the front stair of Clark's store.

He worked as a clerk & real estate agent from 1927 to 1934.

Here he met Marge Mattson Clark's sister Ruth [Ruthie] & married her in 1934.

They lived in Sea View for the next 72 years,

"Bill" passed at the age of 101+.

All photos used in this chapter, except for the Hotel Humarock photo which comes from the author's collection, are from W. Ray Freden collection. Used with permission.

Humarock's Future?

What to do with rocks and other debris that cover Central Ave. and Cliff Road where they meet after monthly tidal surges? What about the silting in of the North and South Rivers? How do we protect the resources of our land for future generations? How can we stop the erosion of the Fourth Cliff? Will devastating fires strike us again? Will the next

generations of committed Humarock residents step forward to pick up the baton left by their fathers and mothers? These and many other questions face us. Can we come together with the will and determination to listen to alternative opinions, respect divergent viewpoints, and arrive at a consensus

for the good of all? Only the future has the answers. Mahatma Gandhi had it right when he said: *"The future depends on what you do today."* — Mahatma Gandhi

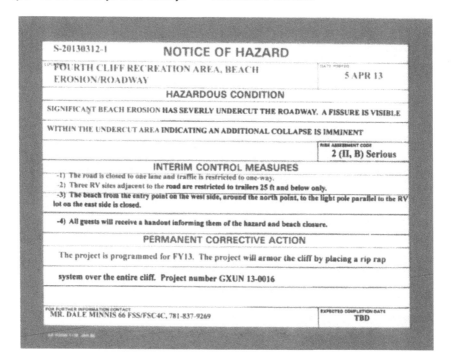

Just as the winter sun majestically sets over Coast Guard Hill, I call to mind Sandeep Shergill's quotation, "Life is all about enjoying every sunset and looking forward for the next Sunrise." Shall we realistically reflect on our sunsets and place our faith and hope in our sunrises.

Change is inevitable. Growth is optional.

Local Humarock and Sea View Gazetteer

Bartlett Island is an island north of Macomber Ridge and connected to Damon's Point Road by raised causeway.

Belangerville is the area that encompassed Victor Belangers Farm which was bordered on the north by Littles Creek, the west Summer Street/ Elm Street intersection, south by Elm Street and east by Ferry Hill Road where the YWCA camp is today.

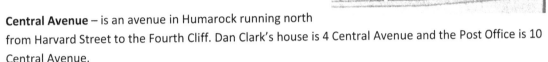

Central Avenue – is an avenue in Humarock running north from Harvard Street to the Fourth Cliff. Dan Clark's house is 4 Central Avenue and the Post Office is 10 Central Avenue.

Coleman Hills or Colman Hills was an east –west terminal moraine on the north side of the Driftway until they were undermined when Boston Sand and Gravel Company transported sand by barges to Boston.

Hanover Flats are called by some the island flats near Fourth Cliff the Hanover Flats or Great Flats.. **(see point of pen.)**

Hatch's Boatyard and Gunning Stand is the area along the South River side of Central Avenue across from the where it is intersects with Seaview Avenue; foundation of large blocks of stone or granite can still be seen. **(see 115 on NSRWA map)**

Hen or Tilden Island is an island east of Summer Street; south of Trouant Island and north of Pine Island.

Holly Hill (Hatch's Hill, Governor's Hill) – hill that is enclosed by Ferry, Church, and Elm streets.

HUMAROCK: Before 1898 - The barrier beach connecting Third and Fourth Cliffs, the beach and hummocks to the Old Mouth. After 1898 - New Inlet, Fourth Cliff, beach and hummocks to boundary with Marshfield at Rexhame Beach at Old Mouth Road.

Littles Creek is the creek that flows into Keene's Pond then under Summer Street to the South River.

New Harbor Marshes along Route 3A going toward Little's Bridge; eastward toward the cliffs; source of much salt marsh hay for early settlers.

New Inlet (Mouth) – is the new mouth of the North and South Rivers between Third and Fourth Cliffs created by the Portland Gale of November, 1898.

Old Mouth – prior to the Portland Gale of 1898 the mouth of the North River was located between Humarock and Rexhame where Old Mouth Road is located today just across from Snake Hill.

Pine Island is a mostly upland parcel of less than 3 acres in the center of a salt marsh now owned by Mass Audubon; lies east of Warren Avenue south of Broad Creek and northwest of Little's Creek. (**see 109 on NSRWA map**)

SEA VIEW: Sea View's boundaries are defined in the street listing of 1894 by the Post Office one used. The Northern line, shows the residences of Summer St. and Flower Hill Lane and went to the Sea View Post Office. The Western line was at about Pleasant Street and Eames Way, they also used the Sea View Post Office. Now, Ferry Hill and Holly Hill are in the village of Sea View, along with Bayberry Point, Julian Street Bridge area to the Coast Guard Station. The Bridgwaye is in Sea View along with Crawford boats and the Yacht Club. They all used the Sea View Post Office. Called in early history Littletown because it was settled by the Little family.

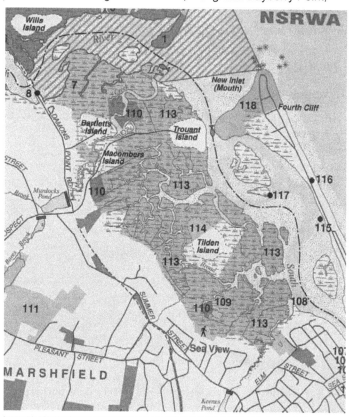

The Public Green is an area of land in Humarock between Marshfield Ave. and Harvard Street north of lots R and Q, south of lots H and I, east of lots C,D, & E and west of lots N,M, L.

The Square is the business area where Marshfield Avenue intersects with Central Avenue and River Street.

The Spit (or Sandy) is a very popular picnic area, especially at low tide. Prior to the 1898 breakthrough during the Portland Gale a roadway over the barrier beach connected Third and Fourth Cliffs. It is habitat for the endangered Piping Plover. (**see 1 on NSRWA map**)

Trouant Island is the island near the mouth of the North River and named for its settler in 1639; part of Marshfield.

White's Ferry – Probably the oldest shipyards existed here, being near the original mouth of the North River. Among those located in this vicinity were both the Hall and Keane yards.

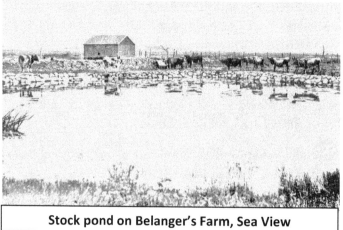

Stock pond on Belanger's Farm, Sea View

CPSIA information can be obtained
at www.ICGtesting.com
Printed in the USA
FSHW012039200220

9 780991 092383